D1558629

Spitfires and Yellow Tail Mustangs

The 52nd Fighter Group in World War Two

Tom Ivie and Paul Ludwig

Also from Hikoki Publications

First published in 2005 by

Hikoki Publications Limited
Friars Gate Farm
Mardens Hill
Crowborough
East Sussex TN6 1XH
England

Email: info@hikokiwarplanes.com
Web: www.hikokiwarplanes.com

Project Editor: Robert Forsyth
Production Management: Chevron Publishing
Design and layout: Tim Brown
Maps: Annette Hunt

ISBN 1 902109 43 0

Printed in Singapore

Spitfires and Yellow Tail Mustangs

The 52nd Fighter Group in World War Two

Tom Ivie and Paul Ludwig

This book is dedicated to the hard working, loyal and extremely dedicated Ground Personnel of the 52nd Fighter Group. Without their long hours at the job keeping the aircraft and base facilities in tip-top order, the pilots could not have established and maintained the outstanding combat record they produced.

CONTENTS

ACKNOWLEDGEMENTS

This history was facilitated by the many contributors mentioned in the Bibliography and Sources. However, it would hardly have been possible to write this book without the help of a few very detailed written records authored by veterans of the 52nd Fighter Group. Important are two books, one by Lawrence Burke and Robert Curtis of the 2nd Fighter Squadron, and another by Carlton Hogue of the Second Fighter Squadron. Emil Torvinen of the 4th Fighter Squadron authored a full, entire war diary. Tom Thacker had, for his friends, printed his history of the 5th Fighter Squadron. From the historical library at Maxwell Air Force Base in Montgomery, Alabama, came the highly detailed official Group and Squadron daily diaries.

GLOSSARY

A/D Airdrome
A-20 American twin-engine attack aircraft
a/c aircraft
ack ack anti-aircraft artillery
AF Air Force, as in Eighth Air Force
AP armor-piercing
ASC Air Service Command
Axis the name the Allies gave to the wartime fascist partnership between Germany and Italy and, later, Japan
B-25 Mitchell, an American twin-engine medium bomber
B-26 Marauder, an American twin-engine medium bomber
"balls out" an expression used by a fighter pilot who throws his entire effort into battle, as in "going balls out"
BBC British Broadcasting Company
'Beau' Bristol Beaufighter – a British twin-engine day- and-night fighter
BC Bomber Command
BG Bomb Group
bivouac a temporary encampment without shelter
bounce an attack in the air by one aircraft upon another, usually two fighters in action
C.202 Italian Macchi Castoldi single-engine fighter
cadre the officers and men necessary to establish and train a military unit
CAVU Clear and Visibility Unlimited
CG Commanding General
CO Commanding Officer
Delousing when fighter aircraft remove an enemy aircraft threat from above a ground battle
DFC Distinguished Flying Cross, a medal of valor won in battle
Djebel or Dj. hill
dinghy rubber life raft
e/a enemy aircraft
E-Boat and F-Boat German torpedo boats
Echelon a military unit regarded as having a distinct function
EM enlisted men
ETO European Theater of Operations
FC Fighter Command
FG Fighter Group
Flak An abbreviation of a series of three German words – Flieger Abwehr Kanone – meaning anti-aircraft artillery.
Flight assignments On missions, squadrons were broken into four ship flights, and each pilot had a designation, the number two pilot in Red Flight would be referred to as 'Red 2' alert when one or more pilots wait in, beside or near their aircraft in readiness for a scramble to intercept nearby enemy aircraft
F/O Flight Officer
Freddie Patrol a mission to prepare for an enemy photo-reconnassiance aircraft coming near
Freelancing taking targets of opportunity
FS Fighter Squadron
FW Fighter Wing
HMS His Majesty's Ship
HQ Headquarters
HSL high-speed launch
Hurribomber A Hawker Hurricane fighter employed as a tactical bomber
IO Intelligence Officer
KIA Killed In Action
Lend-Lease a wartime U.S. governmental organization devoted to exchanges of supplies and equipment between the Allies
line a line-up of aircraft, wingtip to wingtip, out-of-doors, from which all flight operations and some maintenance are conducted
Luftwaffe the German Air Force
Mae West a life jacket giving floatation in water, named for a voluptuous movie star
mess, or Mess relating to food-serving – either an area or a title, as in Mess Sergeant
Me 109 Veterans of World War Two spoke of- and writers refer to the Messerschmitt Bf Me 109 fighter as the 'Me 109' which, technically, is incorrect. In 1927, Prof. Willy Messerschmitt began a cooperation with the Bayerische Flugzeugwerke AG. As Herr Messerschmitt increased his share in the firm, in September 1938 the firm was re-named Messerschmitt AG. Any aircraft produced prior to September 1938 is properly designated 'Bf'. Messerschmitt aircraft types produced during World War Two are designated 'Me', however the Bf Me 109 was designed prior to 1938 as was the Bf 108 and Bf 110. Accordingly, the Me 163, Me 262 and others were designed after 1938. It is impossible to convince an American veteran of the war to refer to the Me 109 in any other fashion, and it would not serve a book written in memory of men of the 52nd Fighter Group to put words in their mouths that were uncommon, such as having them refer to their principle enemy fighter adversary as the 'Bf 109.'
MIA Missing In Action
M/T maritime transport or motor transport
MTO Mediterranean Theater of Operations
M/Y marshalling yard
NATAF North African Tactical Air Force
OSS Office of Strategic Services – forerunner of the CIA
PBY American Navy amphibian aircraft
pool central location for specific interests, as in transportation pool
POW Prisoner of War
PT-17 Primary Trainer – a biplane used for student pilot instruction
RAF Royal Air Force
recon /recce/recco reconnaissance
RR railroad
R & R rest and recreation
SAAF South African Air Forces
scramble when a fighter aircraft and its pilot on a high state of readiness are ordered to get airborne quickly or in an emergency
SM 75, SM 79 and SM 82 Savoia-Marchetti Italian multi-engine aircraft
S/L Squadron Leader, RAF rank
S/Sgt. Staff Sergeant
Sortie a flight by a single aircraft
sweep a fighter aircraft mission flown at low-level over a wide area with intent to lure enemy aircraft into the air and to destroy any enemy aircraft encountered
U-Boat German submarine
U/S unserviceable
USAAF United States Army Air Forces
USO United Services Organization – a civilian organization offering entertainment and relaxation facilities for military personnel
V-mail wartime mail system called Victory Mail
WAAC Women's Auxiliary Air Force
Walrus a British amphibian aircraft used in air/sea rescue
Wing RAF equivalent of a USAAF Group
XII ASC Twelfth Air Support Command
XV FC Fifteenth Fighter Command

Aerial victory claims are noted in this format: destroyed, probably destroyed, damaged: For example, 6-1-2

SPAIN
SARDINIA
SICILY
GIBRALTAR
ALGIERS
BONE
CONSTANTINE
PANTELLERIA
MALTA
ORAN
BISKRA
CASABLANCA
ALGERIA
MOROCCO
TUNISIA
300 MILES

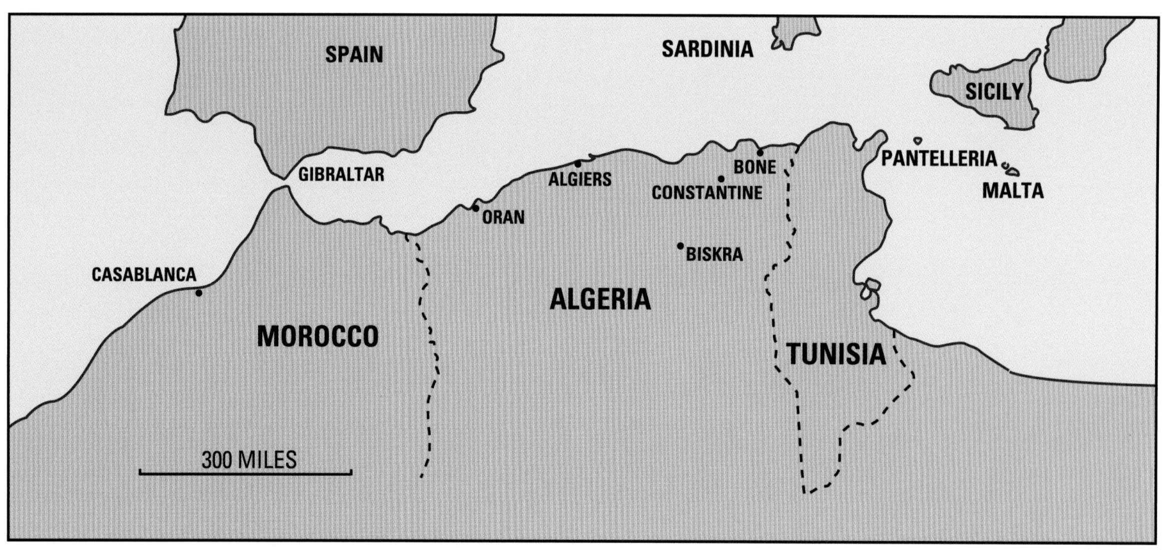

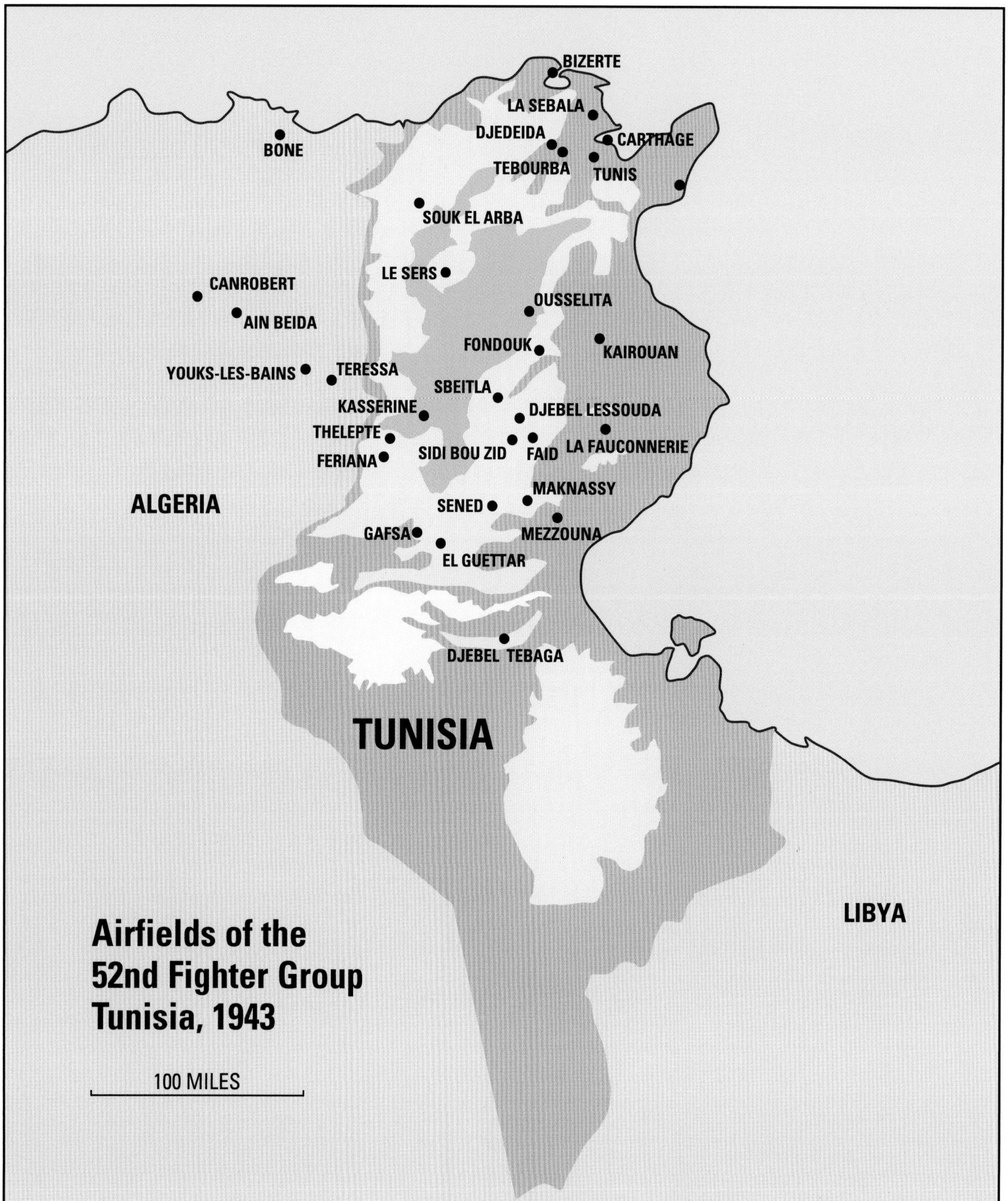

BIZERTE
LA SEBALA
DJEDEIDA
CARTHAGE
BONE
TEBOURBA
TUNIS
SOUK EL ARBA
LE SERS
CANROBERT
OUSSELITA
AIN BEIDA
FONDOUK
KAIROUAN
YOUKS-LES-BAINS
TERESSA
SBEITLA
KASSERINE
DJEBEL LESSOUDA
THELEPTE
FERIANA
SIDI BOU ZID
FAID
LA FAUCONNERIE
MAKNASSY
ALGERIA
SENED
GAFSA
MEZZOUNA
EL GUETTAR
DJEBEL TEBAGA
TUNISIA
LIBYA
Airfields of the
52nd Fighter Group
Tunisia, 1943
100 MILES

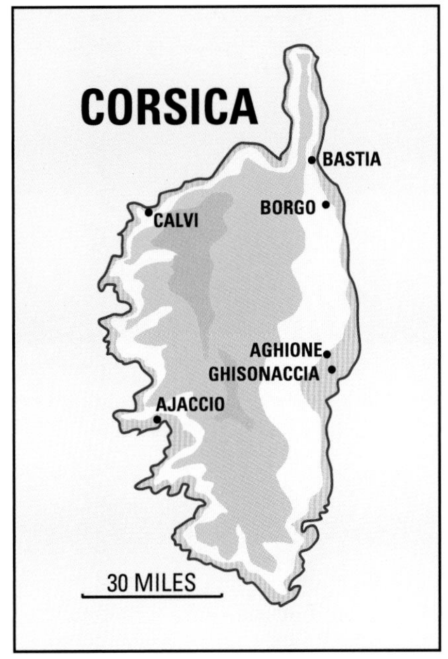

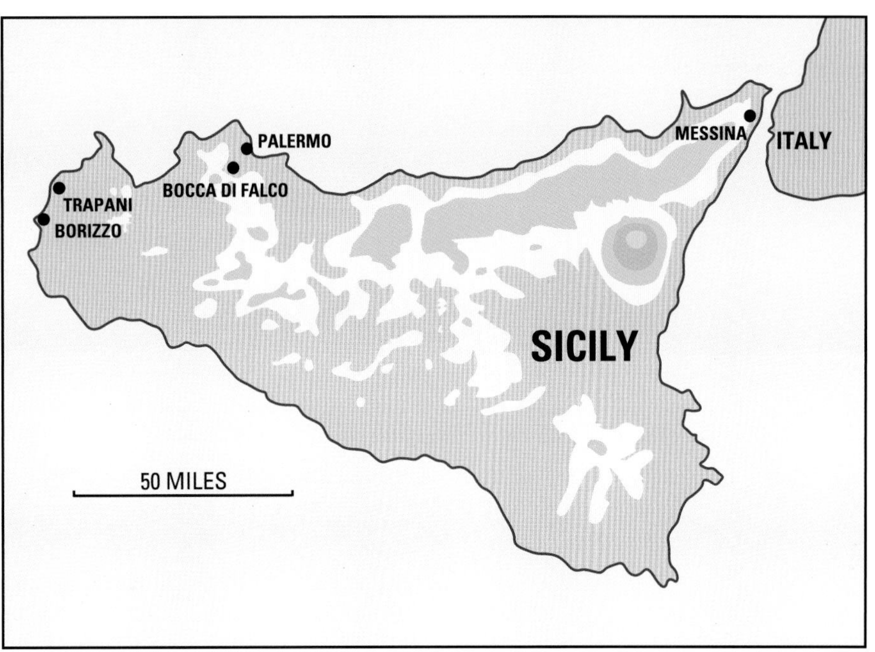

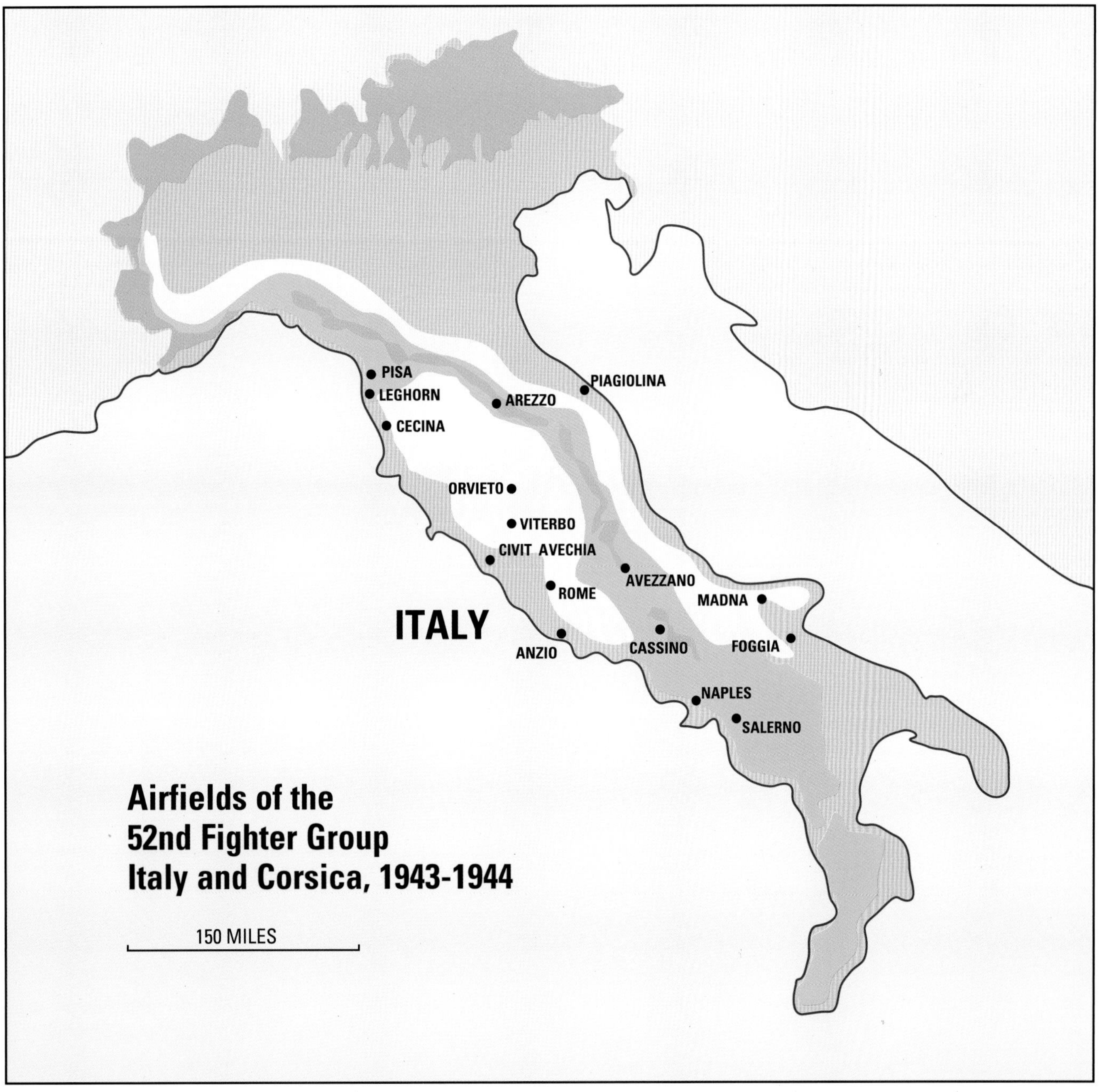

CORSICA
BASTIA
CALVI
BORGO
AGHIONE
GHISONACCIA
AJACCIO
30 MILES

PALERMO
MESSINA
ITALY
TRAPANI
BOCCA DI FALCO
BORIZZO
SICILY
50 MILES

PISA
LEGHORN
CECINA
AREZZO
PIAGIOLINA
ORVIETO
VITERBO
CIVIT AVECHIA
AVEZZANO
ROME
MADNA
ITALY
ANZIO
CASSINO
FOGGIA
NAPLES
SALERNO
150 MILES

Airfields of the 52nd Fighter Group Italy and Corsica, 1943-1944

FOREWORD

by
Robert C. Curtis

former Commanding Officer, 2nd Fighter Squadron, 52nd Fighter Group

Major Robert C. Curtis, Commanding Officer, 2nd Fighter Squadron. This photograph was taken after the then Captain Curtis had scored his twelfth aerial victory. (Credit: Bob Curtis)

My service with the 52nd Fighter Group began in May 1943 when I joined the 2nd Fighter Squadron as a 1st Lieutenant with about 1,100 hours of flying time, most of it in the AT 6 as an instructor in Advanced Flying Training, from August 1941 to January 1943. Then I transferred to fighter training in P 39s at Hamilton Field, California. In April, after 70 hours in the P-39, I was sent to North Africa. At that time I was only a 1st Lieutenant because I had misbehaved twice during my instructing days. First, when buzzing a swamp in Florida my plane's wing hit the limb of a tree and second, I was caught doing a slow roll off the deck at an auxilliary field shortly after such maneuvers had been forbidden.

After about a year flying Spitfires, I became Squadron Commander when we started flying P-51s in May 1944. The Squadron did well and I was promoted to Capt. in June and then to Major in August. I had been a 1st Lieutenant for two years, but was a Capt. for only two months!

I am grateful to Tom Ivie and Paul Ludwig for their condensation of all the material on the World War Two activities of the 52nd Fighter Group into a readable book. It will be enjoyed by all those who were there, as well as by their relatives and friends, and the fans of World War Two fighter pilots. In this regard I want to pay special tribute to Frank Olynyk whose masterful work in digging out the claims and combat reports of these pilots has provided an essential foundation for any history of the air war.

The 52nd was one of two American fighter groups to give up their P-39 Bell Airacobras in the Summer of 1942 and re-equip with the British fighter, the Supermarine Spitfire, for the invasion of North Africa. The other was the 31st Fighter Group. This situation led to rivalry between the two groups, and the pilots of the 52nd were especially upset when, at the end of the North African Campaign, the 52nd was taken out of the Air Support Command and put into the Coastal Command. This meant many boring harbor and convoy patrols during which enemy aircraft were seldom seen. Then, in December 1943, the Group's Spitfires had bomb racks installed so this legendary fighter plane could be used as a dive-bomber, carrying a puny 250 lb. bomb under each wing. This was insult added to injury. But we carried on and did the best we could, relieved that at least the boring patrols became much less frequent.

The Group gave up its Spitfires in the spring of 1944, acquired P-51 Mustangs, transferred from the 12th to the 15th Air Force and started flying escort missions for B-17s and B-24s that were attacking targets in southern and eastern Europe. Although the Group's pilots got their P-51s a month after the pilots of the 31st Fighter Group got theirs, and thus missed out on many encounters with enemy fighters, they felt that, at last, they were truly fighter pilots. They were disappointed again, however, when, after the Invasion of Europe, many of the enemy fighters were transferred north into Eighth Air Force territory, and air combat became much less frequent.

Those pilots who became aces enjoyed the approval and the awards that were showered upon them, but equally prominent in the Groups' story are the many young men killed in accidents or in action, as well as those who became POWs after bailing out or crash-landing in enemy territory. In this regard, the pilots greatly appreciated the services of the personnel of the RAF Air-Sea Rescue squadrons whose Supermarine Walruses rescued many, including me, saving them from death or capture. Finally, and most importantly, the pilots' ability to do their job was completely dependent on the capable and dedicated performance of the support personnel, who greatly outnumbered them, and often worked under deplorable conditions. Together we made our contribution to the winning of the war in Europe.

RC Curtis

Chapter One

"Whiskey, wives, kids and dogs"

Activation and Training

January 1941–June 1942

PT-17s of the 5th Pursuit Squadron at Selfridge Field, Michigan. (Credit: Thomas Thacker)

With war clouds shadowing the world in 1940, it was apparent that America had to prepare for war, and included in the National Defense Act of that year was a requirement for the General Headquarters Air Force to form three new pursuit groups. One of the newly activated units was the 52nd Pursuit Group. The 52nd Pursuit Group – known after May 1942 as the 52nd Fighter Group – was formed on 15 January 1941 at Selfridge Field, Michigan, "*home of the fighters*." To expedite its activation, the 1st Pursuit Group, and 31st Pursuit Group, based at Selfridge, provided the initial complement of personnel for the 52nd. As its ranks grew, Major Earl W. Barnes was named as the 52nd Pursuit Group's first Commanding Officer and it was now composed of a Headquarters Squadron and three fighter squadrons. Its fighter squadrons, the 2nd, 4th and 5th Squadrons, were placed under the command of First Lieutenants Don L. Wilhelm, Jr., J. Francis Taylor, and T. Alan Barnett, respectively.

Even though the 52nd Pursuit Group now had organized into its assigned structure, it was not a stable unit because its headcount fluctuated as its personnel were continuously being transferred out to provide cadres for newly activated units. Nevertheless, the Group began its training schedule on 21 April 1941 when five officers and 22 enlisted men traveled to Camp Skeel near Oscoda, Michigan for gunnery training. After returning to Selfridge on 1 May, Major Robert L. Schoenlein replaced Major Barnes as Group Commanding Officer. During May, the Group's personnel strength became a little more stable and it commenced training exercises

By June the influx of personnel had swollen to the point that Selfridge was so overcrowded that the 5th Squadron was sent to Camp Grayling, Michigan and the 2nd Squadron to Camp Skeel, Michigan for 30 days. The 4th Squadron stayed at Selfridge. Tom Thacker commented on the 5th PS's temporary assignment:

> *"So away we went, in the only reasonable way to enact field problems: completely equipped with our automobiles, whiskey, wives, kids, and dogs. Airplanes were scarce. Three primary trainers were flown from morning until noon under the maintenance supervision of Sergeants Ford Swiney and Peter B. Fralin. From noon on, everybody settled down to beer drinking and poker playing for the rest of the day." The pilots flew three PT-17s putting on an air show and sometimes buzzing the beaches and fishing boats. From early morning until noon, the planes were flown flat out. Afternoons were for maintenance."*

While at Camp Grayling the exuberance of some of the young pilots resulted in some embarrassing incidents. In one case, a pilot buzzed a flock of turkeys causing a stampede of terrified birds that resulted in the death of a number of a local farmer's flock. The pilots pooled money to pay for the dead turkeys. Another buzzing incident resulted in an irate resident putting a .22 caliber bullet through the PT-17 trainer flown by Lt. Dick Long.

The 5th Squadron's adventures at Camp Grayling came to a close on 7 August when it was ordered back to Selfridge. What they found was less than inspiring. Tom Thacker noted:

> *"More men were assigned, but so many were away at schools that numbers on duty didn't increase very much. Some of the pilots were put on detached service, ferrying planes here and there or performing other duties. We had only a handful of trainers to fly, plus a very limited selection of beaten-up P-35s, P-36s, P-39s and P-40s. All of the newer fighter aircraft had been taken by the 31st Group on maneuvers in Louisiana."*

This "*bastard stepchild*" treatment was beginning to irritate the men of the 52nd and was the beginning of a rivalry with the 31st FG that continued throughout the war. To add insult to injury it was decided that all unwanted P-35s and P-36s – no longer front line types and not in flying condition - remaining at Selfridge Field would be turned over to the 52nd. A disgusted Tom Thacker noted in his diary:

> *"We were to collect them, sign for them, and repair them, at which time they would be ferried to other groups at various stations. They eventually turned up in such interesting places as the tall grass behind the Air Corps' supply warehouse, or leaning against the gate of the salvage yard. Wings were off, engines removed, tires blown, instruments missing."*

Mechanics worked to get the aircraft flyable for other groups and wondered how many ever reached their destinations.

On 1 October 1941 seventy-five new pilots, fresh out of training, began to report in to the 52nd and this only increased the frustrations of the Group CO, Lt. Col. Schoenlein, who commented: "*We are now ready for any emergency. Except, of course, that we didn't have any airplanes.*"

That situation was somewhat alleviated later in the month when the 52nd began receiving some early versions of P-39 and P-40 fighters. Soon the skies around the base were filled with these aircraft and of course the fledgling fighter pilots exhibited their skills by performing a few prohibited maneuvers. Lt. Ralph E. "*Gene*" Keyes, who was temporarily in charge of the 2nd FS training noted: "*These early models were not as good as the P-39D but a seven-day week of training started and the pilots flew from dawn until 10 or 11 at night.*"

Tom Thacker added: "*The mark of a daring pilot was to fly under the Blue Water Bridge at Port Huron and not get reported. A few even dared the Ambassador Bridge*" – which connected America with Canada over the Detroit River.

During late 1941, Lt. R.E. Keyes and 19 other pilots were sent to Buffalo, New York to ferry P-39s to the 31st FG at Paine Field in Everett, Washington. This mission turned quite ugly and crashes along the way cost the lives of 2nd Lt. Jack S. Slade, 2nd Lt. Richard N. Long and Lt. William Burrell, and Lt. John H. Pease parachuted to safety, when he ran into dense fog over mountains. In spite of this mission's cost, it was worthwhile training, because by the time Lt. Keyes and other survivors returned to Selfridge, Japan had attacked Pearl Harbor and America was now at war. Pilots would now be required to learn to operate in all kinds of weather!

Now that the nation was at war, the War and Navy Departments embarked on a emergency program to rapidly increase the size and strength of America's armed forces, produce the weapons of war, and build new bases. Incensed and patriotic men began to enlist and the revived draft law increased the flow of young Americans into the military service. They came from all walks of life and upon entry into the Service found that their new world would be much different than what they had experienced previously. For these initial wartime inductees, life would be somewhat chaotic. There were not enough training bases available and hotels had to be requisitioned by the

The convoy of 5th Squadron personnel enroute from Selfridge Field to Long Island, New York, December 1941. (Credit: Everett Jenkins)

Government to house the millions going into uniform, until new bases and new barracks were constructed. Men trained to be pilots knew they would be flying, and generally they had a relatively standard set of base assignments, while men destined to be ground crew were forced into jobs they often knew nothing about and were subject to a variety of strange and rapid base transfers. This situation applied to quite a few of the 52nd Fighter Group's newly assigned personnel.

Emil Torvinen was inducted into the Army in late 1941 in Green Bay, Wisconsin, and from there he went to Camp Grant in Rockford, Illinois, and on to Keesler Field in Biloxi, Mississippi where he was asked what he wanted to be. He chose Mechanics' School and was sent to Newark, New Jersey to the Casey Jones School of Aeronautics in January, 1942 and graduated on 23 May as an aircraft mechanic. Initially ordered into the 2nd PS when it was based temporarily at Wilmington, North Carolina, he worked on P-39s until 19 June when he and others left for Grenier Field.

A somewhat more typical example of how a new recruit's assignment request was handled happened to Carlton H. Hogue. He was asked upon enlistment what his civilian occupation was and Hogue stated *"photographer's assistant."* The Placement Officer responded: *"What do you want to be in the Army, a truck driver or a cook?"* Carl became a dispatcher in the 2nd FS.

When the news of Japan's attack on Pearl Harbor reached the 52nd Fighter Group, a flurry of activity began. Men were issued weapons, aircraft were armed and guards posted. As the excitement rose orders to the men started becoming a little contradictory. First came an order to put all aircraft in the hangar, then later in the day it was changed to disperse all aircraft and post guards. Following these actions everything at Selfridge Field was blacked out. Streetlights were turned off, and windows were painted black. Next came an order to paint the shiny, aluminum aircraft olive drab.

As war hysteria gripped America, authorities believed America's coastline cities were vulnerable to attacks and aerial patrols of the coastlines were begun. The 52nd's first wartime assignment was to play a role in guarding the eastern coastline of the United States. The Group's orders arrived on 16 December sending the 5th Squadron to Floyd Bennett Field, New York, and the 2nd Squadron to Langley Field, Virginia.

Upon his arrival at Floyd Bennett Field Lt. Ward W. Harker, 5th PS Commanding Officer, reported in and stated: *"The squadron has arrived as ordered"*; he was surprised by the response: *"There must be some mistake. We are not expecting you."*

After this bad beginning an arrangement was worked out. The Squadron would bivouac at Fort Tilden and leave its aircraft at Floyd Bennett.

Shortly after, Lt. Norman McDonald graduated from flight school, he was sent to Floyd Bennett Field expecting that, since it was a Navy base, he would be put on a ship to go fight the war against Japan. Instead, he was assigned to the 5th FS that was equipped with three unarmed PT-17 trainers and participated in the defense of New York City. This somewhat dubious mission was carried out during daylight hours primarily to reassure the population that the skies were being patrolled in search of the enemy.

Just after New Year's Day 1942, the 5th Squadron was told that it would receive eight P-43s and the Lancers were waiting for pick-up at the Republic factory. The joy of the Squadron finally receiving new fighter aircraft, however, was short-lived. Concerns began after a hair-raising incident when a P-43 went into an inverted spin from which the pilot somehow managed to correct and land safely Such concerns were compounded by the continuous problem of this machine's tendency to lose lift during landing and set down hard. Needless to say, the Squadron was happy to return them to the factory.

The 5th Fighter Squadron was relieved of its defense of New York duties in mid-January and returned to Selfridge Field by train, arriving on 15 January 1942. The 52nd PG, neither fully trained or staffed, was now to begin a new phase of training that would keep it on the move for some time. During the next few months, the 52nd PG would undergo field training preparatory to overseas movement, requiring a quick series of base transfers and field maneuvers while being organized into a fighting unit.

In February 1942, the Group received additional personnel and some hand-me- down P-39s from the 31st PG. The 52nd was now up to strength and training in the Airacobras began in earnest. As the training progressed, the quirky P-39 began to take a toll of pilots. On 8 February, Lt. Bert S. Sanborn of the 2nd Squadron suffered engine failure during his landing approach and incurred severe burns and injuries after crash landing into some trees. Several days later Lt. John S. White died when his Cobra crashed during a training flight.

While the pilots continued flight training movement orders arrived and on 18 February 1942 the ground echelon of the 52nd PG departed by railroad to Florence, South Carolina while the air echelon waited at Selfridge Field for decent flying weather. A general snowfall was covering the eastern portion of the United States as far south as the Carolinas. In spite of the foul weather and its pilots' lack of instrument training, the 52nd PG pilots were ordered to begin their flight to Florence.

Lt. George Deaton, 5th Squadron Operations Officer, led the formation in its ill-fated cross-

Lt. Robert Rivers, 4th Pursuit Squadron, "cranking the propeller" of his P-39D at Selfridge Field, Michigan, January 1942. (Credit: Robert Rivers)

country flight. Snow and inadequate preparations soon took its toll after the P-39s took off on 19 February. Lt. Norman McDonald, for example, had only three hours of flight time in P-39s when he took off on this flight. McDonald recalled that:

"I had no map – there were not enough maps for everyone. Getting to the destination in poor visibility required staying close to the leader. He was under considerable pressure to deliver the planes. Because of bad weather Deaton took us to Cincinnati and we landed in the snow. After a few hours Deaton decided that we should try again. Shortly after takeoff we ran into a real blizzard."

A few men, including McDonald, dropped out of formation and returned to Cincinnati. Making things worse was the loss of Lt. Edward Wilczewski, who crashed into a hillside. A new leader was designated at Cincinnati. After waiting for good weather the pilots took off for Louisville, a refueling stop, but the new leader took the flight off course and McDonald commented

"...with no radio to communicate with this wild leader, I became very apprehensive about our fate. Afterward we found out that the new leader wanted to buzz his home town, but he got lost and couldn't find it. Everyone was running low on fuel. One pilot chose to bail out rather than crashland. Two pilots, including McDonald, made emergency landings at a field near Fort Blackmore, Virginia, about 30 miles north-west of Bristol, Tennessee, while they still had enough fuel. McDonald needed to go overland on foot to relay his situation to Deaton, but there were no paved roads in the area so McDonald rode a mule along a railroad line to the nearest station where there was a telegraph operator who sent our message to Charlotte, NC. He was told to stay with the aircraft. Two weeks later, trailer trucks arrived to take the aircraft to Florence. McDonald arrived at Florence two weeks after the flight had been scheduled to arrive, and he was told that none of the aircraft got to Florence the day they were due to arrive. Once the aircraft were there the pilots began gunnery practice at Myrtle Beach."

The last day of February 1942 saw a change of command when Colonel Dixon Allison replaced Schoenlein as the Group Commanding Officer. The base at Florence was something of a nightmare as Tom Thacker recalled: *"The airfield had new concrete runways, but was otherwise a sea of drifting sand."*

The sand was murder to aircraft engines and was possibly the cause of some of the accidents that occurred during the Group's two-month stay. One pilot, Lt. Robert Kasper, was killed in flight training at Florence and two enlisted men died in other accidents.

On 27 April 1942, the 2nd Squadron left Florence and moved to the airfield at Wrightsville Beach, near Wilmington, North Carolina. The 4th and 5th Squadrons arrived at Wrightsville a few days later and the entire Group assembled, and training became a little more serious. Early morning calisthenics were added to the training schedule and the men began receiving C and D combat rations for lunch. In the air, the pilots began flying anti-submarine patrols in addition to the scheduled training flights. During the last part of May and early June, the squadrons moved to Grenier Field, near Manchester, New Hampshire for additional training and was finally declared as combat ready.

The stay at Grenier Field was short. It was expected that the 52nd FG would fly its P-39s over the Atlantic with refueling stops in Newfoundland and Northern Ireland. Precedent for mass flights of fighters across the Atlantic Ocean had been set in July 1942 when P-38s flew in formation with B-17s, which acted as navigational aircraft, to England. The training program showed that what had worked for the twin engine Lightnings was not going to be true for the P-39. The test flights quickly demonstrated that the Airacobra, already an unstable aircraft, became a monster when mated with 175-gallon ferry tanks full of fuel. Too much weight, the lack of baffles and the sloshing of fuel in the ferry tank resulted in more instability. Lt. Miles R. Lynn, Jr., 2nd FS, recalled:

"...as the gas in the huge belly tanks was consumed, the remaining gas would swish and swirl about and the plane would slop and slide all over the sky. In the clouds, with a tank half full, the needle, ball and airspeed would have been hysterical – not to mention the airplane and the pilot."

Two P-39s from the 52nd FG crashed killing the pilots - one *"from the landing pattern and the other after going into a spin while on instruments in the clouds."*

Shortly afterwards the plan to ferry P-39s to England was canceled.

The advance echelon of the 4th Fighter Squadron personnel being briefed at Grenier Field, near Manchester, New Hampshire, prior to departure for England, July 1942. (Credit: Everett Jenkins)

Pilots of the 4th Pursuit Squadron at Florence, South Carolina, February 1942. Left to right are Lieutenants R. E. Dawson, Don Jander, Houston, Joe Kelliher, and Sutton. (Credit: Robert Rivers)

P-39s of the 52nd Fighter Group on the flight line at Florence, South Carolina, February 1942. (Credit: Thomas Thacker)

Chapter Two

"Flying down a village street"

Northern Ireland and England

June–October 1942

4th Fighter Squadron pilots relaxing at Goxhill, October 1942. Left to right: First four unknown, Lts. Houston, Vogtle, unknown, Blais, Feld and Rivers. (Credit: Robert Rivers)

The advance echelon consisting of 90 flying officers and 200 enlisted men departed Grenier Field for Fort Dix, New Jersey on 24 June and after a short stay moved to the Brooklyn Port of Embarcation on 30 June. The men sailed the following morning on the British troop ship *Duchess of Bedford* and arrived at Liverpool, England on 12 July where they were sent onward to Eglinton, Northern Ireland two days later.

On 19 July the remainder of the 52nd FG left Grenier Field for Fort Dix and upon arrival they were promptly ferried to Brooklyn Navy Yard and boarded the *Monterey* at midnight. The ship sailed on 6 August and after a stop at Halifax, Nova Scotia where it joined a convoy, headed for Glasgow, Scotland and arrived on the 18th. The following morning the men were transported to Belfast where they were trucked to Eglinton, seven miles from Londonderry.

Now assigned to the fledgling Eighth Air Force, the 52nd Fighter Group began its operational training under the watchful guidance of RAF Wing Commander Jamie Rankin, a Battle of Britain ace. Here the pilots first flew the Miles Magister and then the Supermarine Spitfire.

Detailed flight records were not kept while the Group was in Northern Ireland and England, but it is believed that the 2nd Fighter Squadron flew its first combat mission, a convoy patrol while under the supervision of a Canadian Spitfire squadron, in August 1942. The 4th Fighter Squadron recorded its first combat mission, a convoy patrol, on 19 August, and the 5th recorded its first combat missions during late August. A total of six combat missions (90 sorties) were flown from Northern Ireland.

A Miles Magister I, originally built in 1937 as G-AFBS then BB 661 with the RAF. It was on this type of aircraft on which pilots of the 52nd Fighter Group first trained ahead of their conversion to the Spitfire in the summer of 1942. (Credit: Barry Ketley)

The 52nd FG missed the 'big show' over Dieppe, France on 19 August, a massive but poorly planned effort to test German defenses and to despatch a landing force of mainly Canadian troops. Bad weather prevented the unit from proceeding from Northern Ireland to Biggin Hill. Adding to the disappointment, the Group's rival unit, the 31st FG, did participate in the big air battle over the landing beaches and the English Channel and scored its first victories of the war.

In early September, the 2nd FS moved to Biggin Hill and participated in its first fighter sweep to France on 7 September. The next element to move to England was the 4th FS and it also participated in fighter sweeps over France. By

Lt. Robert Rivers, 4th Fighter Squadron (left), and his crew chief, Sgt. Murray Parker, pose with their Spitfire at Goxhill, England, in October 1942. Note the squadron codes, WD, have not yet been painted on the aircraft. (Credit: Robert Rivers)

13 September 1942, all three squadrons were in England and were based together at the Goxhill RAF Station.

Bert Sanborn commented on his days at Biggin Hill and Goxhill:

> "Biggin Hill was a wonderful large grass air field. We made the usual line-abreast take-offs. The field did have one problem. It was high enough in the middle to screen the other end. One result was a Polish squadron asking for clearance just as a Canadian squadron started to roll from the opposite end. The tower confirmed 'you are clear to take off' and before he could complete the sentence with 'after the other squadron is clear' all the Poles started to roll. Two squadrons coming over that rise head-on made things a bit wild for a short time."

Life as a fighter pilot in England had its luxuries: "We were assigned a batman who woke you up with a cup of hot tea, opened the shades and brought in your shaving water. Most of the flying was with British pilots leading. Flying down a village street was great sport. We had no real combat here and no chance to get in any gunnery. At Goxhill I met a wonderful family who had an estate nearby which resulted in many pleasant afternoons and evenings."

As the 52nd FG continued its operational training in England, other greater events were beginning to unfold. The plan to invade North Africa was quickly taking shape and when the newly activated 12th Air Force arrived in England on 12 September 1942 things began to happen. In order to build its strike force for Operation Torch, the Twelfth Air Force drew heavily from Eighth Air Force units in England. In a four week period starting in mid-September and continuing until mid October, the Twelfth AF acquired the 97th and 301st Heavy Bomb Groups, the 1st, 14th, and 82nd Fighter Groups equipped with P-38s, the 31st and 52nd Fighter Groups equipped with Spitifires, the 81st Fighter Group equipped with P-39s, the 3rd Photo Group equipped with F-4 Lightnings and B-17s, the 15th Light Bomb Group equipped with A-20s and the 60th, 62nd and 64th Troop Carrier Groups equipped with C-47s. Additionally the 350th Fighter Group, equipped with P-39s, was activated in England and assigned to the Twelfth AF.

This massive reorganization brought about some personnel changes in the 52nd FG. Pilots were transferred out and new ones came in, including 22 from the famous Eagle Squadrons replacing 22 going to the newly activated 350th FG. Following these changes were notifications of a move. Lt. Norman McDonald, 2nd FS, recorded that in mid-October, "*...we were informed, in glowing terms, of a lovely, leisurely, luxury ocean cruise to a surprise destination to which we were all invited. The timing of this cruise seemed appropriate.*"

The destination – North Africa – was not mentioned. Sgt. Carl Hogue said rumors flew, and "*...an unknown assignment emanated from the latrine which was the source of all reliable classified information.*"

The Group's destination became a little less uncertain when an order came in late October to send more than 12 pilots to Gibraltar to test fly newly uncrated and reassembled Spitfires and Hurricanes. The small group, led by Major Marvin McNickle of the 31st FG, headed by ship to the island stronghold on 20 October. Upon their arrival they found a huge stash of about 200 Spitfires being prepared for the upcoming invasion, and McNickle was told by the local British commander that: "*You are now in charge of the aerial defense of Gibraltar.*"

The advance party was followed two days later when 75 officers of the 2nd and 4th Fighter Squadrons were sent to Padgate, England along with pilots from the 31st FG and nine RAF squadrons in preparation for a voyage to Gibraltar. The pilots of the 2nd and 4th FSs, along with Capt. George Deaton, Commanding Officer of the 5th FS sailed on 1 November 1942 aboard the *Leinster*. Two days prior to arrival in Gibraltar, the unit received the information that they would be supporting the invasion of North Africa.

WO
W

Chapter Three

"A flip of the coin"

The Invasion of North Africa

November 1942–February 1943

The Anglo-American invasion of North Africa began on 8 November with forces landing at Algiers, Casablanca and Oran. Facing the invading forces were units of the Vichy French forces, and it was hoped that they would not put up a fight. As it transpired, the French resistance at Algiers was negligible, but at Casablanca and Oran a fierce resistance was encountered. This situation was to impact the 52nd FG's entry into the invasion plans. According to Tom Thacker: *"Only a few of the American Spitfires flew that day. The 31st FG was scheduled for Algiers, the 52nd for Oran. The need for Algiers did not develop, but crowded conditions at Gibraltar did not afford much space for changes in plans. So the 31st proceeded to Oran instead. There they encountered some resistance, losing one pilot, but shooting down three French Dewoitine (D-520) fighters. None of our planes actually took off until 9 November when several flights headed for La Senia, the airfield outside Oran."*

On 9 November the 4th FS covered the landing beaches at Oran and then landed at LaSenia. The 2nd FS, led by Lt. Colonel Graham "*Windy*" West, Group Executive Officer, escorted the B-17 carrying the commanding general of the Twelfth Air Force, Major General James Doolittle, to La Senia. Because of severe weather conditions en route, many of the 2nd's Spitfires had to put down at the Tafaraoui airfield. To get their aircraft refueled for the trip to La Senia, the pilots had to use captured French stocks and fill the tanks from five-gallon flimsies ('*jerry cans*'). During the next four days the pilots flew armed recce missions in search of hostile French artillery, and armored car columns, and harbor patrols.

On 10 November, the weather was still somewhat dubious for flying from Gibraltar to North Africa and some of the 4th Squadron's pilots ran into trouble during their flight. Lts. Lee Trowbridge, Edwin Smithers, and Edward Scott drifted off course and were forced down in Spanish Morocco and interned. Capt. "*Beebe*" Booth and Lt. Wallace MacGregor landed in French Morocco. Booth was picked up by Arabs who returned him to his squadron using a donkey for transportation. The Commanding Officer of the 5th FS, Capt. George Deaton, was far more successful in battling the weather and led eleven other Spitfires from Gibraltar to Tafaraoui.

Spitfires of the 52nd Fighter Group, probably belonging to the 2nd Fighter Squadron, on the flight line at La Senia, Algeria. Note the crudely painted American star on the fuselage and lack of code letters. (Credit: Charles G. Jones)

Finally on 11 November, the troop ships carrying some of the Group's ground personnel were able to land at Oran and after a 15 mile march, they entered their new base at La Senia. Others disembarked from ships on 12 November and made their way to Le Senia. On 13 November, negotiations at the highest level between American and French officials reached an agreement by which Vichy forces in Morrocco and Algeria would cease resistance to the invasion and ally themselves with British and American forces. By the 14 November most of the air echelon of the three squadrons had now arrived at Le Senia and began flying patrols and training missions from this airfield.

Not every pilot in the 5th FS flew immediately to North Africa. Lt. Jenkins recalled: *"My log shows that on Nov. 25 we ferried planes to Tafaraoui from Gibraltar."*

Although the 52nd FG was tasked with defense of Gibraltar, Jenkins remembered: *"In all that time on the 'Rock' I was involved in one 45-minute scramble and 2 ten-minute test flights."*

La Senia had been known unofficially as the *'African West Point of the Air'* and its imposingly

Lt. Colonel Graham "Windy" West, one of the 52nd Fighter Group's most trusted leaders. (Credit: USAAF)

A Spitfire Mark Vc of the 5th Fighter Squadron also displaying crude American insignia painted over an RAF roundel, and the letter 'A'. (Credit: Al Gelo)

The barracks at La Senia – "the West Point of Africa" – where the men of the 52nd Fighter Group were housed temporarily in 1942. This photograph was taken 22 December 1942 – it was a warm day! (Credit: Richard Potter)

large and permanent buildings offered what turned out to be the last modern facilities housing the 52nd FG. By the time it had been secured by Allied troops, however, the base had been sabotaged by the retreating French. Tom Thacker reported: *"...the ground was littered with ammunition, guns, bayonets, pistols, knives and swords and there were cars and trucks that had been left stranded by the Vichy French when they left in a hurry."*

The men of the 52nd FG also found and had to dispose of numerous dead bodies.

With groundcrew available, aircraft were fixed and fueled and when ships reached harbor, men off-loaded trucks and equipment belonging to the 52nd FG. There were no air raids because the Germans and Italians were based far to the east of Oran. Pilots from the 2nd and 5th Squadrons flew to Maison Blanche airfield near Algiers, Algeria and ground crews were sent by air to support pilots who flew area defense missions around Algiers. Lt. John Aitken, Jr., 2nd FS, was up on patrol flying wing on Capt. G.V. Williams through a valley at low altitude when he hit a cable. Aitken thought *"the plane was going to explode"* and the Spitfire *"bucked and jerked"* and the airspeed varied between 160-120 mph and Aitken did not know why. The cable had wrapped around his aircraft and knocked out his radio and Williams came up alongside to inspect. Aitken returned to base, landed and the cable dragged across *"telephone lines and hit tents, jeeps and other vehicles in the ground crew's bivouac,"* producing sparks. His Spitfire had 300 yards of cable *"...lodged in the airscoop."*

Lt. Gen. Dwight D. Eisenhower, Commanding General of Allied Forces, ordered that Bone harbor, in extreme north-east Algeria not only be defended, but also that fighter aircraft fly to the airfield there and be employed in air strikes against the Axis in nearby Tunisia. Ground personnel of the 52nd FG had to be moved from La Senia to Bone, via Algiers and the first move took them from Tafaraoui by truck to La Senia where awaiting C-47s prepared to fly them out. The day was cold and rainy and the mud was too deep for flight operations and the flight was aborted. On the following day the C-47s were able to operate and the men were transported to Bone.

There was only enough space at Bone airfield to accommodate one of the 52nd FG's squadrons and Tom Thacker said *"a flip of the coin"* had decided whether pilots of the 4th or 2nd Squadrons flew Spitfires to Bone. The 2nd FS won the toss. Lt. Miles Lynn, 2nd FS, recalled that the harbor *"...was under constant attack; bombs all night and strafing all day."*

On 27 November, four 2nd FS Spitfires led by Lt. Colonel Graham W. West, Executive Officer of the 52nd FG, flew into Bone to reinforce 81 Squadron RAF which had arrived in Bone on 15 November. The reason that only four Spitfires arrived was explained by Lt. John F. Pope, 2nd FS, who reported *"...only four planes got to Bone – the rest were stuck in the mud at Algiers."* Larry Burke and Bob Curtis noted in their book, *The American Beagle Squadron*: *"The guys immediately found themselves in a shooting war. The small airfield at Bone had two short runways, only one of them operational. It was 1,800 feet long and bomb craters were all around the area and the rain turned everything but the steel-mat runway into sticky mud. The harbor was only thirty miles from the enemy lines."*

George V. Williams of the 2nd Fighter Squadron, in the cockpit of his Spitfire. (USAAF)

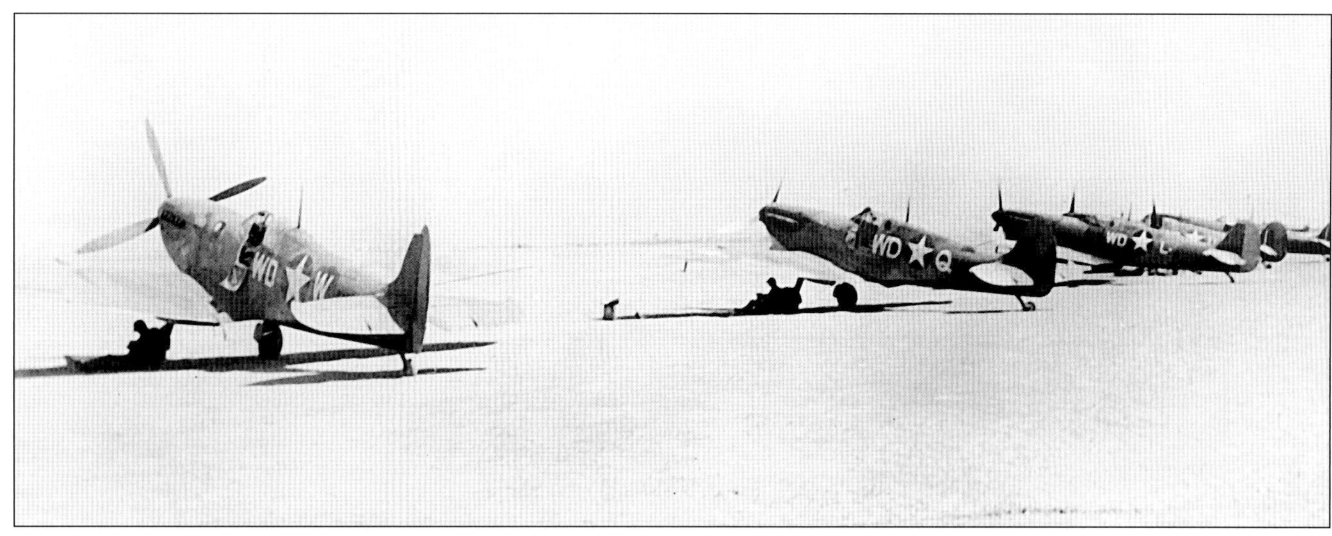

Spitfire MkVs of the 4th Fighter Squadron on the flight line awaiting their next mission during the winter of 1942. (Credit: USAAF)

Lt. Luis Zendegui's Spitfire being run-up by his crew chief. The 2nd Fighter Squadron code "QP" had not been applied at this time. (Credit: Paul Ludwig collection)

This photograph clearly illustrates how the desert heat and sand quickly defaced the paint job on Lt. Short's 2nd Fighter Squadron Spitfire. Posing with the Spitfire are L. Westin and E. Barnes of the 2nd Fighter Squadron. (Credit: Charles Jones and Jeri Sprecher)

The Primary mission at Bone was to protect the harbor and fly top cover for B-17s protected by P-38s. Allied units at Bone were outnumbered in the air, but the worst experiences were on the ground when the *Luftwaffe* bombed, dive-bombed and/or strafed the airfield almost daily and at all hours, (during this period the 5th FS remained at La Senia for the time being and flew harbor patrols, shipping patrols and escorted transports, while the much more combat-ready 4th FS waited at La Senia for its chance to be engaged against the *Luftwaffe* and Italian units.)

When the Spitfires of the 2nd FS arrived at Bone, they became part of 322 Wing RAF, commanded by Wing Commander Petrus H. "*Dutch*" Hugo, Commanding Officer of 81 Squadron, RAF. Immediately after their arrival, the 2nd FS pilots took off on a combat mission and had a *"ring-side seat"* for the air battle that ensued shortly afterwards. During the dogfight, W/C Hugo downed an Me 109 and S/Ldr Ronald *"Razz"* Berry and F/O Rigby shared in another, and provided Lt. Col. Graham West and his pilots a glimpse of things to come.

Seven Ju 88s raided Bone that night, rendering 11 aircraft unserviceable, destroying five Hurricanes and damaging the runway. On the plus side, nine more 2nd FS Spitfires flew in to Bone on the 29 November.

With a full complement of aircraft and pilots now at Bone, the 2nd FS was ready to take on the *Luftwaffe*. The Squadron's first opportunity to test itself in air-to-air combat took place the next day. American-flown Spitfires encountered two Me 109s over Tebourba and Maj. James S. Coward, Commanding Officer of the 2nd FS since 10 November, shot down an Me 109 G east of Bone and Capt. Harold R. *"Ray"* Warren, Jr., accounted for an Me 109 G near Becha, Tunisia. Maj. Coward reported: *"I was on patrol with Breezy flight of 12 ships. We were put onto two Me 109 Gs by ground radio. We spotted the planes at 0900 at about 3,500 feet. We were at about 3,500 feet. We turned into the planes which came toward us, went under us and dove for the deck. My number four man, Lt. Aitken, called the break for my section and I broke to the right and down*

Spitfire Mk Vc, ES353

Captain Jerome S. McCabe,
5th Fighter Squadron,
52nd Fighter Group,
probably La Sebala, Tunisia, June 1943

Captain Jerome McCabe's Spitfire was camouflaged in the standard dark earth and middlestone desert colors and displayed his personal markings of the Cross of Christ with the legend *"Win in this sign"* inscribed along the Cross in Latin under the left windscreen.

Captain James S. McCabe's Spitfire Mk V. The personal emblem on the fuselage is the Cross of Christ lettered in Latin with the inscription "Win in this sign". (Credit: Hahn.)

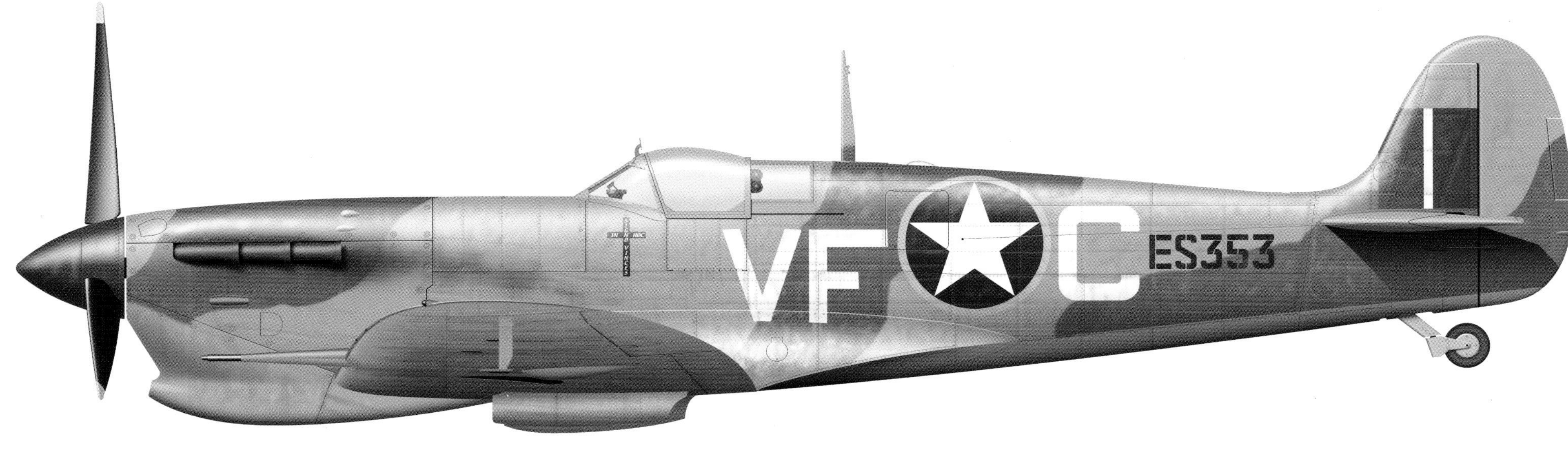

and got onto one of the planes. After two short bursts the Me 109 caught fire and crash-landed in flames."

Lt. Warren then bounced another Me 109 G and reported that he *"...was flying number two man in the right section of a twelve-ship formation. We made a steep turn to the right and I fired my guns every possible chance using all my cannon ammunition. I saw strikes from my .30 caliber machine guns and the e/a finally crashed into a hill bursting into flames."*

The next encounters took place on 1 December when Lt. Colonel West and 1st Lt. McDonald damaged Me 109s two miles east of Djedeida during a sweep of the Tebourba area. On 2 December, it was Capt. Arnold E. Vinson's turn. He downed an Fw 190 west of Mateur, Tunisia, and teamed up with Lt. John F. Pope to damage a Me 109 west of Bizerte. The squadron was flying along the coast west of Mateur when Vinson saw a Me 109. He and Pope chased it through cloud and rain, but lost sight of it. Coming into the clear, he saw another enemy aircraft and at 150 yards he identified it as an Fw 190. He reported: *"I gave the E/A a one second burst. Strikes were seen as the E/A weaved through a valley and I closed to 50 yards striking the engine and it smoked and stopped operating. The prop began windmilling. My next burst hit the wings and the left wing then exploded probably due to HE cannon ammunition and the 190 went into a steep spiral. I stayed with it down to 100 feet from the ground."*

Capt. Vinson continued his scoring spree on 3 December during a sweep of the Tebourba area. Just as the Squadron, along with four RAF Spitfires, were taking off on this mission, three Fw 190s were spotted north of the field. A trio of Spitfires quickly pursued the enemy aircraft and downed one of the Focke-Wulfs. This victory was shared by Capt. Vinson, *"Razz"* Berry and Flt. Sgt. LeHardy, who each received a 1/3rd credit.

Action continued on 4 December when the 2nd FS encountered a formation of Ju 88s escorted by Me 109s during a sweep of the Tebourba area. An air battle ensued and both sides suffered losses in the engagement. Lt. Walter A. Kari was shot down and killed near Bone, the first pilot of the 52nd FG to be killed in aerial combat. The 52nd FG diary recorded the incident: *" Lt. Col. West called for break right and the section broke right but Kari broke left and was last seen being chased by two Me 109s."*

Captain Jerome J. McCabe in the cockpit of his VF – C and a close of his Cross of Christ markings. (Credit: Hahn)

Captain Arnold Vinson who was to become the first American Ace in the North African Theater. (Credit: Robert C. Curtis)

During the melee Lt. Col. West damaged one of the Me 109s five miles north of Tebourba. Lt. Norman McDonald attacked another Me 109 that had slipped in on the tail of Lt. John Pope's Spitfire. McDonald noted in his encounter report: *"I fired a three second burst of cannon and machine guns from point blank range, no more than 50 feet from him. I observed my cannon make a large hole in the center of the fuselage of the Me 109 which flipped on his back just as I passed over him."*

McDonald was credited with a probably destroyed. Lt. Vinson zeroed in on another of the 109Gs and shot it down west of Tebourba. He had scored on three successive days and was the leading scorer in the Group to that point in time.

Lt. Ed Boughton and Capt. J.E. Peck continued the assault on the enemy aircraft and shared in damaging a Ju 88, 25 miles south-east of Tebourba, Tunisia. During this engagement an enemy aircraft moved in and Lt. Fred B. Short's Spitfire received strikes on its engine. Short later reported that: *"I saw strikes on my engine and it started steaming. I did not see the plane that fired on me. I bailed out and landed in a valley, walked east and in about one-half hour was met by a British patrol who was looking for me. I hitch-hiked to Souk-el-Arba where a transport brought me back to Bone."*

Not all the action of 4 December took place in the air. Tom Thacker described the events: *"There was also some drama on the ground. Sgt Myers received the Silver Star sometimes later for taking over an unmanned British ack-ack gun during an attack by enemy dive-bombers. All personnel, whether flying or in support positions, performed most credibly during this difficult period when aerial attacks came almost daily.*

"Some humor came out too, such as the experience of Chaplain Mark Gress while visiting for a couple of days. When the attack began, he headed for the nearest opening in the ground. Finding it safe, but soft, he checked further to discover that it was really a straddle trench normally used for an even more earthy purpose."

There was more action on 6 December when 12 Spitfires met 12 Me 109s over Tebourba and the result was tragic for the 2nd FS which lost two pilots against claims of one enemy aircraft probably destroyed and one damaged. The after action report stated that 1st Lt. Jack M. Shuck, 2nd FS, went missing in action after he *"...was bounced by an Me 109. His plane was last seen dropping toward earth, smoke pouring from the engine."* Lt. Stephen Freel was killed in an unusual manner. His aircraft had been disabled in aerial combat and he flew it over Bone where his friends on the ground saw *"...a large hole about 8 inches in diameter in the fuselage about halfway back."* When Freel put his landing gear and flaps down to land, only one flap came down and the Spitfire *"...did a quick flip to the right and crashed on the field."* His body showed no signs of bullet wounds.

Though of poor quality, this is a rare photograph of Colonel James S. Coward's Spitfire. The code letters are his initials. (Credit: James Empey)

Lt. John Pope and his crew chief, S/Sgt. Lynes, pose with their Spitfire, fall 1942. (Credit: Robert C. Curtis)

On the positive side of this engagement – which took place 10 miles north of Djedeida – Lt. Ed Boughton, 2nd FS, evaded an attack by an Me 109 and recorded: "*I was bounced by 1 Me 109 from above and behind, while in a defensive circle. As he passed me and he climbed for altitude I followed him.*" Boughton blew the enemy aircraft's rudder and elevator off, but had to break off his attack when he was bounced by two Me 109s. Boughton's victim was last seen headed earthward but since he did not see it crash. Boughton was credited with a probable. Norm McDonald damaged another Me 109.

Within the next couple of days the rains moved in and turned most of the airfields into muddy quagmires and for all practical purposes aerial activities were shut down for nearly two weeks. During the lull in the action the 52nd FG labored hard bringing supplies from the ships in the harbor and preparing the aircraft and equipment for future actions which were sure to come.

Finally the skies cleared on 19 December and the 2nd Fighter Squadron returned to the skies. At about 10.40 hrs Capt. J.E. Peck saw three Fw 190s six miles east of Bone flying west. The Fw 190s turned east and Peck flew 30 miles east and saw them again. As Capt. Peck started after them he was spotted. Two Fw 190s hit the deck and Peck chased the one that started to climb. At a range of 600 yards he opened fire with cannon and machine guns and saw strikes on the Focke-Wulf's starboard wing and about three feet of his wing tip blew off. Before he could see if the Fw 190 crashed, Peck was attacked by another enemy aircraft, and he turned for home. He was credited with a damaged enemy aircraft.

Norman McDonald. This photograph was taken after his transfer to the 325th Fighter Group. (Credit: Sanda Ellis)

Chaplain Mark Gress, who mistakenly chose a latrine pit instead of a slit trench to dive into for cover during an air raid on 4 December 1942 (Credit: C. G. Jones.)

By Christmas, according to Tom Thacker, "*...the 52nd was pretty well established, even comfortable, at La Senia. Obviously, it was about time for a move and rumors were flying.*"

During Christmas week there was an alert brought about by the rumor that Spain was about to enter the war on the side of the Axis, but even this did not deter some good old fashioned celebrating around the base.

At Bone on Christmas Day, the 2nd FS celebrated a little differently. 2nd Lt. Jack de Rushe Ludlow and Lt. Luis Zendegui were on harbor patrol when the controller vectored them to enemy aircraft, five miles north of Cap de Fer, and 40 miles west of Bone. Upon arriving at the scene, two Macchi 202 were observed and atacked. Ludlow reported: "*We were both in a dive and I was above him and using deflection and shooting at a range of 100 yards and shot cannon and machine guns until the cannon gave out. From the deflection I was using from the position I was firing from I could not see the e/a or see any strikes. I turned over and looked a second time and I saw the e/a going straight down*" *and when the two descended into cloud, Ludlow peeled off. Later an Arab reported that he saw one aircraft dive into the sea.*"

Lt. Zendegui also accounted for a Macchi C.202 north of Cape de Fer, Algeria.

During the afternoon of 26 December, Spitfires of the 2nd FS and 242 Squadron RAF escorted 'Hurribombers' of 225 Squadron on a strafing mission to Medjez el Bab, and one 242 Squadron aircraft was lost as a result of engine failure. Upon their return to Bone they found the base under attack from eight Fw 190s and eight Me 109s. The Allied flight engaged the enemy aircraft and damaged two of them. Unfortunately during the action, one RAF Spitfire was mistakenly shot down in flames by a 2nd FS pilot, but thankfully its pilot was able to bail out safely.

The 2nd FS was scrambled on 29 December when enemy aircraft were reported heading in the direction of Bone, and it encountered them 25 miles north-east of the airfield. In the brief engagement which followed, Lt. Edwin N. Boughton destroyed one Me 109 and damaged another Me 109. Capt. Harold R. Warren, Jr. also damaged a Me 109, but suffered damage to his own Spitfire in the process when an enemy aircraft shot his right elevator away.

On 30 December the rumors of a move became fact. Tom Thacker recalled "*...the part of the 2nd Fighter Squadron that was not at Bone moved to Orleansville, Algeria – about midway between Oran and Algiers.*"

There the men saw how the French treated Arabs who set up roadside stands to sell things. Carl Hogue noted that "*...French soldiers pass by on horseback and kick those Arab stands over.*"

"Kwitcherdangbitchin", a Spitfire Mk Vc, coded QP-K, awaits its next mission in the desert sun. (credit C. G. Jones)

Lt. Luis Zendegui in a formal pose with his Spitfire which displays a bee as its artwork. (Credit: Robert Curtis)

The Group diarist wrote that Orleansville's airfield "*...was of little use during this monsoon season*" and the strip was *"so far from the front lines that it was of questionable utility with our short-range Spitfires."*

The first few days of 1943 were quite busy and quite hectic for personnel of the 2nd FS based at Bone. Air battles began with a minor skirmish on 1 January when Lt. Allen W. Gross damaged a Me 109. The action took place five miles southeast of Bone when Gross sneaked in behind the enemy aircraft which was flying above a dogfight and delivered some cannon hits on the Me 109's tail surfaces and fuselage. The Messerschmitt rolled and dived away and Lt. Gross was credited with a *'damaged'*.

Bone airdrome was strafed and bombed by enemy aircraft on 1 January and although there was damage done to facilities, there were no casualties. This raid was followed up on 2 January with a bombing attack on Bone Harbor. The attack force was composed of Ju 87s, Me 109s and Fw 190s. The attack had just begun as elements of the 2nd FS arrived over the harbor and its Spitfires quickly joined 81 and 242 Squadrons, RAF, which were also in the air, and waded into the two attacking forces. Capt. Arnold Vinson, 2nd FS, who had scrambled with 242 Squadron observed one 242 pilot down an Fw 190 before he bounced a flight of Stukas. After closing on the enemy aircraft, Vinson hit it with a burst of machine gun and cannon fire and the Stuka literally fell apart in mid-air and crashed into the sea. Next, Lt. John Pope, Vinson's wingman, joined in and quickly sent another Ju 87 crashing into the sea. While this was going on several other 2nd FS pilots engaged the German fighter escort and Capt. James Peck shot down a Fw 190, Before the engagement ended Lts. Norman McDonald, Jerome Simpson, John Aitken, and Luis Zendegui each attacked and damaged a Me 109.

This successful engagement turned out to be the 2nd FS's last from Bone. The 3rd of January was a day of transition at Bone. 81 Sqn, RAF, departed and it was replaced by two new squadrons, 232 and 243 Sqns, and later that day the 2nd FS was transferred to Biskra after the harbor there was attacked by six Ju 88s. Replacing it at Bone was the Major Robert Levine's 4th Fighter Squadron, which would soon be introduced to combat. The flight to Bone by the 4th FS was not without incident, however, since three of its pilots, Capt. James Garvey, and Lts. R. W. Rivers, and Alvin Vogtle vanished during the trip, and were later reported as POWs. The 5th FS remained at Telergma, Algeria, a very cold and miserable base, and continued to miss out on the action.

According to a report written on 17 April 1943 by the 52nd FG's Intelligence Officer, the 4th FS engaged the *Luftwaffe* on 4 January near El Guettar and Lts. John Harvey and Sylvan Feld each destroyed a Ju 88 in aerial combat. For some unknown reason, these victories never appeared in official USAAF records and neither pilot was awarded credit for these victories. The 4th FS scored its first official victory on 6 January when Capt. Donald E. Williams shot down a Fw 190 over Bone Harbor, but it was tempered by the fact that Capt. Williams, moments later, was shot down and killed by another enemy aircraft.

On the same date the 5th FS escorted C-47s from Telergma to Youks-les-Bains, Algeria.

The *Luftwaffe* remained active in the Bone area and on 8 January, Maj. Robert Levine, engaged and destroyed a Fw 190 ten miles south-east of Bone. The 4th's next kill took place five days later when 1st Lt. Norman N.V. Bolle, Jr. was credited with a Me 109 over Cape Rosa, Algeria. On the following day, 2nd Lt. Moss K. Fletcher, 4th FS, downed an Me 109 between Cape Rosa and

Spitfire Mk Vc, ER570

Major Robert Levine,
4th Fighter Squadron,
52nd Fighter Group,
La Sebala, Tunisia, June 1943

Major Robert Levine's aircraft illustrates the early markings of the Group, which included the American flag on the fuselage and non-standard code letters. Major Levine scored three confirmed kills and one probable in this well-maintained Spitfire.

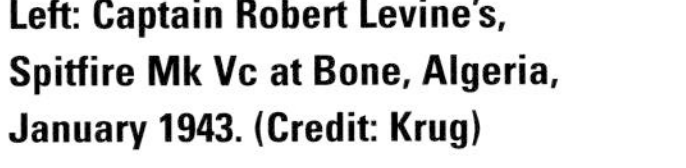

Left: Captain Robert Levine's, Spitfire Mk Vc at Bone, Algeria, January 1943. (Credit: Krug)

Right: Major Robert Levine of the 4th Fighter Squadron, proudly pointing out the Swastika indicating his first aerial victory, 8 January 1943. (Credit: Robert Levine)

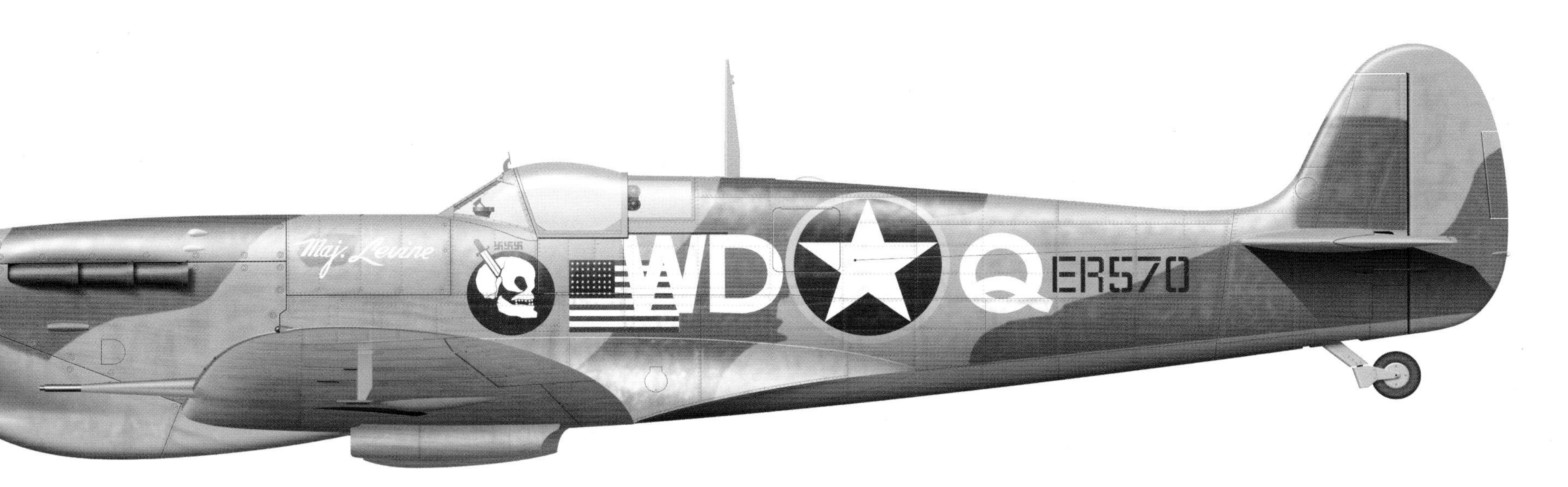

Seen here from left to right are Captain Jim Garvey and Lt Robert Rivers posing with a 4th Fighter Squadron Spitfire Mk Vc at Orleansville, Algeria, January 1943. This photograph was taken shortly before they both became POWs. (Credit: Robert Rivers)

Pilots of the 4th Fighter Squadron at Bone, Algeria, January 1943: In the front row are, left to right, Donnan, Soloman, Armstrong, Blais, Boyce. Second row, from left to right, Fletcher, Houston, Harris, MacGregor, Keyes, Levine, Camp, and Bolle. On the Spitfire, Peterson. (Credit: Robert Klug)

Bone, but his aircraft was hit and he was forced to bail out over friendly territory.

During this period the beloved Ernie Pyle, America's foremost war correspondent, was in the area and wrote some articles about what the men serving in the area of Bone were experiencing. In these articles Pyle provided the news to America that some of its airmen flew and maintained British Spitfires. Pyle added that at Bone, the "*...harbor and its strip were bombed on the average of about every four hours for about three consecutive weeks.*"

The air echelon of the 4th FS followed the pilots to Bone in two transport aircraft on the 10th, but the rains came and the field was too muddy for operations. The rest of the men went by train to Bone on 14 January 1943 and then proceeded onward to Telergma, near Constantine, where the all-weather airport was about one mile from Group HQ. Some men came via Relizane, Algeria and others went onward to Thelepte, Tunisia. Tom Thacker recalled: *"All equipment moved by rail to Relizane, a Troop Carrier base about 40 miles east of Oran. We shoved off on the afternoon of 14 January, 1943 and arrived at Relizane shortly after dark. All equipment had to be unloaded from the train and loaded onto 20 C-47s so that they and the men could take off after dark. The C-47s escorted by our Spitfires, made the trip to Telergma in about three hours and returned to Relizane to be loaded again the following morning. This went on for one solid week and finally the move was complete – 131 loads/trips in all. Telergma was not the place to be in the winter and was probably the worst station for the group."*

The 4th FS continued to fly patrols from Bone while the 5th FS escorted transports from Telergma. During one of these patrols on 24 January, 1st Lt.Robert C. Donnan, 4th FS, destroyed a high-wing Hs 126 on the ground near La Fauconnerie, Tunisia, but credit for ground-kills was not given at that stage of the war. 1st Lt. Newton Boyce, 2nd FS, became a POW on the same day when his Spitfire was struck by Flak and he belly-landed in enemy territory. Through the end of January, 1943 there was little action except to escort transports, cover B-17s, fly patrols, search for paratroops and to scramble for elusive enemy aircraft passing nearby.

A 40 hour inspection being performed on a 4th Fighter Squadron Spitfire Mk Vc, s/n JG778. The assigned pilot for this aircraft was Lt. Scott and S/Sgt Ray was its crew chief. Note the white bear emblem on the vertical stabilizer, and Scott's name on the cowl. (Credit: Fred Wiersna)

Chapter Four

"Aloft–strafing, spying, escorting and patrolling"

The Tunisian Campaign

February–July 1943

Thelepte, Tunisia, February 1943. Two Spitfires of the 5th Fighter Squadron on the line with a P-40 of the 33rd Fighter Group. (Credit: Al Gelo)

Adolf Hitler was determined not only to hold onto Tunisia, but also to push the Allies out of Africa, and when the Allies advanced steadily deeper into the country, they were met with fierce fighting. During February and March, the 52nd FG, nearer to Tunisia than many other US fighter groups, found itself in almost hourly combat action. The Intelligence Section of Headquarters, XII Air Support Command, wrote 'Daily Intelligence Summaries of Missions' for review by the Commanding General of ASC, and the Summaries listed Attack Orders for all groups under XII ASC command. An 'Attack Order' specified which squadron and the number of its aircraft that were dispatched, time off and on, type of mission, the targets, time aloft, and comments, and the 52nd FG was mentioned whenever it was involved in an Attack Order. The 52nd FG Spitfires would now be escorting aircraft such as P-40s of the 33rd FG, P39s of the 81st FG, A-20s of the 47th BG, P-39s and A-20s of the 154th Observation Squadron, P-40's of the Free French *Lafayette Escadrille*, P-39s of the 99th Fighter Squadron, P-39s of the 350th FG, C-47s of the 51st Troop Carrier Wing, 'Hurribombers' of 242 Group (NATAF), A-20s of the 68th OG, B-25s of the 12th BG (NATAF), and escorts for Walrus air/sea rescues.)

February 1943 began with the 52nd FG still on the move. On 2 and 3 February a small contingent of 12 Spitfires from the 4th and 5th Fighter Squadrons, plus a small support crew, were sent to Thelepte, Tunisia to relieve the 33rd FG. The 33rd which had seen constant action and was nearly out of P-40s, needed a chance to rest and re-equip. Upon its arrival at Thelepte, the unit began flying bomber escort and patrols, giving the 5th FS the chance to fly its first true combat missions of the war.

Action was not slow in coming. The 3rd of February was a very busy day and the pilots welcomed it. The 4th FS was involved in Attack Order #1 when 11 Spitfires, six P-40s and six P-39s took off at 07.40 hrs to fly a recon mission to Sened. For Attack Order #6, six Spitfires, five A-20s and seven P-40s hit a 155 mm howitzer east of Ousselita. The 5th FS flew Attack Order #5 when four Spitfires and eight P-40s (*Lafayette Escadrille*) covered a photo plane through Faid Pass. Three Spitfires escorted transports, seven flew a high cover patrol, four covered one A-20 and seven P-40s, two covered six A-20s and six P-40s and eight covered nine A-20s bombing.

In the day's actions Lt. Victor N. Cabas, 4th FS, downed an Me 109, eight miles east of Thelepte and Lts. Harold L. Pederson, 4th FS, and Lt. Frederick Jones, 5th FS, each probably destroyed an Me 109 during other encounters with the *Luftwaffe*.

On 4 February, the 4th and 5th Squadrons were joined for Order #1 when, at 07.30 hrs, 10 Spitfires flew a recon of roads at Gafsa and El Guettar. At 15.45 hrs, Attack Order #6 was carried out, when 12 Spitfires and six P-39s flew a recon via Sbeitla, Fondouk, and return. Spitfires escorted aircraft from Telergma to Biskra, and six flew a recce to Fondouk, four patrolled from Sbeitla to Faid to Lesonde to Sidi Bou Zid, and two patrolled to search for a "*Photo Freddie*" – a high-flying German reconnaissance aircraft which was often at too high an altitude to intercept. During Attack Order 3, Capt. Hugh L. Williamson, 5th FS, was credited with probably destroying one Fw 190 and damaging two others south of Ouselita before having to bail out when his Spitfire was attacked by enemy aircraft. After he bailed out, Lt. Harold L. Pederson, 4th FS, began circling to protect Williamson and was quickly shot down and killed by an Me 109 that sneaked in on him as he shepherded his friend. Williamson became a POW.

The Group's activities would remain somewhat sporadic for several days and Tom Thacker commented on the situation: *"Except for these short operational periods at the front, activities by the Group in this period were fairly normal. Pilots were accruing quite a few flying hours, mainly escorting transports plus now and then accompanying a bombing attack. The limited range of the Spits reduced their suitability for many missions for which P-38s were better suited."*

The air echelon of the 2nd FS stayed at Biskra, a resort for the French, during the first half of February and their activities were much as described by Thacker. Lt. Luis Zendegui, 2nd FS, said of this period: *"Our duties were mainly scrambles and patrols of the airfield. After a month or so of the rest afforded by this duty, the Squadron's personnel began to get bored and were ready to get back to work."*

On 6 February 12 5th FS Spitfires patrolled the area around Thelepte in search of an expected German reconnaissance aircraft, but it did not show up. On another patrol that day, Lt. Harold

A French P-40 from the Lafayette Escadrille at Maison Blanche, Algiers in January 1943. (Credit: Air Force Museum)

A. Taff, 5th FS, engaged and shot down an enemy aircraft, but his victory was never officially confirmed. One day later, pilots came back from Gibraltar with 15 very welcome replacement Spitfires – 12 Vb's and 3 Vc's.

The 13th of February was another day of movement and an advanced detachment of the 2nd FS moved from Biskra to Chateaudun du Rhumel, Algeria, south-west of Constantine, and the 5th FS sent 20 Spitfires to escort transports to Chateaudun du Rhumel.

As if in an omen of bad things to come, 2nd Lt. J.C. Roberts, 5th FS, was killed performing a stunt near Ain M'Lilla, Algeria on 14 February. Coming on the heels of this tragedy was the information that a Panzer unit had broken through Allied lines in the area of Faid Pass. Following the break-though, General Jürgen von Arnim's armored columns pressed on and by 18 February his forces struck several at several locations in Tunisia to include, Sbeitla, Gafsa, Feriana, El Guettar, Kasserine and Thelepte.

Suddenly there was a great need for air support, and the Intelligence Officer of the 52nd FG reported that "*...from February 15 through 18, the 52nd FG was thrown into front line action during the unsuccessful attempt to halt the mid-February drive of German Panzer Units in southern Tunisia. For four hectic days, from February 15-18, all three squadrons fought and fell back, fought again, and fell back again. All day, every day, the Group's pilots were aloft, strafing, spying, escorting and patrolling. Prior to 15 February, pilots prepared for regular missions, but when the crisis erupted, they received orders to move, and during and shortly after the mid-month battles, HQ and the three squadrons were seldom in one place for very long. On 15 February, pilots flew missions from advanced airfields. The method used was to move 12 aircraft from each of the three squadrons forward with a streamlined maintenance section followed by air transport. The 2nd and 4th Squadrons were to operate at Thelepte and the 5th, at Youks-les-Bains, Algeria, a few miles west of the border with Tunisia.*"

15 February: HQ; XII ASC Summary: "*Thelepte airdrome was attacked at 0745 hours by six Me 109G-2's. The 81st FG intercepted the enemy and destroyed three. The 2nd FS sent a dozen Spits over Gafsa and Bou Hamran at 1125 hours. At 1150 hours, 12 Spits from Youks escorted 4 P-39's covering Allied ground troops north of Sbeitla. The 2nd FS was up again at 1410 hours escorting A-20's that bombed trucks three miles north of Gafsa. 12 Spits of the 2nd FS left Thelepte with some P-39's and strafed east of Sbeitla and then dropped back to Youks. 6 Spits of the 4th FS escorted a/c from Telergma to Biskra to Youks and 11 Spits swept Maknassy. Later, 13 Spits escorted a/c to Youks. Some 4th FS Spits at Thelepte beat up a Flak position east of Sbeitla. The air echelon of the 5th FS went via C-47's to Youks, and 4 Spits were immediately dispatched to build up the desired strength at Thelepte No. 1 and to cover our ground forces' retreat from Kasserine Pass. Testifying to the speed of the moves, 8 Spits of the 5th FS up at 1355 hours to escort P-39's on a recce. Attack Order #8: 12 Spits of the 4th FS and 6 P-39's were off at 1545 on a recon of the Gafsa, Maknassy and Bou Hamran region and "strafed a convoy of 8 to 10 vehicles going south.*"

16 February: The Intelligence Officer reported this day was the Group's "*...busiest to date.*" The 4th

Biskra, North Africa, December 1942. From left to right Martin Lucas, Dick Schorse, Vince Reagan and Oscar Sanders, 2nd Fighter Squadron, pose in front of the "Hotel Dorissey" (Credit: Paul Ludwig)

A wrecked 5th Fighter Squadron being stripped for spare parts (Credit: Malcolm Laird)

Pilots of the 4th Fighter Squadron in the desert, early 1943. Seated (left to right) Feld, Tyler, Dougherty, Blythe, Kelly, Puffer, unknown, Dean, Camp. Back: (left to right) Huston, Booth, Levine, Evans, Cabas, Fletcher, Blais, Armstrong, Markley, McGregor. (Credit: John Blythe

Ray Teliczan posing with a Spitfire Mk Vc, VF-L, possibly the replacement aircraft for the wrecked VF-L pictured previously. (Credit: James Empey)

VF-H of the 5th Fighter Squadron at Telergma, winter 1943. (credit: USAAF)

FS was first in action with 12 Spitfires aloft at 08.00 hrs on a recce over Djebel Lesonde, Faid, and Saafria where they spotted eight enemy aircraft which turned away before they came within range. Six Spitfires escorted aircraft from Telergma to Biskra to Youks. 12 more flew a sweep to Sbeitla and 12 flew a sweep to Faid and Sidi Bou Zid, Tunisia. For Attack Order #3, eight Spitfires of the 5th FS and six A-20s were up at 10.50 hrs "*...to bomb two howitzer batteries east of Sbeitla, Tunisia. One of the howitzer batteries was completely knocked out.*"

Two Me 109s appeared but were driven off before they could make an attack. The 4th FS sent 12 Spitfires at 10.55 hrs as cover for A-20s bombing Axis tanks near Melikate. Attack Order #5 ordered 12 Spitfires of the 2nd FS and six P-39s to take off at 11.25 hrs for a recon over Gafsa, Sened and Bou Hamran. On Attack Order #7, 12 Spitfires of the 2nd FS and six A-20s were up at 14.10 hrs to bomb trucks three miles north of Gafsa. Attack Order #8 sent ten Spitfires of the 4th FS and 4 P-39s off at 14.45 hrs to attack 20 German tanks east of Sbeitla. Besides all these missions pilots of the 5th FS flew nine missions of eighteen sorties on airdrome patrols throughout the day.

German artillery fired over Thelepte to Feriana during the night of 16/17 February and every unit at Thelepte began a very hasty retreat at around 02.00 hrs. Personnel were roused from their beds to load equipment and prepare for departure. All flyable aircraft took off at dawn as German artillery was heard close by. The Spitfires were flown to Youks-les-Bains, Algeria except three, which were out of commission and burned. When daylight came, the 4th FS strafed Flak positions and the 2nd FS flew escort for P-39s in the vicinity of Sbeitla which appeared to be the hub of enemy activity. All aircraft returned safely and landed at Youks. The last of the ground personnel was evacuated from Thelepte by 16.00 hrs. The highway was jammed and the column moved slowly but in an orderly manner, and air cover provided some protection from enemy aircraft which could have found excellent hunting. It was nearly dark when the last vehicles arrived at Youks, about 50 miles distant. Defeat of the American ground force at Kasserine Pass and the onrushing German offensive had forced the 52nd FG to retreat.

On 17 February, for Attack Order #1, Capt. Vinson led 12 Spitfires and two P-39s off at 07.15 hrs to fly a recon over Sbeitla, Pichon and Fondouk. On Attack Order #2, eight Spitfires and six P-39s were up at 0815 hrs to strafe in the Sbeitla area: "*Four guns believed knocked out. One tank and 3 trucks destroyed. 20 to 30 trucks strafed and 2 trucks and 1 half-track destroyed.*" On Attack Order #3, 12 Spitfires and four P-39s were off at 11.45 hrs to strafe in the Sbeitla and Kasserine area: "*Attacked 5 trucks, one half-track and one tank all believed were knocked out.*"

The 4th and 5th Squadrons escorted P-39s on a recon mission to Feriana, Tunisia a few miles south of Thelepte. 2nd FS Spitfires escorted A-20s.

The Intelligence Officer wrote of the day's action: "*The best piece of teamwork during the day came in the early afternoon. Eight Spits of the 5th FS and 4 of the 4th FS were escorting two P-39s on reconnaissance and pilots noticed that a key bridge had been blasted by retreating Americans and that Axis motor vehicles of all kinds were backed up in a hopeless tangle on the road leading to it. They reported this observation to their base. Two hours later, at 1550, twelve Spits of the 2nd FS, six A-20s and four P-39s were on their way to the traffic jam, on the road south of Fariana. They dropped bombs and pumped machine gun and cannon fire into every conceivable kind of motor vehicle and tank clogging the road.*"

The day's success was not without cost, however, as the 2nd FS lost a pilot to the intense Flak. Luis Zendegui described what happened: "*That afternoon we flew an escort mission for six A-20s and four P-39s to the area south of Feriana. We were flying very low, under 500 feet because of a low overcast and the heavy ground fire hit two of our planes. Roger Newberry's plane crashed and he was killed; Stan Martin's plane was hit in the prop, the leading edge of a wing and in the horizontal stabilizer.*"

The weather took a turn for the worse on 18 February and hindered, but did not stop, the Group's activities. Tom Thacker reported: "*Ten planes from the 5th Squadron were up for reconnaissance and possible strafing in the Sbeitla area by 0730 hours. Four more from the 4th Squadron were on patrol at 1145 hours when directed to look for three unidentified planes. The weather was becoming increasingly difficult. Lt. Thomas H. Evans, Jr. pulled up suddenly to avoid a mountain peak and disappeared into the overcast. His body was later recovered by our ground troops.*"

By this date the German thrust into Tunisia had been blunted and the Allied air units that covered the battlefield deserved much of the credit for slowing and disrupting the von Arnim offensive. On 19 February, the 52nd FG was ordered to move again. An evidently proud Tom Thacker commented on the skill and dedication of both the pilots and the ground personnel in his diary: "*Activity began at dawn and closed out with darkness, since the strictest blackout was in effect. At night everybody lived in foxholes. Considering the lack of facilities, our mechanics and other support personnel performed miracles. Also the ease of maintaining the Spitfire showed in this period. When word came on 19 February that the emergency appeared to be over and to make plans for a return to Telergma, every one of our planes was in commission. Major credit should go to the 52nd Group in helping stop the Germans soon after they penetrated the Kasserine Pass. This was the high point for the enemy in Tunisia; soon afterward, the tide changed until hostilities in Africa ceased.*"

February 19 began with the onslaught of a "*sirocco*", the violent African wind that raised dust and made flying out of the question. The storm also interrupted the Group's move. It was not until the following day that the 4th and 5th Squadrons went to Telergma and the 2nd Squadron went to Chateaudun du Rhumel. During the day,

In Africa, the destruction of war left this image of Christ on the cross standing while all around it was rubble. (Credit: Cogal)

A very unusually marked Spitfire Mk Vc of the 5th Fighter Squadron. Pilot and coded letters are unknown. (Credit: Charles DeVoe)

5th FS Spitfires escorted transports from Telergma to Youks to Ain Beida and in bad weather the squadron strafed and flew a recon mission to Sbeitla. There was also a little excitement at Youks-les-Bains, Algeria as the 5th FS was preparing for its return to Telergma. Two Me 109s came over the field but were driven off by anti-aircraft fire. As soon as the enemy aircraft departed, loading was resumed. Soon afterwards the maintenance personnel headed back to Telergma, but no sooner were they out of sight, word arrived that the Squadron was to fly a few more missions from Youks! During the next two days, the aircraft were maintained and kept flying by the pilots, cooks, drivers, and administrative personnel.

All went well when the 5th FS flight section began its move on 22 Feburary until Lt. Johnny Kemp, 5th FS, collided on take-off with a Spitfire from the 31st FG which was landing. Lt. Kemp survived the collision and was hospitalized. When well enough to travel he was given a transfer back to the United States. On a much more positive note, three 4th FS pilots, Lieutenants Edwin C. Smithers, Lee M. Trowbridge and Edward M. Scott, who had been interned in Spanish Morocco for three months returned to the Group on 22 February.

By 23 February it was apparent that the German offensive had weakened. XII ASC dispatched A-20s and P-39s on missions without Spitfire escort and the enemy was seen withdrawing to the Kasserine Pass during the night of 22 February. On the same day Spitfires of the 2nd FS flew from Youks to Ain M'Lila as the Squadron left Chateaudun du Rhumel, and Thacker recounted "*...some of these moves – such as the one ten days earlier – were simply to reduce the congestion at Telergma.*"

An escort mission on 24 February turned out to be a very successful day for the 4th Fighter Squadron. The action took place in the vicinity of El Aouina and Emil Torvinen described the events in his diary: "*Lt. Wallace F. MacGregor was escorting medium bombers over Tunis when he sighted a crippled B-26 being repeatedly attacked by the enemy. Not considering the odds he turned to the aid of the bomber and single-handedly broke up three successive attacks, shooting down a Me 109 over El Aouina, probably destroying a Me 109 and dispersing the rest. Even though his fuel and ammunition were low he remained with the bomber.*"

The attacking flight of German fighters suffered additional losses when Lt. Robert C. Donnan and Capt. William M. Houston bounced them over El Aouina. Capt. Houston shot down one Me 109 and damaged another and Lt. Donnan downed another Messerschmitt, giving the squadron a total of 3-1-1 claims for the day.

The Allies regained control of Kasserine by 25 February and things in the Group began to return to normal, but only for a short time. The 52nd FG celebrated Colonel Dixon Allison's first anniversary as Group Commanding Officer on 27 February, only to learn two days later that he was being replaced by Lt. Colonel Graham W. West. A few days after the change of command, the 52nd FG found itself on the move again. The move back to Youks-Les Bains began on 8 March and was completed on 17 March. Unfortunately, the rains had come and the Group found a very unpleasant surprise awaiting it at the new base. Rains had made the regular airstrip unserviceable and a makeshift landing ground on top of a hill was used. Tom Thacker recorded the situation in his diary: "*Rains had fallen since we were last there and the field was muddy despite the 'all-weather' steel matting which had been installed and which was sinking into the mire. It had just been learned that matting was effective only with a compact gravel base. A strip was laid out on higher ground. This site was as rolling as a Missouri cornfield. Planes landing or taking off disappeared from sight a couple of times during which the observer could only speculate as to whether it would ever appear again. Planes were nosing up quite regularly and the mortality rate for props was very high.*"

The 4th of March turned out to be a rough day for the 2nd FS when accidents cost the life of one of it pilots – and a flock of sheep. Lt. Jay A. Baldwin died in a crash at Ain M'lila when he tried to do a low-altitude roll over the field. The second accident occurred when a flock of sheep ran onto the runway as Capt. G.V. Williams was

Wallace MacGregor's Spitfire Mk Vc, coded WD-M. Note the winter clothing the unidentified men are wearing in the desert. (Credit: Robert Levine)

Spitfires of the 4th Fighter Squadron wait their next mission from a desolate desert airstrip. (Credit: Richard Potter)

landing at Telergma. Norm McDonald recalled: *"His plane went into a flock of sheep and mutton chops and other choice cuts went flying all over the place."*

The *Afrika Korps* attempted to renew its offensive against British-held positions on 6 March, but its attack was blunted by the stubborn defense of the ground forces supported by an aerial umbrella. The last gasp offensive against British lines had cost the Germans almost one third of its tanks, and sent it in retreat back to the Mareth Line. As the Allies continued to push German forces toward the sea the 52nd FG assisted with battlefield coverage for the ground forces. On 10 March, its Spitfires flew two reconnaissance patrols, the first to La Fauconnerie and later in the day carried out the second recce mission in support of the 1st Armored Division.

On the following day ten Spitfires and four P-39s took off at 07.30 hrs on an offensive recon over Faid, Sidi Bou Zid and Djebel Lesonde, but were forced to abort when encountering bad weather. The 12th ASC wanted a repeat mission and Attack Order #1A sent ten Spitfires and four P-39s aloft at 11.30 hrs to fly the same mission as

One of the 4th Fighter Squadron's Flying Sergeants and his crew pose with Spitfire WD-O. Left to right are Sgt. Robertson, Sgt. Miller (pilot), S/Sgt Steel, S/Sgt Wirsmith and S/Sgt Katz. (Credit: Fred Wiersma)

#1. Attack Order #2 put ten Spitfires and four P-39s aloft at 14.20 hrs to drop leaflets over Pichon, Fondouk and Faid, and Attack Order #3 dispatched nine Spitfires and four P-39s to take off at 16.25 hrs to fly an offensive recon to Faid.

On one of the missions, 2nd Lt. John *"Jack"* Ludlow claimed an unusual victory: *"I noticed that my gas gauge showed only 25 gallons and I reported on the radio to Capt.Vinson that I was leaving and heading for home. I saw three twin-engined planes heading south flying very low. I thought they were friendly."*

Ludlow wanted to land and refuel and he flew toward the planes looking for the field they might have used and he opened his canopy and *"…the rear gunner of one of the planes shot the canopy off, cutting one of my hands slightly."*

The enemy aircraft made a sharp left turn and he lost sight of them. Ludlow flew around a knoll and met the aircraft coming around the other way at 90 degrees to him; *"When they saw me they made a sharp left turn. The leading plane crowded the inside plane so much in the turn that it crashed on the ground but did not burn."*

After he landed he claimed one enemy aircraft destroyed but did not receive official credit for it; (in Frank J. Olynyk's *USAAF (Mediterranean Theater) Credits for the Destruction of Enemy Aircraft In Air To Air Combat World War II* [1987] Ludlow is given credit for this kill).

Although the XII ASC report for 12 March stated that enemy aircraft were active over the entire sector throughout the day, the 52nd FG was involved only in Attack Order #1 when eight Spitfires and two P-39s were off at 07.45 hrs to fly an offensive recon to Faid. The men on the ground however, suffered an attack from three Me 109s which strafed the base on this date. One of the attacking aircraft was downed by anti-aircraft fire and the pilot was captured when he bailed out over the field.

On 13 March, Capt. Arnold Vinson led 10 Spitfires of the 2nd FS on an escort mission to the Sbeitla-Sidi Naceur-La Fouconnerie area. As the formation approached the target two Me 109s bounced the P-39s they were escorting. Vinson and his wingman quickly intercepted the enemy aircraft and Vinson managed to score several cannon hits on the wing and fuselage of one of them before the enemy aircraft got away.

On 17 March the Group participated in both bomber escort and ground support missions. Attack Order #2 sent 23 Spitfires of the 2nd FS to Gafsa as an escort for 18 B-25s,This attack was followed up two hours later when Attack Order #8 dispatched 12 Spitfires and three P-39s to attack a column moving south-east from Gafsa.

During the next several days the 52nd FG pilots continued flying a mixture of escort and ground support missions. In the air German aircraft were somewhat scarce but targets on the ground were plentiful. Strafing attacks by the Group's Spitfires took a deadly toll of German vehicles and personnel. Maintaining the aircraft and preparing them for these missions was a real struggle for the maintenance personnel because of severe supply problems. Tom Thacker recalled the seriousness of the situation during this period: *"Life was maintained by scrounging and stealing and begging and padding the ration account. Planes were operated by stripping one to keep three in the air. Practices which normally would result in a courts martial were not only tolerated, they were encouraged."*

The size and intensity of the 52nd FG's missions began to increase on 21 March and quietly signaled the beginning of a very active period for the Group. The day began with 12 Spitfires escorting six P-39s on an armed recon over German lines, and continued with two large-scale bomber escort missions. On the second of the escort missions, enemy fighters were encountered over Mezzouna airfield and during the ensuing engagements Lt. Norman Bolle, 4th FS, damaged a Me 109. The 4th FS, however, did not escape unscathed from this air battle and Lt. Glenn St. Germain was shot down a Me 109, six miles south-west of Sened, Tunisia. The after action report stated that: *"His Spitfire rolled over and dived through cloud, not to be seen again."*

On 22 March, air activity intensified considerably and the first engagement of the day took place at 08.45 hrs when Lt Cowell Van Deventer, 4th FS, shot down two Fw 190s over Mezzouna airfield. Ernie Pyle's article in *The Stars and Stripes* about the fighting on 22 March mentioned Cowell Van Deventer's role in the day's encounters with the *Luftwaffe*. In his article Pyle stated that Lt. Van Deventer *"…spotted a German airdrome just as some German fighter pilots were taking off and he swooped over the top of one Hun fighter who was just off the ground, and disposed of him in short order. Then he kicked his plane over on one wing to make a fast turn, and as he did so his wingtip ran smack into another German fighter who was just taking off and whom he hadn't seen at all. Van's wing tip went right through the German's cockpit, killing the pilot, and the plane hit the ground instantly and blew all to pieces."*

Next to engage the *Luftwaffe* was the 5th FS. During the squadron's armed recce mission to the Maknassy area, Lt. Gilbert Montour probably destroyed a Me 109 and Lts. John Carey and Eugene Steinbrenner claimed a Messerschmitt as damaged giving a the Group a total in the morning's actions of 2-1-2.

The major action of the day, however, took

VF-D of the 5th Fighter Squadron ends it life as a "hangar queen", supplying desperately needed parts to keep other Spitfires in the air. (Credit: USAAF)

place during the afternoon over Mezzouna airfield and resulted in the 4th FS's most successful mission to date. The big air battle broke out over Mezzouna airfield at approximately 15.10 hrs and Lieutenants Moss K. Fletcher, Robert E. Armstrong, Jr., Sylvan Feld, Victor Cabas and John Harvey each destroyed a 109. Lt. Bob Armstrong also damaged two other Me 109s and Capt. Robert R. Booth and 1st Lt. Donald M. Markley each damaged a Me 109.

The action was renewed a few minutes later as Capt. Norm McDonald and Lt. Bill Beard, 2nd FS, were returning from a reconnaissance flight over Mezzouna. McDonald detailed the action in his report: "*On our return trip Lt Beard called out two Ju 88s directly above us heading southeast. We were at this time at about 2,000 feet in the area of T5053. I saw the e/a at about a 1,000 feet above us and I climbed directly up at them. They were flying a two ship formation slightly echeloned to the right. I leveled off behind and slightly below their #2 ship. From 50 yards with 5 degrees deflection to the right I opened up with cannon and machine guns. My first cannon shells knocked his right motor out and the engine caught fire. Then the cannon shells exploded in the cockpit and along the fuselage and the whole ship seemed to explode in mid air. It went down burning. In all I gave him about 4 seconds of cannon and machine gun. I then closed on the #1 aircraft who apparently had not seen me yet and from a range of 25 yards I opened up with cannon and machine guns with a 4 second burst. I set his right motor on fire, his right wing dropped and my cannon fire hit his left motor setting it on fire also. Then I saw several other strikes of cannon fire along his fuselage. The plane went into a spin toward the ground. I then looked around and saw the first Ju 88 hit the ground in flames. I looked back and saw a second Spitfire following the second Ju 88 to the ground. This afterward was found to be S/Sgt Pilot James Butler. Time down 1635. Claim – 2 Ju 88s destroyed.*"

With these victories the 52nd FG's totals for the day increased to 9-1-7. One pilot, Lt. Norman Bolle, 4th FS, was lost during the afternoon engagement and became a POW.

The day had been a great one for USAAF units in North Africa. The 52nd, 79th and 82nd Fighter Groups claimed at total of 21-5-12 enemy aircraft, which at this stage of the war was the best one-day score run up by USAAF pilots in the war against Germany and her allies.

Heavy fighting between the tank forces of Generals George Patton and Jürgen von Arnim was taking place on 23 March near El Guettar on and Patton's need for aerial support drew the 52nd FG into one of its busiest days. The day began with Attack Order #2 sending 24 Spitfires at 06.35 hrs on a fighter sweep over the El Guettar-Mezzouna area. Order #4 sent 13 Spitfires and four P-39s off at 09.15 hrs to fly a recon over El Guettar. Attack Order #8 provided 24 Spitfires and four P-39s aloft at 11.00 hrs to escort B-25s bombing El Guettar. After lunch, Attack Order #12 put 24 Spitfires and 12 'Hurribombers' up at 13.40 hrs to bomb tanks and vehicles and in mid-afternoon, Attack Order #18 sent 24 Spitfires and six P-39s up at 15.40 hrs to bomb and strafe south-east of El Guettar. 2nd Lt. John S. White, Jr., 5th FS, damaged an Me 109 south-east of Gafsa, Tunisia.

The pilots participating in Attack Order 4 were bounced from out of the sun by a flight of four or five Me 109s and the ensuing engagement was costly for both sides. The action in which Capt. Theodore R. *"Sweetie"* Sweetland, 2nd FS, was credited with a victory and lost his life was described by Major Ralph Keyes: *"I was flying Yellow*

A poor, but rare, photograph of Lt. Sylvan "Sid" Feld and his Spitfire Mk Vc taken prior to his first aerial victory on 22 March 1943. (Credit: E. Torvinen)

S/Sgt. James E. Butler of the 2nd Fighter Squadron who scored 4.5 aerial victories before being killed in action (Credit: Robert C. Curtis)

5 when someone called break, whereupon I immediately broke to the right. A moment later I saw a Me 109 open up on a Spitfire from about 250 yards. Smoke began streaming from the Spitifire which continued on for a second or two, then turned sharply upward and to the left directly into the path of an oncoming Me 109. A crash occurred and both planes went down in flames from about 2000 feet. Though I followed the descent of neither plane to the ground, I did see two flaming spots on the ground where the two planes had obviously just crashed. I saw these spots before the crash of Capt. Williamson's Spitfire, which had been hit and from which he bailed out. Whether the crash of Capt. Sweetland's plane – I learned later that this Spitfire was Capt. Sweetland's – with the Me 109 was owing to a deliberate action or a reflex action resulting from being hit, I do not know, but knowing Capt. Sweetland, I believe he deliberately crashed into the Me 109 after having been, perhaps, fatally shot."

The Me 109 G-6 that Sweetland crashed into was piloted by the leading German ace *Major* Joachim Müncheberg, *Kommodore* of *Jagdgeschwader* 77 who was credited with 134 victories and wore the Knights Cross with Oak Leaves. Both men died in the collision. Capt. Hugh L. Williamson parachuted safely from his burning Spitfire and became a POW.

Missions of 24 March were again in support of Patton's forces and the 52nd FG found numerous targets in the air and on the ground. The first encounter of the day took place at 1250 hours when Lt. John W. Watson, of the 5th FS, downed an Me 109 in the Gafsa area for his and the Squadron's first confirmed victory.

Three more enemy aircraft fell during the late afternoon when the 2nd FS encountered a flight of nine Ju 88s escorted by Fw 190s and Me 109s east of Maknassy. When the enemy aircraft saw Spitfires, they dived and Capt. Arnold Vinson chased an Fw 190, closed to 25 yards and put cannon strikes onto the top of the fuselage and the right wing. The Fw 190 lost speed and caught fire. Vinson reported: *"The enemy aircraft lost speed very quickly and caught on fire, emitting a volume of black smoke out of the exhausts. I pulled away after almost colliding with it."* With this kill Vinson's total score was now 4.33. Capt. Zendegui chased a Me 109 and destroyed it *"...after diving from 7,000 feet to the deck. I fired two short bursts and saw strikes on the engine and the cockpit, then heavy black smoke from its exhaust. The combat took place about 10 to 20 feet above the ground."* The Squadron's third kill was scored by Lt. Warren Williams who got behind an Me 109 and shot it down. Lt. Williams later reported: *"The enemy aircraft seemed to stop in mid-air and then went down landing on its belly and I flew right over him."*

Captain Theodore Sweetland, who lost his life when his Spitfire crashed into an Me 109 flown by the German ace, Major Joachim Müncheberg, the Kommodore of Jagdgeschwader 77. (Credit: Robert C. Curtis)

The Luftwaffe ace Major Joachim Müncheberg, Kommodore of JG 77 was credited with 134 victories and wore the Knights Cross with Oak Leaves. On 23 March 1944 he collided with the Spitfire flown by Captain Theodore Sweetland of 2nd FS.

During the remainder of March 1943 the 52nd FG continued its escort and strafing missions in support of the Allied thrust into Tunisia. Each day was extremely busy for the Group, which flew an average of five to six missions a day, and no day went exactly as scheduled.

On 27 March, for example, the 52nd FG had already been assigned missions when a call for help came over the teletype at Thelepte from the 1st Armored Division. The message stated that a field artillery unit, in the vicinity of Maknassy, was being blasted by German guns and it had suffered 300 casualties. Hearing this, Lt. Col. West sent 24 Spitfires from the 2nd and 4th Squadrons to escort 12 Hurribombers to the target. The target was hit and the German shelling ceased. Next 24 Spitfires of the Group escorted nine 'Hurribombers' on a mission to bomb a machine gun emplacement. The last two missions of the day sent Spitfires, escorting Hurribombers, to attack rail and troop positions. Attack Order #4 despatched 12 Spitfires and five 'Hurribombers' off at 09.00 hrs to bomb railroad cars at Mezzouna. The last Attack Order of the day was Number #9 which sent 25 Spitfires and 12 'Hurribombers' up at 14.50 hrs to bomb enemy positions at Djebel Naemia.

On 30 March, the 52nd FG dispatched a flight of 36 Spitfires to escort 18 A-20s to bomb La Fouconnerie. During this early morning mission the *Luftwaffe* was encountered and the 4th FS added two more confirmed victories and one probable to its scoreboard. The action took place 15 miles west of La Fouconnerie at 08.10 hrs and when it was over Lts. Robert Donnan and Donald Markley had each destroyed an Me 109 and Lt. Edward Scott claimed a third Me 109 as a probable.

With so much flying taking place, one day seemed to run into another but pilots and ground crew kept up with all the attack orders, and – 31 March – saw no let up. During this day the Group flew an armed recce mission and five fighter sweeps over enemy terriitory. Lt. Cowan, 5th FS Engineering Officer, up early to help out, put it succinctly: *"Up at 5:30 and damn near froze. The boys strafed a lot of German trucks and destroyed about 20. On another mission they got a lot more trucks."*

April 1943 began with a day of numerous missions and intense aerial combat by the 52nd FG. In the first encounter of the day pilots of the Group battled Fw 190s and Me 109s and came out on the short end. Lt. Ed Boughton of 5th FS, was shot down and killed. Up to this fateful mission Lt. Boughton was considered to be living a charmed existance. At Goxhill he had escaped a bad crash-landing and another incident in North Africa that Ernie Pyle wrote about. During a mission from Bone his canopy was jammed shut by a hit from enemy fire. He had tried unsuccessfully to open the canopy to bail out and was forced to nurse his crippled Spitfire back to

Spitfire Mk Vc, VF-A, and two unidentified crewman. Note the "Spittin Kitten" emblem on the nose. (Credit: Thomas Thacker)

base. When finally freed from his aircraft, Lt. Boughton found that half his parachute was shot away, and if he had jumped it would have not opened. His luck finally ran out on 1 April and American ground forces later verified that Lt. Boughton had been killed in action.

During the afternoon of 1 April, pilots of the 2nd and 4th Fighter Squadrons were able to able to enact a measure of revenge by attacking and destroying enemy aircraft on two separate missions. The first encounter took place at 1245 hours south of Hamadt and S/Sgt James Butler shot up a Fw 190, claiming it as a probable, and Lt. Jerome Simpson damaged a Me 109. S/Sgt. Jim Butler was Red 4 on a cover mission for ground troops in the El Guettar area when he saw bombs explode on the ground near American troops. It was known that enemy aircraft were in the area and as Butler cast a quick glance upward he saw an Fw 190 "*...that immediately rolled over and started down on me. I pulled my nose up and fired a short burst and he went down to the deck.*"

After a very long chase through hills at very low altitude, Butler got another shot at it and saw hits and smoke pour out. Butler had to pull up to avoid the hills and he "*...kept looking back and he did not come out. The enemy aircraft would have had to climb a hill to get out, and from where I was watching I could have seen him if he came over the hill.*"

Butler was credited with a probably destroyed. 1st Lt. Jerome Simpson was in that engagement and saw four Me 109s at six o'clock at about 4,000 feet. He recalled: "*One of the Me 109s dove at me and I turned into him, both of us firing head-on. He passed over me and as he did so I flipped over and from a range of about 150 yards I gave him a 2-second burst and saw strikes on his right wing midway between the cockpit and the very tip. As he was in a dive and I saw I could not catch him I broke off combat.*"

The final and most decisive encounter of the day took place at 17.30 hrs when pilots of the 2nd and 4th Squadrons bounced some Ju 88s in the vicinity of El Guettar and destroyed five of them. The 2nd FS kills were shared by Captains Norm McDonald and G.V. Williams (one Ju 88) and Lt. Bert Sanborn and S/Sgt James Butler (one Ju 88). Lt. Bert Sanborn reported that he "*...was Blue 2 in a squadron sweep to cover the ground troops in the El Guettar section. Take-off was 1605 hours. While patrolling I saw two Ju 88s east of us as we were going north. They were at about 3,500 feet and about level with us. I broke right and made directly for one of them. He made a sharp turn to the left and I swung in behind him. From about 150 yards I fired a two-second burst, using about ten degrees deflection. I did not see strikes but his right engine started emitting greyish smoke.*"

The Ju 88 went into cloud and Sandy remained beneath the cloud but he saw the "*...silhouette and when he came out I fired a two-second burst at about 45 degrees.*"

The rear gunner shot at Sanborn who let loose another short burst and Sanborn saw "*chunks fly off.*" S/Sgt. Jim Butler joined in on the kill and "*...the enemy aircraft went into a spin and crashed into a mountain and exploded just south of Djebel Hamadt.*"

The remaining three Ju 88s were shot down by the 4th FS with individual victories credited to Lts Sylvan Feld, John Harvey and Donald Markley, giving the Group a total 5-1-1 for the day.

Aerial action diminished on 2 April and the entire USAAF fighter forces in North Africa claimed only 4-0-2 during the day. From available records it appears that the 52nd FG flew only two missions on this date, both late afternoon fighter sweeps over El Guettar. In spite of the lack of combat on this date the 52nd FG (and other units) was about to face the wrath of another formidable foe, General George S. Patton, Jr. Even though Allied Air Forces had flown continual front line missions his troops were still being subjected to constant attacks and harassment from German dive-bombers. According to Tom Thacker: "*General Patton blamed the AAF for failing to provide total protection for his troops from air attack. The difficulty was that Ju 87 Stukas were being used in the area and were based as close to the front lines as we were. Thus no matter how hard they tried, there was no positive method for preventing them from slipping through, bombing, and then dashing safely home.*"

As if to personally challenge Patton's accusations, the 2nd FS responded in an outstanding manner on 3 April 1943. During a late afternoon patrol the Squadron encountered a flight of Ju 87s and attacked with an intensity that would have made "*Old Blood and Guts*" smile! When the smoke had cleared the 2nd FS had destroyed 13 Stukas, probably destroyed three and damaged two. Norm McDonald, leading Blue Flight sounded the alarm and led the attack. His encounter report stated: "*15-20 Stukas were sighted just as they were dive-bombing American concentrations. As my flight was nearest the Stukas, we went after the farthest formation. They were very slow, so we caught them easily. I closed to within 25-30 yards of the trailing Ju87, opened up with both cannon and machine guns, using about five degrees right deflection. A two to three second burst was sufficient. The motor belched black smoke and slight flame. The aircraft dove down and left into the ground from about 1000 feet. I closed on the next Stuka same distance and deflection, opened up with both cannon and machine guns, 2 or 3 second burst. The aircraft burst into flames, broke into pieces in the air. This combat took place at about 1000 feet.*

"*The third victim was about 500 yards ahead. I closed on him easily. He was in a slight climb. Again my range was no more than 35 yards, very slight right deflection from slightly below. The rear gunner was*

Lt Warren Williams of the 2nd Fighter Squadron, posing with his Spitfire which is marked with a Swastika indicating his victory of 23 March 1943. (Credit: R. Klug)

Spitfire Mk Vc, serial number unknown, *Irish* (left side)/*Helen Louise* (right side)

**Captain John Blythe,
4th Fighter Squadron, 52nd Fighter Group,
North Africa, February 1943.**

John Blythe's Spitfire featured the standard desert camouflage scheme and was decorated, in addition to its name, with the 4th Fighter Squadron emblem under the left windscreen, Blythe's name forward of the left windscreen, and mission markers under the exhaust stacks. On the right side, it displayed the name Helen Louise over the state flag of Texas for Crew Chief, S/Sgt Kormos, girlfriend and home state.

Left: Lt. John Blythe's Spitfire Mk IX coded WD-F. The name on the nose is "Irish" (Credit: John Blythe)

Right: The other side of Captain Blythe's Spitfire Mk IX carried an additional name and artwork. His crew chief, S/Sgt Robert Kormos, added the flag of Texas and his girlfriend's name, and later commented to Blythe: "Sir, those Germans will think another country has declared war on them." (Credit: John Blythe)

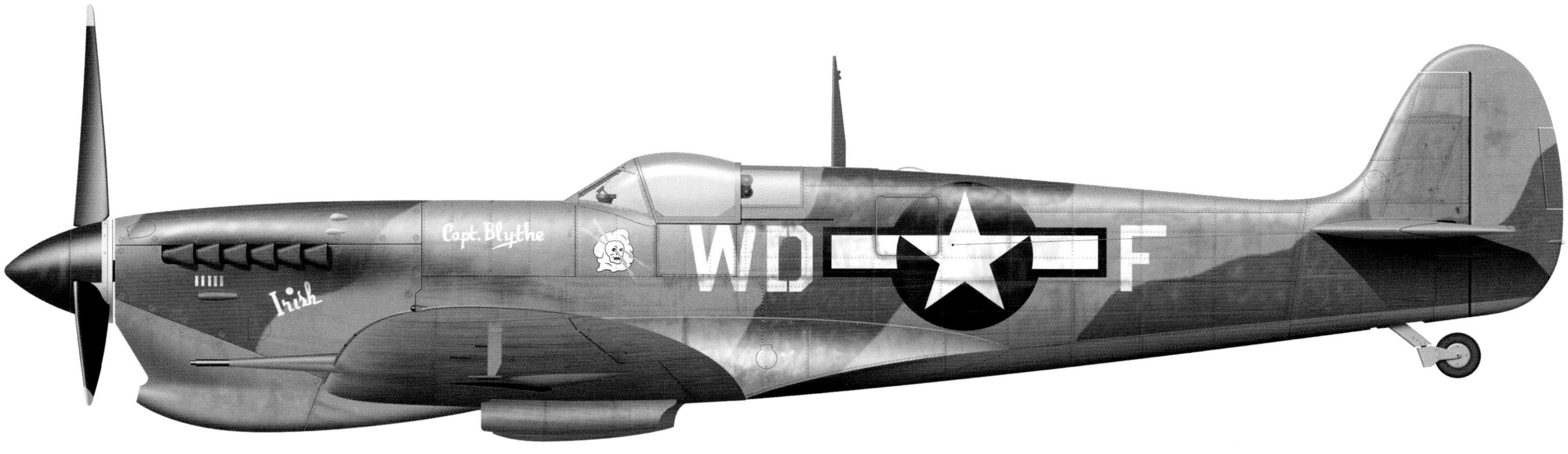

Lt. Bert Sanborn of the 2nd Fighter Squadron. (Credit: Robert C. Curtis)

General George S. Patton, Commanding General, II Corps, expressed his displeasure about his troops being harrassed by Stukas in early April 1943, and blamed the AAF. The 2nd FS answered his complaint by downing 13 Ju 87s on 3 April 1943. (Credit: USAAF)

firing intensely at me. I opened up with cannon and machine guns, about a three-second burst. Just as we entered a cloud great chunks of his propeller and parts of the plane flew back, just missing me. When I came out of the cloud the Stuka was spinning into the ground, and emitting much smoke and pieces still flying off. This combat took place at about 1500 feet, cloud base. Of the three e/a, only the latter seemed to take any evasive action, and he just tried to beat me to cloud cover. I was only conscious of return fire from the third aircraft."

McDonald claimed three enemy aircraft destroyed in this action.

As the turkey shoot continued, Capt. McDonald joined in the attack on another flight of three Ju 87s and claimed a probable before having to evade an attack by Me 109s. His 3-1-0 claims for the day raised his total confirmed victories to 5.5 and he was now an Ace. Right behind McDonald with two Stukas each were Lieutenants Bill Beard, John Pope, Jerome Simpson, and S/Sgt James Butler. The remaining confirmed kills went to Captains Arnold Vinson and George Williams. Vinson's victory raised his totals to 5.33 kills, but sadly, he did not make it back to base. His Spitfire was apparently hit by return fire from the Stukas or one of the escorting Me 109s, and Capt. Vinson crashed to his death. Witness said that Capt. Vinson was pursuing the Me 109s on Capt. McDonald's tail when he was shot down.

The loss of Capt. Arnold E. Vinson hit hard. The Group diarist recorded that Vinson was "*...coming to the aid of Capt. McDonald who had been jumped by three enemy aircraft. When McDonald called back to say that everything was okay again, he received no reply from Capt. Vinson, nor was the latter ever seen again.*"

Lt. Miles Lynn, 2nd FS, recalled: "*Vinson had superior vision, but we used to kid him about carrying opera glasses because he could identify distant enemy aircraft which were just flies in the sky to the rest of us. He never denied it, but just smiled at our joking. I was with Vinson when we were jumped by 109s. He had already shot down one Stuka; I called a break but he was hit as we turned. We all felt bad about Vinson, especially me, since I was his wingman. But I felt I did my part.*"

Back on the ground, McDonald praised Vinson, the man and pilot, recording "*...his leadership talents lay dormant for a while, probably because he was so self-effacing. To those who flew with him as their leader, he was the best. Cool is the most accurate word to describe his behavior. On fighter sweeps into enemy territory he always knew where he was geographically and had the mission objectives in proper priority. Respect for his leadership, in the air or on the ground, was so great that no one would question a decision or order of his.*"

The popular leader of the 2nd FS was replaced that evening with the appointment of Capt. George V. Williams as Squadron Commander. An interesting sidelight to the events of 3 April 1943 was presented by Craven and Cate in their *The Army Air Forces in World War II* (University of Chicago Press, [1948 to 1953]) when they noted "*...that shortly after this date, and to the regret of Allied pilots, the Stuka was withdrawn from North Africa.*"

Aerial encounters continued on 4 April but not to the degree of the previous day. The 2nd FS flew an uneventful sweep, while the 4th FS had a more active day when it engaged Me 109s near La Fauconnerie. A dogfight broke out and when it was over Capt. Frank B. Camp and Lieutenants Wallace F. MacGregor and Philip J. Fox, each shot down an Me 109. The 4th FS lost one pilot in the engagement. Lt. Richard I. East, who had been in the 4th FS for only one month, was killed in action when several Me 109s jumped his flight. His body was found two weeks later by British forces beside his wrecked Spitfire.

The 5th of April 1943 turned out to be a banner day for USAAF units in North Africa when Operation Flax began. The purpose of Operation Flax was to destroy the German aerial supply

Captain Norman McDonald of the 2nd Fighter Squadron. (Credit: American Beagle Squadron Assn)

caravans flying into Tunisia from Italy, Sicily and Sardinia, and the opening day of this operation was a roaring success. US fighters shot down 47 enemy aircraft that day and certainly disrupted the German supply chain. The 52nd FG, however, was not invited to this party and its pilots had to be satisfied with the downing of one Me 109 near El Guettar by Lt. John Carey, 5th FS. In addition to Carey's victory Lt. Robert Q. Kelly of 4th FS, damaged an Me 109 near Lake Buhira, Tunisia.

On 6 April, a large convoy of trucks showed up at Thelepte at breakfast time and nobody in the 52nd FG knew why. Tom Thacker hunted down the officer in charge of the trucks who said: "*We're the trucks to move you to your new base.*" Moments later Col. Graham "*Windy*" West came striding across the field, hurriedly pulling his jacket on; '*Just got a call from General Williams to tell us we're supposed to move today. We go farther front about 50 miles to a place called Sbeitla Number Two and we should be operating out of there by 1300 hours.*'

Camp was broken, the trucks were loaded, aircraft serviced and the Group headed for the new base. The air echelons of the HQ Detachment and those of the three squadrons moved to Sbeitla, Tunisia and the men who had been at Thelepte No. 2 went to Sbeitla while the balance stayed at Youks. By mid-month other men were ordered to go to Gidem. Thacker recalled Sbeitla "*...was covered by dust several inches thick.*" The airfield was located about 25 miles from the German lines and it was at Sbeitla that the group received its first Mark IX Spitfires. The sudden move to Sbeitla was not the only exasperating and disheartening event that day. Adding to the misery was the loss of several pilots and aircraft.

The severe losses on 6 April were a result of both Flak and enemy aircraft, with Flak taking the heaviest toll. The 5th FS lost four aircraft, flown by Lieutenants John White, Gilbert Montour, John Carey, and John Nangle, to Flak. Of the four, White was listed missing in action, Montour

Captain Miles Lynn of the 2nd Fighter Squadron. (Credit: American Beagle Squadron Assn)

Spitfire Mk Vb, WD-P flown by Captain Frank Camp of the 4th Fighter Squadron. (Credit: Toppen)

taken POW and Nangle and Carey were returned to the Squadron. The 4th FS lost two Spitfires, but both pilots Lts James Doughtery and Don Markley survived and were returned to their squadron. Lt. Markley was the only one of the six to be shot down by enemy aircraft and was wounded during the attack but crash landed in friendly territory and extricated himself from the aircraft. Arabs found him the following morning and took him to an Allied unit where he was given first aid and sent to a hospital.

The *Luftwaffe* was encountered again on 7 April by the 2nd and 5th Fighter Squadrons and the 2nd FS fared much better than the 5th FS – the *"Spittin Kittens."* In an air battle near La Fouconnerie, Lts. John Aitken and Maurice Langberg, 2nd FS, each shot down a Me 109 and the Squadron suffered no casualties. At about the same time, Lt. Terrell E. Yon, 5th FS, damaged a Me 109 south of La Fouconnerie, but 1st Lt. James A. Marshall, 5th FS, was last seen over Melikate, Tunisia after passing over a Flak bed. He was listed as missing in action.

The following day, 8 April, the Group's pilots had another successful day against the *Luftwaffe*. Lt. Sylvan Feld of 4th FS, scored his third victory, a Me 109, 10 miles north-west of Kairouan at 16.50 hrs. In another encounter that took place 50 minutes earlier Capt. Jerome J. McCabe, Jr. Lt.. Edwin J. Odom, 5th FS, each damaged a Me 109 west of Kairouan. During the 5th Squadron's mission, Lt. John W. Watson felt his Spitfire shudder but experienced no problems with the operation of the aircraft. When he returned to base, he found that AA fire had, in fact, hit his ship. Shrapnel had gone up through the belly and came to rest in the parachute he was sitting on. Sometime after that date, Sgt. Hogue said Watson *"....was preparing for a mission when his orders were received to go home. This wise fellow unfastened his parachute harness, flung his jacket over his shoulder and got into the transport without so much as a trip to his tent to pick up his belongings."*

Tom Thacker recalled that *"....during the period from 17 March through 9 April, the Group scored almost 50 per cent of all victories of the XII ASC and boasted a total of 52 enemy aircraft destroyed. Lord only knows how many vehicles, personnel, locomotives, buildings, bridges, communications centers, etc., were destroyed on strafing and dive-bombing missions. The price paid was 13 air combat losses. Of these, about half turned up later as prisoners of war and were eventually returned home."*

While at Sbeitla the 52nd FG received 15 replacements pilots, eight of which were flying Staff Sergeants. Needless to say the timing was perfect in order to provide relief from the pilot shortage. (Shortly afterward all eight of the flying sergeants received a commission that promoted them to the rank of Flight Officer or 2nd Lieutenant.)

On 9 April the 2nd and 4th Fighter Squadrons flew a fighter sweep and encountered a formation of 12 Ju 88s west of Kairouan. For the German bombers, it was a day of pure hell. Norman McDonald, leading the 2nd FS, sighted the Ju 88s, instructed the 4th FS to fly high cover, and led his squadron down to a devastating attack. In the initial attack six Ju 88s fell to the guns of the 2nd FS. Lts. Fred F. Ohr, Maurice Langberg, Luis Zendegui and S/Sgt. Butler, each destroyed a Ju 88 and S/Sgt Butler also shared another with Lt. Aitken. The 2nd FS's sixth and final victory was scored when Lts. Miles Lynn and Stanley Martin teamed up and shared in the destruction of an Ju 88. As the 2nd FS completed its attack the shattered German formation was bounced by the 4th FS and three more Ju 88s fell to the earth. Lts. Sid Feld and Victor Cabas each shot down a Ju 88 at Kairouan, while Lt. Lee Trowbridge shared another Ju 88 with Lt. Cabas. In addition to the nine confirmed kills, Lt. Edward Scott of 4th FS, claimed another Ju 88 as a probable. In a separate action Lt. Edwin Gardner of 5th FS, damaged a Me 109. The 2nd FS lost one aircraft when Lt. Langberg was forced down due to hits on his engine, but he was able to safely return to the squadron.

Lt. McDonald also had a narrow escape from death on this mission when he slid in behind a Ju 88. He related the story as follows: *"I fired my cannon and I saw hits on the right engine, which then caught fire. But then all hell broke loose in and around my cockpit. I instinctively pushed the stick forward and to the right and felt something drop onto my lap. I was a bit foggy, feeling like somebody had hit me upside the head. When I could think clearly I put the Spitfire into a tight 360 right turn, to check for enemy aircraft on my tail. All was clear."*

The dogfight was over but enemy fire had *"...torn off a piece about ten inches long from the front steel reinforcement of the canopy and then ricocheted towards my head, grazing my helmet and knocking the earphone off it."*

Another moment of note about this mission was that it provided the first of six victories that would later give Lt. Fred Ohr the title of 'Ace'. Ohr, from Fairview, Oregon, whose original name was Oh, is America's only Ace of Korean-American ancestry.

The *Luftwaffe* took another fierce pounding from American fighters on 10 and 11 April as Operation FLAX continued. The *Luftwaffe* lost 78 aircraft and two others were claimed as probably destroyed by USAAF P-38s and P-40s. RAF and South African fighters claims even increased the total German losses. Again, to its dismay, the 52nd FG was not made a part of the attack force. The only claim mustered by the 52nd FG during this two-day period was made by Lt. Leonard V. Helton of 5th FS, who possibly shot down a Me 109. Wartime records credit him with a kill, but Olynyk's authoritative study does not.

While on a reconnaissance mission on 12 April

Spitfire Mk Vc ,WD-C, flown by Captain Robert Booth of the 4th Fighter Squadron. (Credit: R. Levine)

John Nangle of the 5th Fighter Squadron, posing with his Spitfire Mk Vc, "Maddy". (Credit: Charles DeVoe)

Spitfires of the 5th Fighter Squadron. (Credit: Frank Sherman)

Sgt. Bond of the 5th Fighter Squadron posing with Spitfire Mk Vc, VF-F. (Credit: James Empey)

The wreckage of Lt. Maurice Blais's Spitfire. Blais was taking off on a scramble when his aircraft collided with another Spitfire coming in for a landing (Credit: Robert Rivers)

a flight of 5th FS Spitfires including an aircraft flown by Lt. Morris A. Dodd, observed American tanks in a battle with German armour. The fire-fight was taking place at a position far forward of where the American ground forces commanders thought they were. When the pilots landed they reported what they saw, and a report immediately went up the chain of command to XII ASC, whose reaction was one of disbelief. The ground forces commander called and asked that the pilots be re-interrogated, stating "*...it was impossible for a tank battle to be occurring at that place, and more than likely this location was a German bivouac area.*"

Lt. Dodd responded: "*If this was a German bivouac area, the Germans were certainly having a lot of fun shooting at each other with the 75 mm cannon in their tanks.*"

XII ASC reported to the ground forces' commander that it was convinced a tank battle was occurring at the time and place reported. Later, American ground forces confirmed through XII ASC what the 5th FS pilots had reported. That evening XII ASC notified the 52nd FG that its pilots were first in notifying the headquarters of the ground forces that their tanks had penetrated German positions to this point.

During the latter part of April some of the USAAF units in North Africa were already beginning to carry out attacks against targets in Sicily and other Mediterranean island targets in preparation for future Allied invasions. Others, including the 52nd FG continued to support the drive into Tunisia. To better support the final campaign against the Germans in Tunisia, elements of the 52nd FG moved to Sbeitla and Gidem, better known as Le Sers, located 80 miles south-west of Tunis, during mid-April. Sgt. Hogue said the move to Le Sers "*...represented the first time the entire group was based in Tunisia.*"

The Group did not see much opposition from the *Luftwaffe* on 16 April, but did manage one unconfirmed damaged credit. The damage claim occurred when Lt. Bob Armstrong, Jr., 4th FS, engaged an Me 109 at Oudna. The down side of the day occurred when Lt. Maurice B. Blais, 5th FS, was killed while taking off from Le Sers airfield. As Blais was heading down the strip, his Spitfire became stuck in a gravel bank made by a grader. A cloud of dust covered him, and Lt. Fox, not seeing him, proceeded on his take-off. His wing hit the cockpit of Lt. Blais' aircraft knocking him unconscious, and Lt. Blais died on the way to the hospital.

The date of 18 April is famous in the history of the North African campaign. On that date Allied fighters, as part of Operation Flax, took such a toll of the *Luftwaffe*'s slow moving transport aircraft flying over the Mediterranean to Tunisia that the incident has forever been known as the "*Palm Sunday Massacre.*" As in the previous Flax operations the 52nd FG did not participate and it had to settle for one victory during the day, a Fw 190 downed by Lt. Feld south-west of Tunis. This victory raised Lt. Feld's total to five and he was now the Group's newest Ace.

Things picked up considerably for the 52nd FG on 19 April and both the 2nd and 4th Squadrons engaged German fighters. The first encounters took place at 10.40 hrs when Capt. George

Spitfire Mk IX, EN447, *Kay III*

Lt. Victor Cabas,
4th Fighter Squadron,
52nd Fighter Group,
spring 1943

Victor Cabas' aircraft displayed four white Swastikas and the name Kay III, on the left side fueslage which was finished in the standard desert scheme. It still retained the RAF roundels on the the wing undersides and the fin flash on the vertical stabilizer.

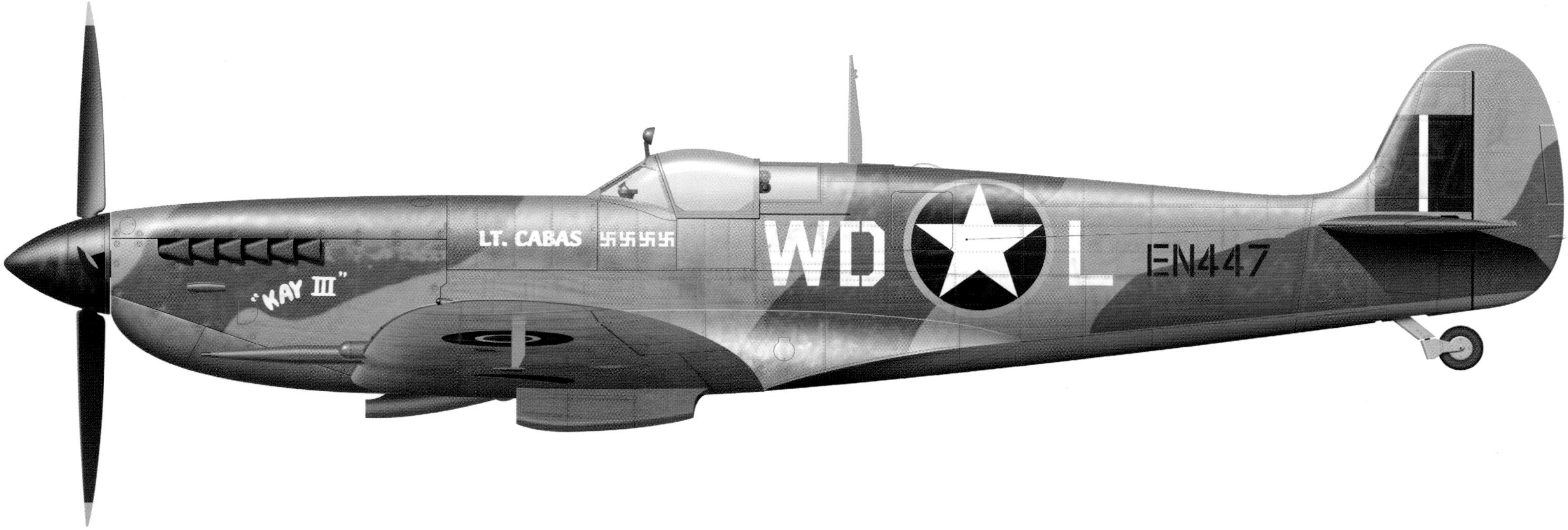

An unidentified groundcrewman poses with Lt. Victor Cabas' Spitfire Mk IX. The aircraft was named "Kay III" and coded WD-L, serial number EN447 (Credit: Fred Wiersma)

Lt. John Blythe of the 4th Fighter Squadron, posing with F/O Montgomery's Spitfire, "The Impatient Virgin". (Credit: John Blythe)

Lt. Moss Fletcher's Spitfire Mk Vc WD-O. Note the artwork of a cowboy on a bucking mule. (Credit: Paul Ludwig collection)

Pre-flight of a Spitfire Mk Vc of 4th Fighter Squadron. It required three men to hang onto the aircraft's tail to keep it down on an engine run-up. (Credit: Richard Potter)

Williams and Lt. Maurice K. Langberg each damaged a Me 109, but unfortunately Langberg's Spitfire was hit by gunfire from pursuing Me 109s and he was forced down. The mission summary lists him as 'MIA', but the book *American Beagle Squadron* states that Langberg was killed.

The 4th FS fared somewhat better during an encounter which took place at 15.50 hrs, 15 miles north of Tunis. In this dogfight Lt. Sylvan Feld downed a Fw 190 and a Me 109, Major Robert Levine destroyed a Messerschmitt, and Lts. John Blythe and Vic Cabas shared another Me 109. Even with its fine showing, the 4th FS did not escape loss. 2nd Lt. Edwin C. Smithers was lost eight miles south-east of Mateur, Tunisia. The Group diarist recorded that Lt. Feld, who had shot an enemy aircraft off Smithers' tail, "*...heard the latter call on the RT stating that he had been hit in the glycol system and would have to crash land*" and that Smithers bellied it in near Mateur.

Adolf Hitler's birthday, 20 April, was *"celebrated"* by 52nd FG pilots by further reducing the strength of the *Luftwaffe* in North Africa, but it was a very costly victory. All of the action took place between 09.00 and 09.30 hrs when all three of the 52nd FG's squadrons engaged the *Luftwaffe* north and north-west of Tunis. First blood was drawn at 09.15 hrs when Lt. Jerome Simpson downed an Me 109 and an Fw 190 was damaged by Lt. Bill Beard, both of the 2nd FS. At about the same time, Lts. Terry Yon and Morris Dodd of the 5th FS sent another Messerschmitt limping away from the encounter. The Germans, in turn, shot down Lt. William Higgins, F/O Letcher Williamson and S/Sgt James Butler, all of the 2nd FS. Butler was killed and the other two became POWs.

Another dogfight took place five minutes later when the 4th FS entered the fray. The 4th managed to destroy six enemy aircraft and probably destroyed two others, but lost two of its own in the process. Capt. Frank B. Camp downed an Fw 190 and an Me 109 north of Tunis but was lost while chasing a Me 109 out toward the sea and listed as 'MIA'. Moss Fletcher also downed two enemy aircraft and tied Capt. Camp for scoring honors of the day. Right behind them was Major Levine with one confirmed and one probable, Lt. Leonard Helton chipped in with one kill and Lt. Bob Armstrong claimed a probable. During this engagement Lt. John Harvey was last seen chasing an Me 109 with a second Messerschmitt on his tail. Lt. Puffer radioed a warning to Harvey to break, but apparently too late. Harvey did not rejoin the Squadron nor return to the base and was reported 'MIA'.

The 22nd of April was the last day of 'Flax' and the 52nd FG was still disappointed about being left out of the action. Lt. Bert Sanborn, 2nd FS, recalled: *"We missed the big turkey shoot when the Germans made the mass flight out. We had been covering this area each morning but were taken off flight operations that morning. I still think it was to keep Spitfires from making headlines."*

To further dampen the morale a hail storm hit the base and inflicted considerable damage. Lt. Marshall Cowan, 5th FS related that the base suffered "*...a terrific hail storm with hail stones the size of oranges (no exaggeration). All the elevators on the ships got holes in them and the wings picked up a few dents. Some made holes in tents.*"

The only bright spot in an otherwise dismal day was that Lt. Douglas C. Wolfe, 5th FS, damaged a Me 109 north-west of Tunis.

Troubles continued into the next day. Cpl. Paul A. Johnson became the first Enlisted Man from the 52nd FG to be killed in the war zone. He was sitting on the tail of an aircraft taxiing to the line to prevent the machine from nosing over in the high wind when tragedy struck. Another Spitfire had just landed and its pilot was blinded by the dust and rammed the aircraft upon which Johnson was sitting.

Easter Sunday, 25 April, was a day of limited action with American pilots scoring only three victories during the day. One of victories was of significance to the 2nd FS, however, as Norm McDonald became the top-scoring pilot in the Squadron with a victory over a Fw 190. His score now stood at 6.5 kills. The weather still seemed to be pro-German on this date because the base was again hit by a damaging hail storm. The hail, according to one witness was the size of billiard balls and hit the men, ripped more holes in tents and put more Spitfires out of commission.

Tom Thacker noticed "*...a marked change in the attitude of the men and in the operation of all planes in the Group because the war was being won and there was a release of tension.*" He remembered that the Germans began to drop "*...everything and sought anyone to whom they could surrender.*"

The end of the North African campaign was near and aerial combats became less frequent. The

Sgt. Shoenike posing with a Spitfire Mk IX of the 4th Fighter Squadron which displays its newly applied code letters and touched up paint. (Credit: Toppen)

This Mk IX Spitfire of the 5th Fighter Squadron displays a crudely painted national insignia applied over an RAF roundel. It is coded 'AA' denoting that it is the second Spitfire in the squadron coded 'A'. It is an alert aircraft and the start cart is waiting under the wing. (Credit: Thomas Thacker)

Captain Eugene Steinbrenner in the cockpit of his Spitfire Mk Vc VF-Z. (Credit: Thomas Thacker)

inactivity was, to a degree, broken on 5 May when Lt. Robert Q. Kelly, 4th FS, damaged a Me 109 near Lake Bahira. A few encounters occurred on 6 May when Lt. Allen W. Gross, 2nd FS, probably destroyed an Me 109 west of Tunis. In other engagements that day Capt. McDonald, 2nd FS damaged a Me 109 in a brief engagement between Tebourba and Tunis, Lt. MacGregor of 4th FS, damaged a Fw 190 over St. Cyprian Island, Tunisia and Lt. John Carey, 5th FS damaged a Fw 190 10 miles north-west of Tunis. In the last encounter of the day, at 18.00 hrs, three 5th FS pilots, Lieutenants Morris Dodd, Eugene Steinbrenner and Ernest Gebhart, teamed up to damage a Me 109 in a skirmish 10 miles south-west of Tunis.

Now that the campaign in Tunisia was drawing to a close, morale in the Group seemed to become a little more somber. This was primarily due to the way the unit, in spite of its excellent record to date, was improperly utilized by the planners at XII ASC.

Lt. Norman McDonald recalled: *"The 52nd Fighter Group, and especially the 2nd Squadron, whether they were taking the war to the enemy or the enemy was bringing it to them, never received the recognition they so rightly deserved. We were a bit like born-out-of-wedlock children of the US Army Air Corps and the British Royal Air Force, shunned by both parents. If the famous war correspondent, Ernie Pyle, had not spent a couple of days with us in North Africa, nobody in the States, other than our families, would have known that American Spitfire groups existed. For about seven months after the invasion of North Africa, our pilots and ground personnel endured living and flying conditions as tough as the worst experienced by any American fighter squadron during the war. We were, literally, the infantry of the air war on many occasions."*

Lt. Lynn remembered: *"We were always fighting a defensive war against the Me 109s and Fw 190s, which could out-climb, out-dive and outrun the Spitfire V, and had more power at high altitude. The Spitfire could out-turn these aircraft, but this was not much help because they were usually above us and we seldom had dogfights, where tight turns were a help. The Group welcomed the few Spitfire IXs it received, but it never was assigned a full squadron of them. The Spitfire IXs arrived late in the campaign. We were always close to the front lines, never more than thirty miles and at times only 15 miles and at Thelepte #1 we were being fired upon by German artillery from a few miles away. The P-38s were based near Algiers and would fly for two hours before getting into enemy territory and log five hours for a mission, whereas we would be in enemy territory shortly after takeoff and logged an hour or two at the most. During the final days of the (Tunisian) campaign the Germans evacuated as many personnel as possible by air and by ships and small boats."*

Miles Lynn was *"on a mission in a flight of four that strafed and sank several small boats."*

Lt. Luis T. Zendegui recalled that *"...as many as four missions a day were flown to escort bombers, A-20s or P-39s."*

The 5th FS had its biggest day so far on 8 May

Spitfire Mk Vb, serial number unknown, *Minnie Mk II*

Lt. Terry Yon,
5th Fighter Squadron,
52nd Fighter Group,
fall 1943

Terry Yon's Spitfire showed evidence of heavy use. Its desert camouflage scheme was weathered badly which made its red bordered US national insignia stand out prominently

"Minnie Mk II", Spitfire Mk Vb VF-P was flown by Lt. Terry Yon of the 5th Fighter Squadron. (Credit: Al Gelo)

Spitfire Mk Vb, ES276

**Lt. Sylvan Feld,
4th Fighter Squadron,
52nd Fighter Group,
La Sebala, Tunisia, June 1943**

Lt. Sylvan "Sid" Feld was the highest scoring Spitfire Ace in the 52nd Fighter Group with a total of 9-0-1 victories, seven of which were scored in the Spitfire Mk V. This profile shows his Spitfire as it would have appeared after he scored his final two victories on 6 June 1943.

Lt. Sylvan "Sid" Feld of the 4th Fighter Squadron, with nine victories in the Spitfire, was the top scoring USAAF Spitfire Ace. (Credit: John Blythe)

Lt. Sylvan Feld's Spitfire displaying all nine victory symbols, two of which are on the door that is folded down. (Credit: Paul Ludwig collection)

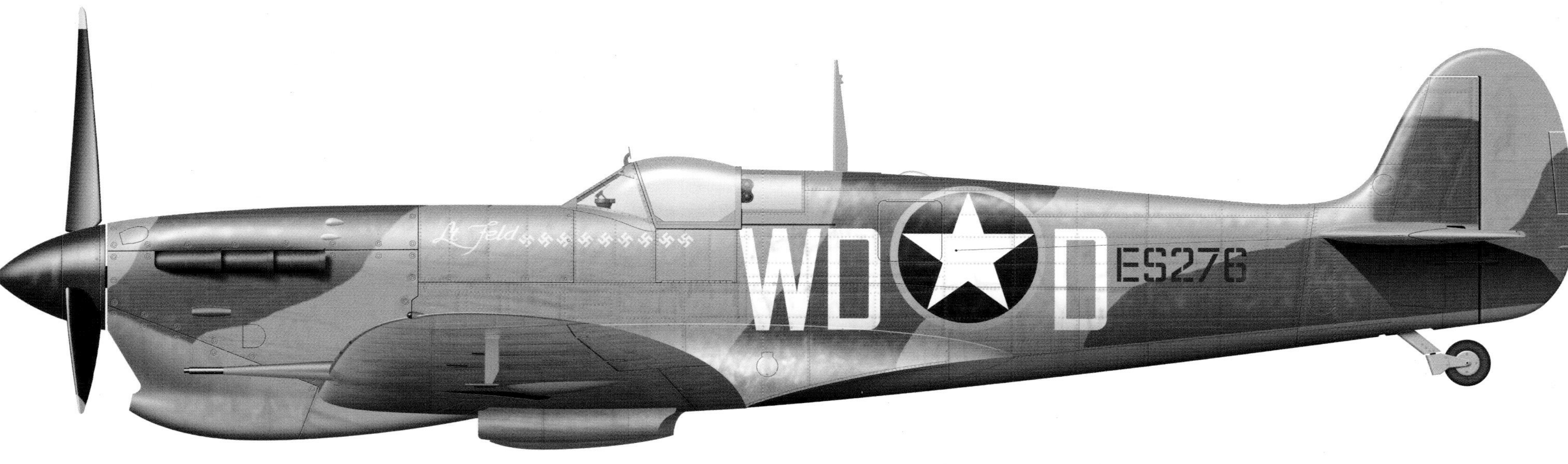

Lt. Leonard V. Helton's Spitfire Mk IX "Doris June II" at rest at La Sebala airdrome. (Credit: Robert Klug)

Lt. Robert E. Armstrong of the 4th Fighter Squadron posing with his Spitfire Mk Vc which displays three Swastikas, and which dates this photograph on or about 12 June 1943. (Credit: Marvin Haskins)

Lt. Marvin Haskins of the 2nd Fighter Squadron, and his Spitfire Mk Vc at La Sers airdrome. (Credit: Marvin Haskins)

when its pilots claimed 6-1-1 during a late morning air battle. 1st Lt. John Carey shot down an Me 109 east of Beni Khalled, Tunisia. 1st Lt. John T. Nangle had a probable victory over an Me 109 at Soliman, Tunisia. Lt. Walter L. Morgan destroyed two Me 109s over Soliman, Lt. Morris A. Dodd flamed an Me 109 over Soliman; and 1st Lt. Terrell E. Yon got a shared kill with 1st Lt. Carey who, after that action, was shot down. 2nd Lt. Robert W. Hine shared in a Me 109 north of Nabeul, Tunisia with 1st Lt. Gene Steinbrenner, but Hine's aircraft was hit by Flak and he crash-landed south of Tunis.

Once on the ground, Hine reported that he *"...walked out of the dry lake and was picked up by Arabs who gave me a ride on a donkey leading to northeast Tunis where I met a couple of Britishers. A Major induced me to take a double scotch and took me to Medjez el Bab where I caught a ride to my base."*

John Carey had a very unusual experience after he was shot down by Flak. He did not remember crash-landing or getting out or running away fast and the first thing he remembered was *"looking backward from a small hill-top and seeing my plane about two or three hundred yards away."*

Carey also met with an Arab and his donkey and Carey paid for a ride to friendly territory, but the ride ended at an Arab hut and after he was given some food, Carey started walking again and was noticed by a German/Italian patrol which came after him. Carey headed away from the patrol and came upon a British Bren Gun Carrier and its crew captured the enemy patrol. One of the Germans gave the location of some 90 Italian troops who were voluntarily awaiting capture. The British subsequently captured them and took them to Tunis. After Carey was back in friendly hands, Brig. Gen. Paul Williams awarded him the Silver Star for gallantry in action.

In spite of the successful air battle the day ended on a sad note for the 52nd FG. Lt. Albert A. Alenius, a new arrival in the 4th FS, was killed when he tried a slow roll coming home from a mission, spun out and crashed into a mountain.

British and American ground forces took Tunis and Bizerte on 8 May and although German and Italian units held out until the 13th, the war in North Africa was at an end. The squadrons made a change-of-station flight in mid-May from Le Sers to La Sebala, and the hot season began. Near the end of the campaign, the Commanding Officer of the Group sent a message to the Commanding General of XII FC stating: *"The 52nd's Spits supported General Patton's ground forces at Kasserine, El Guettar and the eventual advance through Tunisia to the final defeat of the enemy at Cape Bon. By shooting down 13 Ju 87s in one evening of aerial combat, the Group was credited with performing the outstanding aerial feat in the battle for El Guettar, and throughout the Tunisian campaign led all fighter groups in the number of enemy planes destroyed."*

In his article for *The Stars and Stripes* of 13 May, Ernie Pyle wrote *"My old Spitfire Group that I visited in Northern Ireland, and strong again in Africa a few weeks ago, is going stronger than ever these days."*

The British author Christopher F. Shores noted that the 52nd FG was well ahead of the 31st FG in scores at the end of the campaign – 88 and one-third to 46 for the 31st FG. The 52nd FG also claimed 17 probably destroyed and 47 damaged. Shores asserts it was at this point in time that the 52nd FG nearly ceased to be active as a front line fighter group, and Lt. Curtis pinpointed the reason why, saying the Group *"...was taken out of the Air Support Command and put into the Coastal Command"* effective 20 May 1943. Curtis added that *"...as we know, not all the enemies are on the other side."*

Following transfer to the North African Coastal Air Force, an article in *The Stars And Stripes* praised the fine record of *"Second Squadron of an American flown Spitfire outfit"* and of Capt. Arnold Vinson, without mentioning that the 52nd FG was now part of the NACAF.

The NACAF, commanded initially by Group Capt. G.G. Barrett who was soon relieved by Air Vice Marshal Hugh P. Lloyd, *"was made responsible for the air defense of North Africa, for air-sea reconnaissance, for anti-submarine operations and for protection of friendly and destruction of enemy shipping."*

Other than the 52nd FG, the NACAF was composed of the US 81st and 350th Fighter Groups flying P-39s, three RAF Wings, two air defense commands and the US 1st and 2nd anti-submarine Squadrons and some miscellaneous units. The NACAF really was no place for a top-scoring fighter group, but orders were orders. Air combat and aerial victories fell away to nothing almost overnight while other US fighter groups fought over Sicily and, soon, Italy.

Lt. Lynn recalled: *"Immediately after the German surrender Lt. Albert C. Adams, Jr., and I were sent to Cape Bon to find housing for officers."*

When they reached Korba on the south-east shore of Cape Bon, the two officers were told that the Group would not be moving to Korba. Tom Thacker recalled that he and others moved to Korba on 15 May, then to Le Sers on 18 May and then to La Sebala on 21 May. He remembered that *"...after scouting for the best airfield, La Sebala, ten miles northwest of Tunis, was chosen and most of the men of the 52nd FG departed for La Sebala on 22 May"* by a convoy of trucks.

The Group's scoring for the month of May 1943 was closed out on 30 May when Lt. Edwin J. Odem, 5th FS, probably destroyed a Ju 88 and damaged another.

With the war in North Africa now over the 52nd FG would remain at La Sebala, far from the fighting from 22 May to 1 August, flying coastal patrols while others carried out pre-invasion attacks in preparation of the scheduled assault on Sicily. This was a bitter pill for the Group to swallow.

Lt. Bob Curtis, 2nd FS, was on one of his first sea convoy patrol missions on 1 June, with 12 to 14 Spitfires providing cover for a British cruiser and destroyers. Above the 2nd Squadron was a formation of Me 109s and Fw 190s and Curtis saw the enemy aircraft high above him and with their height advantage he *"felt vulnerable"*; however they did not attack. After the war he recalled his Squadron *"...encountered enemy aircraft only once during its two months and ten days at La Sebala and this was the first time I saw a formation of German fighters. I was flying at about 4,000 feet as wingman to Lt. Albert McCraw. The rest of our planes were much higher, at 10,000 to 12,000 feet, with two Spitfire 9's even higher, as top cover."*

Lt. Bill Beard spotted the Germans and Lt. Marvin Haskins who was at 10,000 feet reported that the Germans *"...dropped their belly tanks when they saw our planes and that we did the same, although I do not remember doing so or even having a belly tank. I was very nervous, not knowing what to expect."*

There was no dogfight but when Curtis landed at his home base his *"...leather A-2 jacket was soaked through with sweat."*

On 2 June, 1st Lt. Thompson D. Litchfield, 5th FS, damaged a Ju 88 over the Bay of Bizerte. Lt. Sid Feld shot down an Fw 190 on 3 June, 20 miles northeast of Cape Bon, and three days later, Feld downed an Me 109 west of Pantelleria and damaged another in the same area, for his final victories. With nine kills Sylvan Feld is the USAAF's highest scoring Spitfire Ace. Soon afterwards he was transferred out of the Group and in September 1943 Feld was reassigned to the 410th FS, 373rd FG. The 373rd was later deployed to the Ninth Air Force in England, and during his short combat tour with this Group, Major Feld destroyed 3.5 German aircraft on the ground. On 13 August 1944 Feld's P-47 was brought down by Flak, and seven days later, as a POW, he was mortally wounded during a USAAF bombing attack, and died the next day in Petit Quevilly, France. Major Feld was buried as *"an unknown German soldier"* and it was not until 1959 that the German War Graves Commission unearthed the remains and found American military clothing and Major Feld's dogtags. His remains were re-interred in the Ardennes American Cemetery in Belgium.

A snapshot of King George VI and his driver during his visit to the 52nd Fighter Group. (Credit: Thomas Thacker)

Lt. Colonel Graham West. (Credit: Thomas Thacker)

Aerial action during the convoy patrols of 7 and 8 June was sparse, but successful for the 4th and 5th Fighter Squadrons. On 7 June Lt. Bill Canning and F/O Jim Montgomery, 4th FS, shared in the destruction of an Me 109 over Cape Bon, and on 8 June Lt. Morris Dodd, 5th FS, shot down an Italian MC 200 west of Pantelleria. Tragedy struck on 9 June when Lt. Donald Markley, 4th FS, was killed in a landing accident upon his return from the mission. What made the incident even sadder was that Markley had already completed his required missons, and had volunteered for this one. The Group diary noted that *"...he was returning from a mission and in his first attempt to land, he overshot the field. He climbed to an altitude of 200 to 300 feet and then, with his flaps down, began a left bank. His ship lost flying speed and his motor cut out. The plane went straight into the ground."*

Allied air power continued to pound the island of Pantelleria on 11 June as the invasion fleet approached. The 52nd participated in the aerial umbrella covering the fleet and encountered some German opposition. The *Luftwaffe* tried

Lt. Marvin Haskins proudly posing with his Spitfire which now displays the 'American Beagle Squadron' emblem on its cowling. (Credit: Marvin Haskins)

Seen from left to right: Sgt. Harry Greenburg, Crew Chief, and Lt. Charles T.O.'Conner and their Spitfire. (Credit: Thomas Thacker)

desperately to fend off the invading forces, and lost 17 aircraft in the attempt. The 4th Squadron played a part in blunting the Germans' efforts and claimed 1-0-2 of the total claims of 17-2-4. The credits went to Lt. Robert Armstrong who shot down an Fw 190 north-northeast of the island and damaged an Me 109 in the same area. The third claim was credited to Lt. Dale Anderson who damaged an Me 109 north of Pantelleria.

The highlight of 11 June, however, was the sight of a white cross of surrender on the airfield at Pantelleria. Air power alone had brought about the surrender of the island.

Action over the island continued on 12 June as German aircraft again tried to interfere with Allied operations. As the 52nd FG flew a protective cover over the ships, a gaggle of Fw 190s flew into the 4th FS zone and paid for their intrusion. Three Focke-Wulfs were quickly dispatched into the sea, and Lts. Bob Armstrong, Robert Burnett III and James O. Tyler were each credited with one victory. Armstrong also managed to damage another enemy aircraft before it fled the area.

At about this point in time Lt. Luis Zendegui had an unusual and very memorable experience with a German reconnaissance aircraft. The Germans often flew photo recce missions over Allied positions at altitudes which meant they were beyond the reach of the 52nd FG's Spitfire Mk Vs. The Allies nicknamed the German recce ships *"Photo Freddies"* and one day the 52nd FG prepared a surprise for them in the form of one of the Group's new Spitfire Mk IXs. Lt. Zendegui was chosen to intercept the German recce flight and waited in his Spitfire for the for the approach of the enemy aircraft. The German, however, was late this time so Zendegui climbed out of his aircraft and took off his flight jacket and relaxed. As he relaxed in the warm desert sun the German aircraft was spotted and Zendegui was alerted to go after him. Without thinking he leaped into his Spitfire IX without the benefit of his warm flight jacket and soon afterwards was chasing the German at 37,000 feet where the temperature could reach 60 degrees below zero. To add insult to injury, the *"Photo Freddie"* got away and Lt. Zendegui came home "*...so thoroughly chilled that I didn't fly again for about five days.*"

Captain Everett Jenkins and Sgt. Richard C. Brown posing with their Spitfire Mk IX. (Credit: Everett Jenkins)

Another of the 4th Fighter Squadron's Spitfire Mk IXs on alert status. In this case the photographer was able to confirm that the aircraft was painted in a mottled brown on its uppersurfaces and blue on the undersurfaces. The pilot in the cockpit is Lt. James Puffer and his Crew Chief is resting under its left wing. (Credit: John Blythe)

Spitfire Mk IX coded WD-QQ of the 4th Fighter Squadron on alert in Tunisia. Note the aircraft is finished in a one color upper surface with Azure blue undersurfaces. The upper surface is probably the High Altitude Medium Sea Grey scheme, but some of the 52nd FG's Mk IXs uppersurfaces were painted light brown. (Credit: Fred Wiersma)

On 17 June, King George VI and Winston Churchill visited La Sebala. The King reviewed the troops, and quite unexpectedly, presented Lt. Colonel James Coward with the British Distinguished Flying Cross. Two days later the scene at La Sebala changed from one of ceremonies to one of a very somber nature. Motor accidents killed three crew chiefs, T/Sgts. Edgar Barnes and Donald Empey, and S/Sgt George McDaniel, and injured nine other enlisted men. On the following day, 20 June, things continued to go very badly beginning with the men fighting a wheat field fire which was threatening the base. It took an hour to extinguish. Following that incident, the Group Commanding Officer, Lt. Col. Graham West, Capt. Ralph Thomas, Lt. Howard Brians and Sgt Bernard Schreiber took a water truck to extinguish a fire in an abandoned Ju 52 that had been in the path of the fire. As the men began to spray water on the burning transport, which unknown to them was booby-trapped, it exploded. Lt Brians and Sgt. Schreiber were killed instantly and Graham West's legs were mutilated so badly that they required amputation. Following this tragic incident James Coward became the Group's Commanding Officer, and the 4th FS's Commanding Officer, Major Robert Levine was made Group Administrative Officer. Capt. William Houston took over as Commanding Officer of the 4th Fighter Squadron.

Capt. Norman McDonald paid tribute to *"Windy"* West, noting that West came from the 20th PG and was Commanding Officer of the 2nd FS for a while before moving up to Group Ops and then Group Commanding Officer: "*'Windy' led us and the 5th Squadron to Algiers. The Fifth was stationed there and 'Windy' took us on to Bone Harbor airport, where we saw five weeks of real action. 'Windy' flew with us on many missions, leading our twelve-plane formations. On one of our first sweeps into enemy territory, he clobbered an Me 109. None of us saw it go in; we were all under attack at the time. So 'Windy' only claimed that it was damaged, adhering to the strict RAF code that the e/a must disintegrate, someone must see the pilot bail out or the plane crash, if its destruction is to be confirmed. He was a man of great integrity, who led and inspired by example."*

When Lt. Gen. Carl A. Spaatz visited him at the base hospital, West continued to demonstrate his leadership qualities and Col. West told Spaatz: *"I can fly again."* An article printed in the *New York Times* on 22 August compared America's own legless fighter pilot to Britain's legless Squadron Leader, Douglas Bader. Spaatz told an aide to get West fixed up with artificial legs and when West recovered, he was assigned to England where he did liaison duty between British and American units.

Lt. Miles Lynn took some pilots overland to the former German radar station at Bizerte. While they were there learning more about radar, which the Allies had put to use, they saw echoes on the screen of a Ju 88 with a Spitfire which was flown by Lt. Charles Hoover, 4th FS, attacking it. The two shot each other down. On 21 June, Capt. Bill Houston, 4th FS, damaged an Fw 190 east of Bizerte.

On 26 June the Germans attempted to launch a major attack off Cape Bon on the Allied invasion fleet heading toward Sicily. Over 100 Ju 88s, Fw 190s and Cant Z1007s attacked the fleet but were driven off before doing much damage by the covering convoy patrols consisting of RAF and USAAF fighters. During the air battle, six *Luftwaffe* aircraft were shot down, and none of the ships suffered serious damage. Lt. Albert Adams, Jr., 2nd FS, shot down one of the Fw 190s north of Pantelleria and damaged another Focke-Wulf in the same area. The official history of the USAAF reported that on that day "*...the enemy failed in a major effort to sink Allied shipping bringing supplies for the later invasion of Sicily*."

Sometime in June 1943, the 2nd FS was given the nickname, *"The American Beagle Squadron."* This nickname expressed the feelings of tent-mates, Armstrong, Curtis, Haskins and Macmillan about their role as American Spitfire pilots, like those of the American Eagle Squadrons in England, but reduced to doing *"dog work"* of harbor and convoy patrols. Armstrong had trained in the RAF, but transferred to the USAAF, thought of the name and Haskins drew a suitable emblem which many pilots painted on their aircraft and/or flight jackets. This name and unofficial emblem have persisted and the name recently was officially adopted by the present 2nd FS, along with a modified version of the emblem.

The date of 1 July marked one year of foreign service for the Group and 1st Lt. John Carey, 5th FS, marked the occasion by downing two Fw 190s northeast of Cape Bon. Carey's flight latched onto the tails of a flight of two Fw 190s and a Me 109 G and as he disposed of the two Focke-Wulfs, Lt. Charles T. O'Connor, Jr., 5th FS, downed the Me 109. About an hour after this engagement, Lt. Irwin Gottlieb downed another Fw 190 20 miles north east of Bizerte, giving the 5th FS four confirmed kills for the day.

Lt. Connor shared the story of his victory in a letter to his family: "*Well now I shall give you a first hand account of my er... ok, a triumph, (as you so naively put it) of the past month. Excuse me while I light up a cigar first. Ahem, brsfsk!! Ahhhh – it all began by my being up on an alert since dawn. Shortly after seven a scramble was called and Capt. Carey and I roared off into the blue in a big cloud of dust, noise, excitement and a vector. In this war better than 98 per cent of all (missions) an airplane's movements are controlled by radar, which, beyond a doubt, is one of the greatest inventions devised by man.*

"We were vectored onto a heading and climbed to 32,000 feet where we began to patrol. We made a turn and I saw a flash of sunlight on someone's canopy which turned out to be a 'Jerry'. Capt. Carey was above me and quite a distance ahead due to the turn when all of a sudden two Fw 190s and a Me 109 G came out of the sun and above us, and apparently they had not seen us for they made a 90-degree turn away from us. We 'firewalled' everything, moved in behind them and started in. Capt. Carey picked the nearest 190 and opened fire on him. About that time the Me 109 half-rolled and started for Sicily so I half -rolled after him and away we went. He was doing a steep turn down and to the left when I closed to about 200 yards and gave him a quick burst of cannon and machine gun fire. My first burst then, was a deflection shot of approximately 30 degrees and I noticed strikes on his left wing." (Unfortunately the last page of Lt. O'Conner's letter has been lost, but he was credited with the destruction of this Me 109 over Cape Bon.)

Contact with the Axis air forces diminished for the Group during the next several days, and then a brief flourish of activity began on 5 July. On that date Lt. Robert L. Confer and 1st Lt. David W. McMillan, 2nd FS, shared in downing a Me 109 near Abmar. Two days later Lt. John C. Burchfield, 4th FS, damaged an Fw 190 north-east of Zombra Island.

On 8 July a Ju 88 *"Photo Freddie"* , appeared overhead and 1st Lt. Robert E. Armstrong, Jr., 4th FS, took off as 'Digwell Red 1 in a Spitfire IX on a Freddie scramble', and shot the Ju 88 down west of Bizerte. In doing so Armstrong had held course in the face of the rear-gunner's heavy fire and his Spitfire was shot up by return fire. He bailed out at 40,000 feet and free-fell to 10,000 feet before he pulled the rip cord, landed and walked three miles into friendly hands. He and the German pilot, Lt. Herman Schmick, were taken to the 114th Service Hospital and Armstrong *"got a Luger from his enemy friend."* He also got the DFC.

Sicily was invaded on 9 July and with the exception of the 52nd Fighter Group, Allied fighters saw heavy action during the period of 9-11 July and claimed a toll of 51-13-16 enemy aircraft. The 52nd FG, serving its Coastal Command duties, did manage to engage and down a pair of enemy aircraft on 12 July, which helped slightly to soothe its frustration in being left out of the big events. On that date, Lt. Irwin Gottleib, and F/O Louis M. Weynandt, 5th FS, each shot down a Me 109 F in dogfights occurring north of Bizerte.

An accident claimed another of the Group's pilots on 19 July. Lt. George L. Bailey, 2nd FS, was lost when he and 2nd Lt. Norman English were up practicing gunnery runs. As English flew over the sea to create a shadow on the water, and Bailey, using the shadow as a moving target, dove and shot at it. Bailey experienced target fixation and flew into the water. Pilots flew a search for the dinghy but found nothing.

A few days later, rumors of a move were verified and excitement spread rapidly when the men were told they would move to bases in Sicily at the end of the month. Tom Thacker recalled "*Beginning on 28 July, 56 officers and 168 enlisted men of the 2nd and 4th Squadrons departed by air, and our planes flew to Bocca di Falco airdrome on the outskirts of Palermo, Sicily. The balance of the squadrons arrived in early August on an LST. The 5th FS was to be based at Bo Rizzo, Sicily, near Trapani on the far west coast*."

But the squadron did not leave La Sebala right away. On 30 July, the air echelon of the 2nd FS moved to Palermo, Sicily and the ground echelon moved on 2 August. On 30 July, while still based in Tunisia, 1st Lt. Franklin A. Everett and 1st Lt. Everett K. Jenkins, Jr., both from the 5th FS, both got Fw 190s north-east of Bizerte.

Chapter Five

"Sitting on our duffs doing nothing for the war effort"

Sicily – A period of frustration

July–December 1943

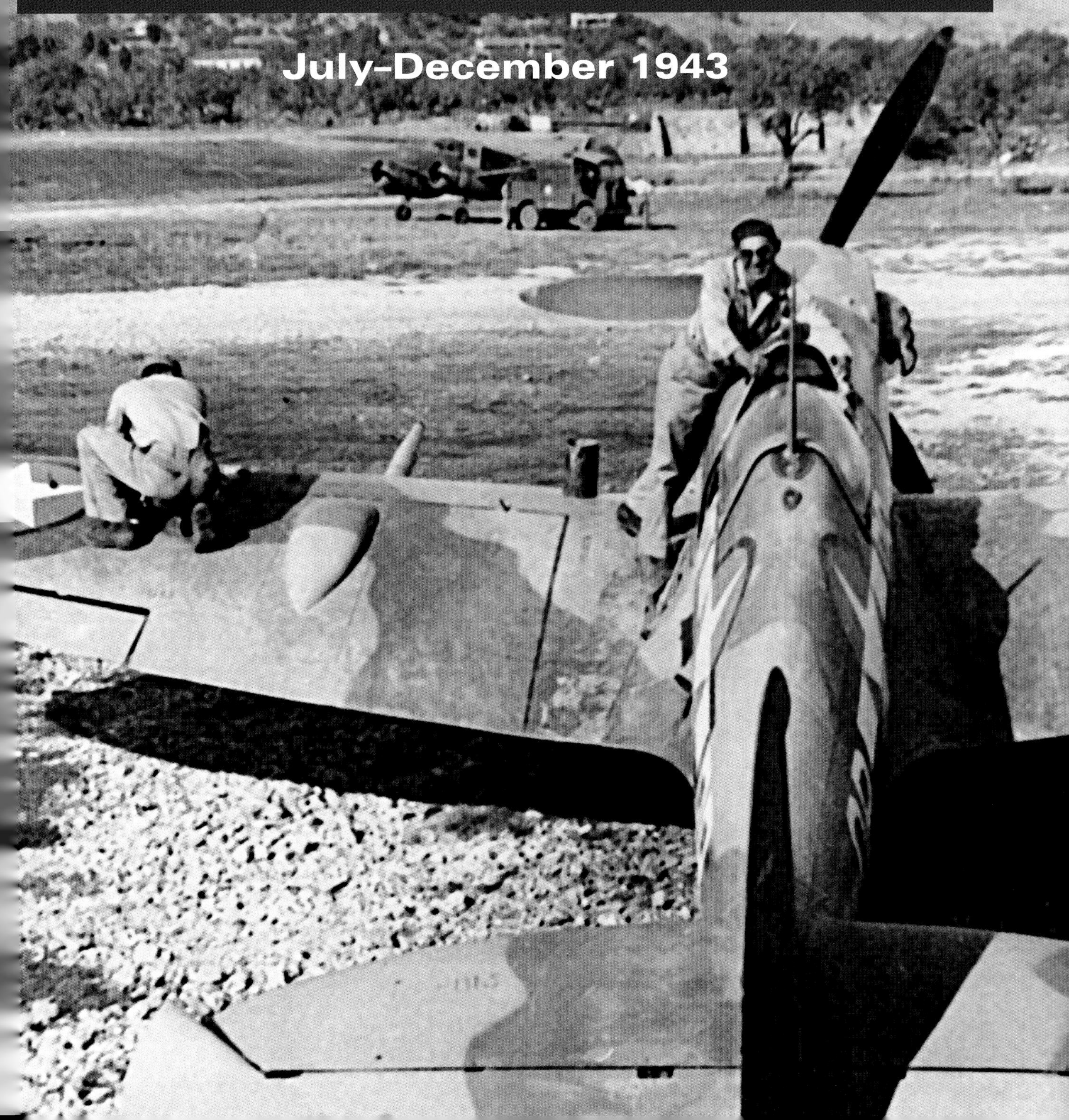

A 2nd Fighter Squadron Spitfire Mk VIII awaiting its next mission at Palermo, Sicily, August 1943. (Credit: Paul Ludwig)

On the last day of July, the 2nd FS air echelon flew to Palermo, Sicily, and immediately after arriving, flew two harbor patrols and two convoy patrols. An Allied cruiser shelled enemy shore positions and when Fw 190s attempted to dive-bomb it, the 2nd FS scrambled Spitfires which drove the Germans off, but did not catch them. Maj. G.V. Williams damaged an Fw 190 near Caronia, Sicily while leading Red Section on a cover over a cruiser and two destroyers shelling Caronia. Williams spotted four Fw 190s as they were dive-bombing these ships and Williams and attacked one of them, firing at it three times, but not closing the gap. On his third burst Williams saw a cannon strike on the left side of the fuselage.

Capt. Norm McDonald, 2nd FS recalled: *"The morning after the air echelon arrived, an hour or two before dawn, German bombers raided Palermo harbor."* The night raids continued all week. McDonald decided to set up a two-aircraft section which would surprise the nocturnal raiders as they approached the field at the prescribed time, always two hours before dawn. Miles Lynn and McDonald got into a conversation with two other men one evening over drinks and McDonald commented he *"would love to take a crack at those bombers but he was afraid our ack-ack might do a job on me."* One of the other men said he knew he could make one phone call and silence Allied anti-aircraft artillery if needed. McDonald's plan called for his section to take off before the bombers made their appearance and wait for them, but he would need some kind of runway lighting to get airborne. Lt. Lynn and Lt. Fred B. 'Fireball' Short volunteered to man a Jeep one on each side of the take-off strip and turn on the headlights long enough to see the direction of takeoff.

McDonald and Lt. Norman English scrambled aloft in the early morning hours of 1 August 1943 and flew out to sea, climbed to 10,000 feet, and flew a racetrack pattern and waited, while McDonald pondered how to get two Spitfires back on the ground in the dark. As dawn broke and with low fuel, McDonald spotted two enemy bombers 2,000 feet above him, climbed and shot down a Do 217 15 miles northeast of the island of Stromboli.

The second Do 217 was shot down by Lt. English who described the kill in his encounter report: *"I was Red Two and shortly before dawn as we were standing by to take off on harbor patrol I heard an e/a overhead, so I took off immediately at 0540 hours. As I reached 5,000 feet I sighted what I afterwards identified as a Dornier 217 flying due east over the harbor of Palermo at 15,000 feet."*

Climbing and approaching the target, English was not seen by the *Luftwaffe* crew and *"....closed to within 100 yards and gave him a five second burst. The top turret gunner started firing at me."*

English answered his fire with another burst and the top gunner stopped firing and the left motor began to smoke. After a few more bursts from English's guns, the enemy aircraft began to slow down, pieces flew off and he jettisoned his canopy and one of the crewmen bailed out. The aircraft kept dropping and crashed into the water about 60 miles due north of Salina Island.

Another lull in action lasted until 6 August when F/O James H. Montgomery, Jr. and Lt. Leonard V. Helton attempted to shoot down a high-flying *"Photo Freddie"* escorted by three Me 109s. The action ended in a tie. Lt. Helton downed one of the Messerschmitts, and another German pilot evened the score by shooting Montgomery out of the sky.

The events that unfolded after he bailed out earned F/O Montgomery the title of *"Robinson Crusoe of American Spitfire Pilots."*The Me 109 pilot hit Montgomery's Spitfire with cannon shells that exploded on the canopy of the cockpit, blackening his eyes. Otherwise he was completely unscathed. Montgomery recounted what happened in a terse *"a-b-c"* chronology: *"(a.) losta fight to a Messerschmitt; (b.) bailed out after such a fast dive that I didn't open my parachute until I was only*

F/O James Montgomery's Spitfire Mk IX "The Impatient Virgin" which was coded WD-A. (Credit: Robert Klug)

1,000 feet above the Mediterranean; (c.) climbed into my inflated rubber dinghy and drifted all night; (d.) speared a fish with a knife and ate it on the theory that it might quench my thirst. 'It wasn't so good' he added later; and (e.) I saw a large turtle and poked it in the nose in order to avoid a maritime traffic crash; and (f.) hailed a British Walrus rescue plane and climbed aboard it after almost twenty-four hours on the sea."

While HQ 52nd FG and the 2nd and 4th Fighter Squadrons were operating from their new base at Bocca di Falco near Palermo, the 5th Fighter Squadron continued to operate from Tunisia, while its new base at Bo Rizzo, near Trapani, was being readied. During its last few days in Tunisia the Squadron chalked up its last kills in North Africa, when on 12 August Lt. Taylor Malone, Jr., and F/O Robert M. Moore shared a Fw 190 northeast of Bizerte. Malone also damaged an Fw 190 in the same area. The air echelon of the 5th FS finally made the move to Sicily on 17 August. Tom Thacker noted: *"The engineers required extra time to clean up a flying field at Bo Rizzo, near Trapini at the west end of the island of Sicily so the 5th Squadron planes had remained behind in Africa. On August 17th, they flew over and landed among the vineyards and wrecked Macchi aircraft that were abundant in the area. The mission of the 5th was not particularly glamorous, as it was mainly to provide protection for shipping along the north-east coast of Sicily. Strategically, it was important but yielded few victories. However, morale was high as is traditional among units operating separately."*

In August a change in command took place in the 2nd Fighter Squadron and Capt. Bert S. Sanborn replaced Major George Williams, who departed for an assignment at 62nd Fighter Wing. On 20 August, German bombers bombed Palermo harbor and some bombs landed near Bocca di Falco field, but Beaufighter nightfighters shot down four of the enemy aircraft. For the pilots of the 2nd and 4th Fighter Squadrons, however, enemy aircraft were nowhere to be found.

When 2nd FS pilots next fired their guns on 27 August, the encounter turned out to be a tragic mistake. An element of the 2nd Squadron spotted what they thought was a 'Ju 88' but which was, in reality, a Beaufighter, and the two pilots attacked. The first pilot hit the Beaufighter, killing its observer, and then the second pilot swooped in and fired, hitting the British aircraft again. As he pulled up he realized that they had made a terrible mistake and called out to his wingman to break off the attack. It was too late, the stricken Beaufighter plunged into the sea below and its entire crew was killed. (When reporting the incident one of the pilots stated: *"The Beaufighter's horizontal tailplane has some dihedral while the Ju 88s had none. Why neither (name omitted) nor I saw this I will never know."* In correspondence in September 2000, Bob Curtis offered a possible explanation stating: *"...the horizontal tailplane of early Beaufighters had no dihedral and it is possible that it was of these aircraft they shot down."*) Several days later both pilots were transferred out of the Group to Twelfth Air Force headquarters for disposition of their cases. Here General Pete Quesada *"dressed them down"* and sent them to an aircraft recognition class with the warning that they would be given a tough aircraft recognition exam and if they failed to get a perfect score they would be thrown out of the AAF. Both pilots, to their relief, passed and were reassigned to the 31st Fighter Group. The incident also cost the Group Commander, Lt. Colonel James Coward, his job. Lt. Colonel Richard Ames was named as temporary Commanding Officer and on 6 September he turned command of the 52nd over to Lt. Colonel Marvin McNickle.

A Bristol Beaufighter used by an American nightfighter squadron photographed in the 4th Fighter Squadron area of the field at La Sebala. It was an aircraft similar to this one that was accidentally shot down by 2nd Fighter Squadron pilots on 27 August 1943. (Credit: C.G. Jones)

At Bocca di Falco the result of this tragedy was that aircraft recognition tests, not often given previously, were given very frequently throughout the year. Another low point for the Group during the last few days of August 1943 was that they were again missing out on some major engagements with the *Luftwaffe*. During the three-day period of 28-30 August, US fighters claimed 34-14-27 victories, but the Group could only take credit for two of them. Lt. Robert W. Hine, 5th FS, downed an Me 109G south of Naples on 28 August and the next day, 1st Lt. Edwin J. Odom, 5th FS, received credit for an Me 410 south of Utica. Beyond this, the pilots only could look forward toward to endless and boring harbor patrols or convoy patrols periodically broken by an occasional but usually fruitless scramble. One aircraft was written off during this period when Lt. William Bryan, Jr., 2nd FS, lost an engine on 28 August while flying over Sicily and he crash-landed, hitting a stone wall. Bryan received some painful injuries, but recovered and returned to duty.

This Spitfire Mk Vc, VF-AA of the 5th Fighter Squadron came to grief at La Sebala in August 1943 after a new pilot blundered his landing approach. (Credit: Toppen)

The unit witnessed an event on 30 August that was to become part of a major moment in history when Lt. Lynn led a flight to Salerno, Italy to escort an Italian transport aircraft carrying senior government officials back to Bocca di Falco. The aircraft landed at about 16.30 hrs, and there to the surprise of everyone, were the senior Italian officers that participated in the meetings which led to the surrender of Italian forces to the Allies on 8 September 1943.

The Germans evacuated Sicily in mid-August, leaving the 52nd FG based in the far western half of the island flying fighters that did not have the range to operate over Italy, so the Group continued flying convoy and harbor patrols. The battle-tried American fighter group was out of the fight. There was so little flying to do that the 2nd FS alternated patrols with the 4th FS and 1 September was a day off for the 2nd Squadron. The diarist for the 5th FS misdiagnosed the ugly mood at Bo Rizzo airdrome recording: *"...the pilots are happy. They are getting to do quite a bit of flying. Convoy patrol is their main duty."* On 2 September the 5th Squadron diarist reassessed the mood at Bo Rizzo:*"the mechanics on the line are unhappy at having to sit alert all day without having their planes fly."*

In August several new flight officers were assigned to the Group including F/O Robert *"Bob"* Hoover who introduced himself by looping a P-39 off the deck while at Casablanca. (F/O Hoover was later to become the post-war world's foremost aerobatic pilot, and perhaps this was his premier air show performance.)

On 3 September, British and Canadian troops invaded Italy across the Strait of Messina, and again the Group found itself missing out on the activity over the beaches and began a long dry spell that lasted until 7 December 1943 when Jim Tyler finally broke the Group scoring drought. Further frustrating the 52nd FG, was the lack of newer and more modern replacement aircraft. Despite long-time mass production of Mark IX Spitfires, two outdated Spitfire Vc's were flown in to the 2nd FS to relieve an aircraft shortage. Tom Thacker recalled: *"We were losing more airplanes during this period from landing accidents than from combat."* Bocca di Falco had a short runway that was rough, sloping and was approached through a treacherous mountain pass. On 6 September, Capt. Dougherty was taking off and his Spitfire *"...ran into a pile of rocks at the end of the runway and flipped over onto its back."* Dougherty *"...escaped without a scratch."*

During the three day period of 6-8 September, the unit's diaries revealed a mixture of grumbling and pride. The 5th FS of 6 September complained that: *"We feel we are sitting on our duffs doing nothing for the war effort..."* – but the entries for HQ and all of the squadrons of the next two days reflected how proud they were of the protection the pilots provided for the invasion convoys and in the work of the maintenance crews that supported the missions.

Accidents continued during this period, largely due to worn out aircraft and a parts shortage. A rash of accidents in the 4th FS began on 6 September when Capt. Dougherty's Spitfire failed to get airborne. A week later another two more accidents occurred, on 12 and 13 September. The 4th FS diarist stated: *"Lt. Roy W. Smith had a narrow escape today when his left tire blew out on takeoff. The fuselage of his aircraft was broken in two places, but Lt. Smith was uninjured."* The very next day Lt. Walton's Spitfire failed to get airborne, crashed and was demolished at the end of the runway. Somehow Walton escaped with only a small cut. On this date, in an effort to get aircraft back in good conditions some of the Group's pilots flew to North Africa to get replacement tail wheels, *"...the lack of which made our status board look like a sick call."*

The 2nd FS flew dawn and dusk patrols on 14 September, and 15 September was such a do-nothing day that a squadron diarist said *"Practically no work today. This is certainly a dead sector. We haven't had a scramble in weeks."* Two days later, there were more dawn and dusk patrols, convoy patrols and convoy searches. In the 5th FS *"...No flying was done at all which further makes the Squadron think they are doing no good what-so-ever."* On 18 September, the 2nd FS covered three convoys, flew one scramble but the enemy aircraft on the radar plot faded and got away. The 5th FS was inactive.

The 2nd FS escorted convoys, flew one scramble, and served as an escort for a B-25 in distress on the 19th. The air war had grown so mundane for the pilots that events on the ground gained in importance. The 4th Squadron diarist noted, for example: *"Lt. Paine, 4th FS, the new Armament Officer, was in the States only two weeks ago and he has been smothered with questions about life in America."* On the same date the HQ 52nd FG diarist stated: *"In the afternoon a group of officers and a truck load of enlisted men went to the Red Cross Beach Club to swim, sail play bridge and otherwise enjoy themselves."*

Some other forms of relieving boredom were tried as evidenced in this extract from Lt. Charles O'Connor's letter, dated 18 September 1943, to his brother. *"Do you remember that little 25 caliber 'Eyetie' rifle I told you I picked up? A bunch of us have located some Jerry concrete pillboxes and some 90 MM and 155 MM shells – the 90 MM for anti-aircraft fire and the 155 MM for a howitzer. We very carefully lug the shells down a hill and place them in the pillbox doorway, withdraw about 200 yards, taking a good sheltered spot in a slit trench (that's spelled right too- you dope!) or a fox hole, and commence to blaze away. Boy, do those things make a racket when they go off!! We've managed to blast quite a bit of the doorway to pieces, but those pillboxes were really built for endurance – they're solid!"*

The entry for 20 September in the HQ diary was somewhat more positive. *"Covered five convoys – business was pretty good today – and had one scramble without incidents. Also routine dawn and dusk*

A Ju 88 T, known to the personnel of the 52nd FG as a 'Photo Freddie', of 1.(F)/123 in Italy in 1944. The aircraft has just landed and its film container is being taken away for development.

The SM-79 bomber that brought the Italian surrender delegation to Palermo being viewed with interest by members of the 52nd Fighter Group. (Credit: Robert Klug)

QP-BB, one of the Mk Vc Spitfires still in use on Sicily by the 2nd Fighter Squadron during the summer of 1943. (Credit: Marvin Haskins)

Spitfire Mk Vc QP-K of the 2nd Fighter Squadron returning from a patrol to its base at Palermo, Sicily. (Credit: Paul Ludwig)

Edwin Fuller posing with his Spitfire which was damaged by Sully Varnell's propeller during a landing accident. (Credit: Robert C. Curtis)

The Red Cross donut girls and their "Clubmobile" were a positive morale factor for the troops in the field. (Credit: Cogal)

harbor patrols. It is noted that the pilots were in a much better mood today. This was probably due to the fact that they were all able to put some operational time on the books."

On 22 September, the 2nd FS flew the daily dawn and dusk patrols, covered three convoys and flew three scrambles. Things had gone well until now, but the Group diary then reported: *"Upon landing after one mission, the plane flown by Lt. James S. Varnell, ran up the rear of the plane piloted by Lt. Edwin W. Fuller breaking off the entire tail assembly and part of the canopy."*

It did not end there. While taxiing in after landing, Lt. Clyde S. Cleveland's Spitfire hit a rock on the runway and it lost a tail wheel and the Group diarist recorded: *"Immediately thereafter, Group ordered all planes to land on the other side of the field."*

The diarist reported that the most newsworthy that happened on 23 September was that a detail of enlisted men cleared the side of the runway of all rocks and the *"mail arrived"* and *"morale is high."* The 24th of September was similar in that dawn and dusk patrols and convoy patrols were the only flying done. The 5th Squadron held an aircraft recognition class in the early evening in the courtyard of the Officers' villa.

The next day there was some activity and an unusual victory was scored when Lt. Bob Curtis shot down a barrage balloon. Several sorties, to include dawn and dusk patrols, convoys escorts, and a *"Photo Freddie"* patrol, were flown during the day but even this activity didn't totally relieve the boredom. To combat the doldrums some of the men of the 4th FS made a speedboat by squaring off the back end of a float from an Italian seaplane and they rigged up a motor from a battery cart for power.

The 5th FS reported that on 27 September *"...quite a bit of flying was done today. Most of it consisted of convoy patrols. This is a dull and drab*

Lt. "Sully" Varnell and his Spitfire Mk IX at Palermo. (Credit: Robert C. Curtis)

Lt. Bob Curtis and the Spitfire Mk Vc that he shared with Marv Haskins on Sicily. (Credit: Robert C. Curtis)

existence for the outfit these days. Everyone wants a change." Next day – 28 September – the 2nd Squadron flew a dawn harbor patrol, covered two convoys, flew escort for a Walrus and launched one scramble, but bad weather prevented further missions. The 5th FS diarist reported: *"...today we had our first good rain since coming to Sicily"* and pilots attended an aircraft identification class. There were rumors of a move. On the 29th, the 5th was inactive. A day later, after pilots flew a dawn patrol and covered one convoy, the 5th FS diarist said *"...today, was, as usual, a boring and uninteresting day."*

The 52nd FG scored no aerial or ground victories in the month of September. XII ASC put a good face on the dullness saying: *"During the month of September, not one combat mission was flown; the first such month since November, 1942. The flying was confined solely to sea patrol and convoy duty, the most important of which was escorting convoys passing through our sector on their way to the Salerno invasion point."*

In spite of the lack of combat operations, Lt. Charles O'Connor of the 5th FS answered his brother's questions about flying the Spitfire with an obvious pride: *"As for any information as to what models of Spitfires we're flying over here, that's taboo. All I can say is that we've got the very latest and best models. These planes are more maneuverable and speedier than any plane we have been up against. Makes a P-38 look silly and boy, believe me that P-38 is a (illegible) piece of machinery. I don't know how it would stack up against a 47 because a 47 and our Spits are both high altitude fighters and from what I've heard a 47 is a going concern after it gets over 15,000'. Just the same though I'd match a Spitfire against it."*

On 1 October, rainy weather rendered Bocca di Falco field for the 2nd FS into a muddy mess; the 4th FS flew convoy patrols and for the 5th FS at Bo Rizzo, *"...eighteen convoy protection sorties were flown today. (A mediocre day.)"* A freak windstorm hit the area on 2 October and the diarist reported: *"Planes of all sizes were tossed around like straws. A B-24 that had landed here for minor repairs after a raid deep into enemy territory was blown through a fence and badly damaged."* It landed on top of a Walrus.

"Many of our Spitfires were blown onto the runway. A couple crashed together and one went under the tail of a transport."

Even though the weather was dreadful, the 2nd FS flew a dawn patrol and the 5th FS flew a convoy protection mission.

On 3 October, the diarist wrote that the field for the 4th FS at Bocca di Falco *"...is too muddy for fighters to land on today"* and the 5th FS at Bo Rizzo closed the field for part of the day but flew a convoy protection mission. On 4 October, in the 4th Squadron's area, *"a terrible accident happened around 1 o'clock. A gas burner exploded in the kitchen" and Cpl. Edward T. York, Cpl. Ralph Brahmer and two Italian workers were all badly burned."*The 5th FS flew six sorties and convoy patrols. A recognition quiz was held and a final exam was scheduled for the next day and out of the 30 pilots taking part only three failed. On 7 October, the 4th FS undertook its first flying in six days. To liven up the atmosphere, Lt. Fraser, Special Services Officer, sponsored classes for the men and Capt. Westbrook taught recognition, while Capt. Steinbrenner taught a class in the German language.

The Italian Breda 15S rebuilt and coded WD-4F by the 4th Fighter Squadron. The aircraft was used as a hack by the Squadron for a while. (Credit: Fred Wiersma)

Italian and French troops took the city of Bastia, Corsica on 4 October and the island fell under Allied control, paving the way for a move for the Group. On 8 October, the 5th FS flew convoy patrols. Four days later, officers and men of the 4th FS finished *"...putting an Italian high wing monoplane together and they say it will fly tomorrow."* The little aircraft was coded *'WD 4F'* – when describing a man's fitness for service, *'4F'* denoted *'unfit'*! There was no activity in the 5th FS areas.

On 13 October, for the first time in months the 52nd FG lost one of its pilots when Lt

Bob Hoover (left) and Ted Bullock (right) pose with Spitfire WD-W. (Credit: Ted Bullock)

A very scenic photograph of QP-R landing at Palermo after a mission with the mountains Sicily as a backdrop.
(Credit: Paul Ludwig collection)

2nd Fighter Squadron personnel performing maintenance on a Spitfire Mk Vc at Palermo. Note the UC-78 Bobcat in the background, and the extremely weathered and faded national insignia on the Spitfire. The dark surround is where the red outline has been over painted in insignia blue.
(Credit: Paul Ludwig collection)

Ferdinand W. *"Herky" Holmberg, 5th FS, went in from 10,000 feet while on a training mission."* The wreckage of the Spitfire IX was found a few miles west of Marsala. On the 15th a few pilots from the 4th FS flew for the first time in five days and F/O Robert Hoover put on an air show for the men. The 4th FS diarist described Hoover's aerial display: *"F/O Hoover has been testing a P-38, and has put on a real show over the field, with his diving, looping and doing slow rolls with one engine. He ended up the show with a dogfight with a Spitfire V, flown by Lt. John Meyers of the 2nd FS, and proved the P-38 is definitely a good airplane. In the 5th FS there was no operational flying. This is a dead sector."*

Pessimists believe accidents come in threes, and there was another fatal accident on 19 October when, during a six-ship formation training flight, Lts. Atkins and Donald K. Monk, both in the 5th FS, collided when one of them ran into the prop wash of a big B-24 bomber which threw one of the Spitfires sideways into the other. Lt. Atkins was able to land his disabled Spitfire, with minor injuries but Lt. Donald K. Monk was killed in the crash. The 4th FS was inactive while the 2nd FS escorted Henry Morgenthau, Secretary of the Treasury, to Naples and Allied Headquarters.

The 2nd FS flew 12 sorties on 20 October and took part in an Army Cooperation mission with the 2nd Armored Division and the 4th Squadron. During a practice flight, a wingman motioned to Capt. Edward M. Scott, 4th FS, that smoke was trailing from his aircraft. Capt. Scott attempted to bring his Spitfire in for a landing, but his engine stopped a short distance from the field, and Scott hit a telephone pole. The aircraft burst into flame, hit the ground and overturned. Sadly, he was unable to exit the overturned aircraft and burned to death. The diarist commented on his loss: *"Capt. Scott was one of the three remaining pilots who came over*

A pair of Spitfire Mk Vcs of the 2nd Fighter Squadron seen parked inside concrete and earthen revetments at Palermo. (Credit: Paul Ludwig)

from the States with the squadron, and his death was a blow to all of us." The 4th FS diary entry for 21 October stated: *"Today was a busy day for flying and it was a good thing, because all of the officers and men are feeling rather blue over the death of Capt. Scott."*

Twelve operational sorties were flown by the 2nd FS on 22 October but it was still not the needed *"tonic"* for the squadron. The diarist lamented: *"Although the squadron had twelve operational sorties today, the pilots and men on the ground are getting tired of just hanging around the 'line' with comparatively nothing to do. A little action would be an excellent tonic for what ails them."*

There was virtually no activity by any of the squadrons during the remainder of October. The weather turned cold on the 29th, and the 4th FS diarist noted, *"...all kinds of gasoline and electric heaters have been brought into the officers' quarters..."* but few men felt warm.

Morale continued to slip as a result of inactivity

S/Sgt Ellis of the 4th Fighter Squadron looking over one of the new Merlin engines received by the Squadron. (Credit: E. Torvinen)

and the worsening weather, as evidenced by the Group diarist's entry for 30 October: *"The words 'Rainy Season' certainly have a very real meaning here. Group activity has actually ceased to exist. It seems almost useless to report for work with nothing to do. Everyone is now desperate in his hope that we'll move on."*

On the last day of the month, rain made fields unuseable. The 5th FS diarist recorded that despite predictions, the new, hard-surfaced landing strip at Bocca di Falco was not completed and that *"...the pilots would probably be highly insulted if asked to earn their pay by flying now, for they're completely out of the habit."*

November began the way October ended. Staff officers of the 52nd went to Naples, Italy and Algiers on 2 November to learn if there was to be a move and, if so, to where. The 4th FS flew 26 uneventful sorties as convoy escorts on this date. On 3 November, HQ reported that *"...rain and mud are with us again, but the completion of the new paved runway has made the weather far less important."* The 4th FS had a day off and the 5th FS reported no activity. The HQ diarist reported that *"...the sabotage of telephone lines has increased noticeably. In one recent case a fifty foot section was cut out from the line to the officers' quarters. The communications men spliced in a section to replace the missing one only to discover the next day that the new fifty foot section had been removed."*

A steady rain made the day very unpleasant and there was no activity in the 4th and 5th FS.

On 5 November, the 2nd FS had a busy day, flying 20 sorties, but it was quiet in the other two squadrons. Despite rain and inactivity, there was no shortage of equipment, and the diary noted: *"The Group has had better success with supplies on Sicily than it had in Africa. Our mobile radio station is now operating full time on several channels, but the weather channel is being jammed by the enemy."*

Sometime between 3 and 7 November, Lt. Marshall Cowan, 5th FS Engineering Officer, noted *"11 Macchi 200's" in the 5th FS parking area which meant they were flown in by Italian pilots friendly to the Allies escaping German control and stopping at Sicily before heading south."*

By 10 November, the weather had cleared and it was a busy day for 4th FS pilots who escorted convoys and provided a continuous patrol over Palermo harbor. The 4th FS diary related that: *"It was the first pretty day we have had in almost a week and they were all glad to have the chance to fly again."*

The ground echelon of the 5th FS was ordered to move to Palermo and the men packed up in readiness for a move by truck, but no one knew what the move meant. On 11 November flying was non-existent in the Group since the supply of oxygen for Spitfires was inadequate. The diarist reported: *"...we've been getting French and Italian oxygen under the necessary 1,800 pounds pressure. If there were more British mobile units we'd be able to get an adequate supply."* The weather was clear and the 2nd FS flew more intensive operations.

The 4th FS flew more boring convoy patrols on 12 November, and the squadron diary closed out the day's entry with this comment: *"Everyone is getting tired of Palermo and we are anxious to move to another spot."*

Morale took a tremendous jump on 17 November when Colonel McNickle returned from his conference in Algiers and told the 52nd FG to get ready for its move to Corsica. The Group diarist noted: *"The men feel we will be seeing some action again and look forward to it, even though they know some may get hurt. The Group, beginning today is now relieved of its assignment to the 62nd Wing and is now under the 63rd Wing. For the first time in two months we received a shipment of new Merlin engines. The need had approached the emergency state and the arrival of thirteen new engines has enabled us to make some necessary engine changes. A request for 731 bales of straw for the men's mattress covers had to be refused by the medical authorities because of the presence of fleas and lice in the straw over here."*

On the 18th, rumors began to circulate that bomb racks were to be fitted to the Group's Spitfires and the unit would soon commence dive-bombing operations. Lt. Miles Lynn and Col. McNickle flew to Corsica to pick suitable fields for the squadrons at Calvi and Borgo. The 4th FS was assigned to Calvi and the 2nd and 5th Squadrons would go to Borgo. The move to Corsica was underway.

On 19 November, Major Houston, Commanding Officer of the 4th FS and Lt. Tyler returned from Malta today, with a 250 lb. bomb fitted under each wing of their Spitfires. According to the 4th FS diary: *"This converted the disbelievers and confirmed the rumor that the 4th Squadron would soon be dive-bombing, but the pilots*

Some of the Mc200s that flew in and surrendered at Palermo during early November 1943.

Spitfire Mk IX, serial number unknown

**Lt. Fred Ohr,
2nd Fighter Squadron,
52nd Fighter Group,
Palermo, Sicily, August 1943**

This profile shows another of the color schemes used on the 52nd Fighter Group's aircraft – time the RAF high-altitude scheme of medium sea gray upper surfaces and PRU blue undersurfaces. Fred Ohr finished his tour of duty as an Ace with six victories, one of which was scored in a Spitfire.

Lt. Fred Ohr prepares for a mission from Sicily in his Spitfire Mk IX coded QP-N. (Credit: John Fawcett)

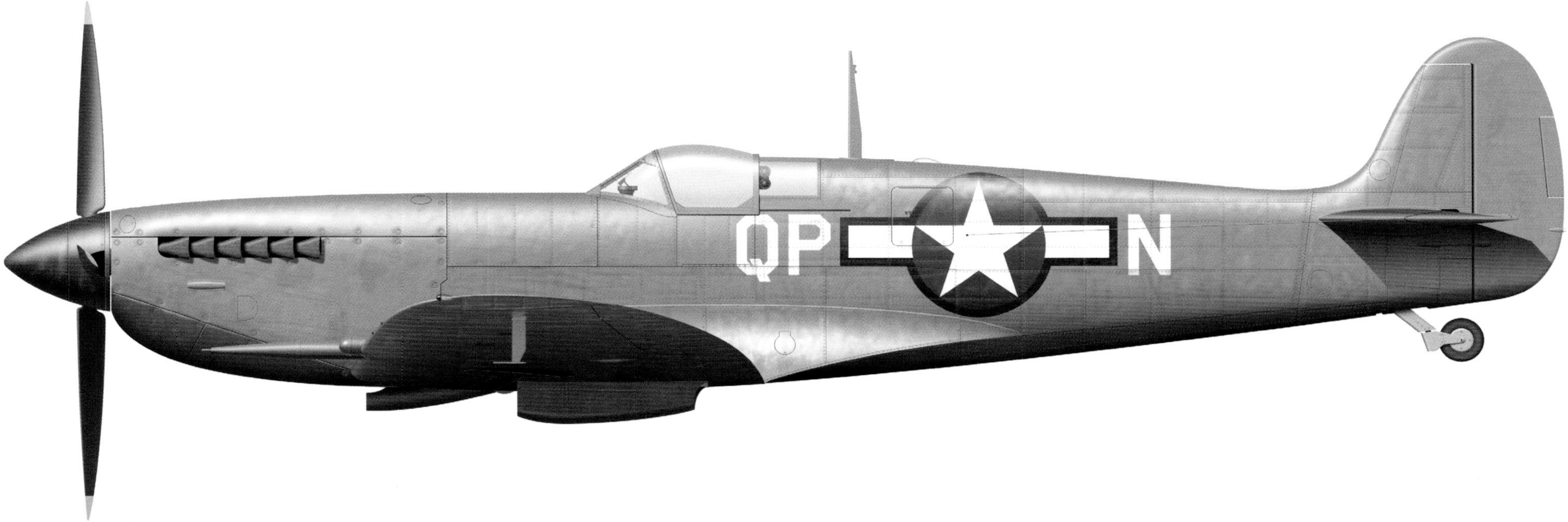

"Georgia III", flown by Lt. Anderson of the 4th Fighter Squadron, bombed up and ready to deliver the message inscribed on the bomb. (Credit: Fred Wiersma)

still don't seem to think it is a very good idea."

On 22 November, *"...several men went to Algiers today to learn how to install bomb racks on Spitfires... Lieutenants English and Williams, 2nd FS, flew to Algiers to have bomb racks installed on their planes. Pilots are enthusiastic about the prospect of bombing. The 4th FS flew a few convoy missions but rain and poor visibility caused the pilots to have a hard time getting close to the convoys. Orders prepared part of the 5th FS ground echelon to move to Corsica tomorrow."*

The 4th FS flew practice dive-bombing missions on 23 November while Capt. Westbrook, 5th FS, and seven men went to Bastia, Corsica to look over the new base. A delay in route of 15 minutes during the trip turned out to be a lifesaver. Because they were 15 minutes late, they missed being killed in the bombing which destroyed the building where these men were to be billeted. On the 24th, high winds suspended all operational flying. On Thanksgiving Day, the troops were treated to what was described as *"the finest dinner we've had since leaving the States."*

Finally, on 26 November, the 52nd FG received its movement orders and began its transfer to Corsica. The impending return to a war zone prompted a new training program. The 2nd FS, for example, had a very full day. The training included aircraft identification lectures for the pilots; a sex morality lecture to officers by Maj. Alexander; practice flights and a shipping recognition lecture by Squadron Leader Metcalf. There was no activity in the 5th FS on 27 November, other than the arrival of eight Spitfires from Sicily. Maj. Houston flew to the new base on Corsica to inspect it and make arrangements for his squadron.

A potential glitch in the dive-bombing assignment occurred on 29 November when a serious complication arose while converting the Group's Spitfire MkVs to dive- bombers. An examination of the Mark Vc Spitfires, based upon tests set out by the British at Malta, disclosed that 22 of the 51 aircraft in this class were unfit for the installation of bomb racks. While this situation was being attended to, Sgt. Hogue recalled that: *"...personnel visited Malta to see the installation of bomb racks, then they went to Algiers where the initial work was done and where the necessary tools and supplies were obtained."*

Lt. Mike Encinias and his Spitfire Mk VIII at Palermo. (Credit: John Fawcett)

The change to convert Spitfires fighters into dive-bombers had to be undertaken before moving to Corsica, and assembly lines were set up at Bocca di Falco. Under the direction of Maj. Ralph Thomas, Lt. Spangler and M/Sgt. Hall, along with men from all three squadrons, the Group was transformed into the first American Spitfire dive-bombing group.

The last day of November 1943 turned out to be the opening day of the move, and within a week the 52nd was flying combat missions from Corsica.

There were no victories in November – the third month in a row.

As at the last day of November 1943, Tom Thacker reported the scores for the Group after one year of combat were:

	Destroyed	Probables	Damaged	Totals
HQ Det.22			2	2
2nd FS	46⅓	7	22	75⅓
4th FS	47	6	17	70
5th FS	20	5	17	42
Group Totals	113⅓	18	58	189⅓

The 4th Fighter Squadron Officer's Mess Hall at Palermo. The bar itself was "midnight requisitioned" from a local hotel as was much of the 'booze'. The Spitfire and the nude were painted by the Squadron artist. The hotel supplies were also used to set up a similar bar for the NCOs and enlisted Squadron members. (Credit: John Blythe)

Chapter Six

"We are all wondering just how a Spitfire is going to take off with a 250 lb bomb under each wing"

Corsica and a New Begining

December 1943–May 1944

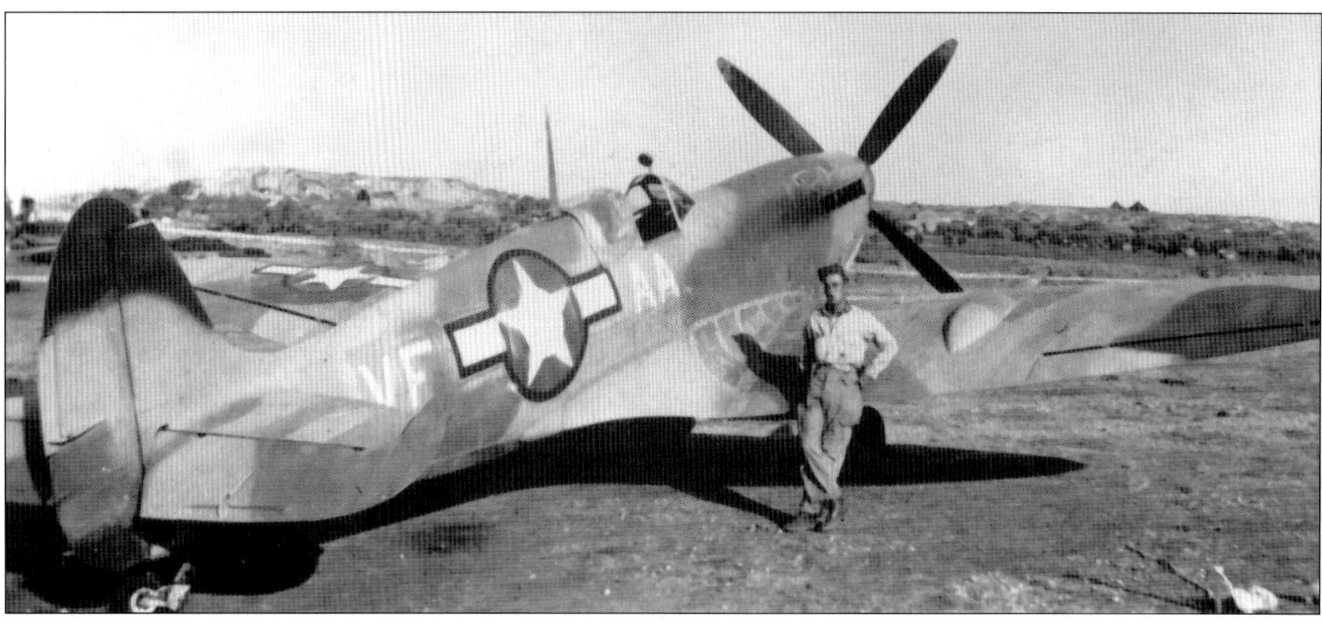

VF-AA of the 5th Fighter Squadron on alert status at its new base on Corsica. (Credit: James Empey)

With the move to Corsica the months of frustration and inactivity were about to end. This was a welcome relief to the 52nd Fighter Group which felt deeply that its talent and experience had been totally wasted during its tour of duty within Coastal Command.

The first few days of the month were spent primarily bringing in the aircraft and maintenance personnel in order to become operational as quickly as possible. The complete movement of the Group's personnel and equipment would take nearly a month to complete.

On 1 December, ten transports moved personnel from Sicily and on 3 December more of the vehicles and personnel embarked in two LSTs for the trip to Corsica. Pilots flew into Borgo and Calvi ahead of the arrival of personnel and equipment. Lt. James W. Bickford, a new pilot who wanted to be first to do anything new, flew an airfield patrol at Borgo on 3 December.

The ships carrying 52nd FG personnel and equipment arrived on at Ajaccio on the west coast of Corsica 6 December and the following day, convoys delivered the HQ Detachment and the 2nd and 5th Squadrons to Borgo, Corsica, and the 4th FS to Calvi. Borgo is approximately eight miles south of Bastia and a mile inland and Calvi is on the northwest coast facing southern France across the Ligurian Sea. From Borgo, the German-occupied island of Elba, and the west coast of Italy, 70 miles away, could be seen on a clear day. The south coast of France is 150 miles away to the north.

Capt. Everett K. Jenkins, the 5th FS's newly appointed Commanding Officer, arrived on Corsica on 1 December with a force of two Spitfire IXs and 9 Spitfire Vs. One Spitfire, piloted by Lt. DeVoe, was damaged when a strong crosswind during the landing caused it to groundloop. Anxious to get back into action, 5th FS flew 12 operational and six combat sorties on 2 December, one of which was a Walrus escort near the coast of northern Italy.

The air echelon of the 2nd FS landed in Corsica on 3 December and was followed by the 4th FS the next day. During its move the 5th continued to fly missions from Borgo and on 3 and 4 December flew a total of 47 sorties.

The 2nd FS flew its first mission from Corsica on 5 December. The honor went to Lts. Jack R. Schneider and Harry O. Schellhase, who flew a shipping reconnaissance mission along the Italian coastline. The 5th Squadron did not fly because it was the 2nd Squadron's day for alert. The limitation on flying was, in part, due to a gasoline shortage on Corsica. The 4th FS diary stated: *"Gasoline for Spitfires didn't arrive on time and there is only enough gasoline to service two airplanes and after that is used, we will just have to sit and watch whatever the Germans send over."*

On 6 December two truckloads of gasoline arrived which solved one problem, but another surfaced: *"We are now short of oil."*

Problems of a totally different nature occurred for the 4th Squadron on 7 December. An alert was sounded at 03.00 hrs because of a suspected German commando raid but it turned out to be a false alarm. At 10.00 hrs, the base was alerted that enemy aircraft were approaching and Lts. James O. Tyler and Lt. W.E. LaBarge were scrambled to intercept them. The intruder turned out to be an Me 210 and after spending a few minutes chasing it in and out of clouds Tyler shot down it down 20 miles southeast of Calvi. Lt. La Barge's day, however, was not as successful. Something went wrong during his landing approach and he crashed on the muddy field. His aircraft overturned, knocking a wing completely off causing the aircraft severe damage. LaBarge was extricated by medics and was dazed and unhurt except for shock. Tyler's victory was the first for the 52nd FG in over three months.

Maj. Sanborn led a flight of six 2nd FS Spitfires

Seen from left to right: Lts. Charles DeVoe and Boyd. (Credit: Charles DeVoe)

on a sweep over the Italian coast on 8 December and strafed a number of ground targets, to include rail targets, seaplanes and barges. Capt. Lee Trowbridge, 4th FS, led a three-aircraft sweep to southern France and he was lucky to have survived the mission. Trowbridge, F/O Bob Hoover and another pilot had just dive-bombed power plants and rail targets when Capt. Trowbridge began a strafing run on a locomotive: The 4th FS diary reported the strange story which followed: *"While attempting to shoot up a locomotive, Trowbridge's right wing hit a three inch pipe that was sticking up from a building. About fifteen feet of the pipe took root in the wing and although it cut almost a quarter of the way into the wing, Capt. Trowbridge flew back to base and belly-landed."*

The pipe was removed and kept outside the Operations shack as an icon of battle. The 5th FS flew seven combat missions that were mostly recce for shipping along the Italian coast near Spezia and Genoa.

On 9 December, 2nd FS pilots strafed some E-boats on the coast in the morning for their first real action in a long time. In the afternoon the rains came. Talks at Teheran between Roosevelt, Churchill and Stalin concluded on the 7th and resulted in Roosevelt stopping at Sicily on his way home. Eight Spitfires from the 5th FS covered the presidential landing on 8 December.

The Group's first escort mission in over three months was scheduled for 10 December and as morale zoomed upward momentarily, the mission was canceled. This was a real disappointment since sixteen aircraft from the 2nd and 5th Squadrons had been waiting for an hour and a half to escort a formation of B-26s when the mission was scrubbed. On 11 December, despite bad weather, Maj. Levine and Lt. William D. Gahagen flew a recce mission over Genoa harbor where they saw and noted shipping, which formed promising targets for their new role as dive-bombers.

The 12th, 13th and 14th of December were days marked by rain, and Calvi's airfield was too muddy for use. During this time frame Capt. Miles Lynn, 2nd FS, finished his tour of duty was assigned home leave. On the 14th, Lynn departed in a Jeep with Lt. Marvin *"Pappy"* Haskins, Capt. Beard and Lt. Williams. During the trip the Jeep turned over while rounding a curve. Haskins recalled that: *"...it threw us all out all over the so-called road and luckily it flipped over into the side of the mountain – luckily, because a nice 1,500 feet drop was the other way."*

Haskins was knocked out and Lynn suffered severe concussion. Fortunately they were able to flag down a French jeep and continue the trip to Ajaccio, where both Beard and Lynn were hospitalized because of their injuries.

The incessant rains which had virtually eliminated flying during the following days ended on 17 December and there was a little excitement when a Ju 88 was seen flying on the deck a mile east of the 2nd FS's base. Lieutenants McCraw and Schneider were scrambled but the Ju 88 got away. The rains returned on the 18th and the men busied themselves with needed construction work around the bases.

A 5th Fighter Squadron Spitfire Mk Vc beautifully silhouetted against the clouds as it flies a patrol from Corsica. (Credit: Al Gelo)

Captain Lee Trowbridge of the 4th Fighter Squadron and his heavily damaged Spitfire after their return from his hair-raising mission of 8 December 1943. (Credit: R. Klug)

Seen from left to right, Lts. Elmer Boney, Mason Armstrong, and Miles Lynn of the 2nd Fighter Squadron. (Credit: C. G. Jones)

F/O Albert McCraw's "Fascinating Bitchy", a Spitfire VIII or IX of the 2nd Fighter Squadron. (Credit: Marvin Haskins)

Lt. Louis Weynandt of the 5th Fighter Squadron. (Credit: Charles DeVoe)

Clear skies greeted the Group on 19 December and in spite of very muddy fields a few missions were flown. Things went okay for the 5th FS which dispatched two aircraft on shipping reconnaissance, but it was a day of disaster for the 4th FS. Runway conditions, was probably the reason why Lt. Hugh W. Dorland, 4th FS, crashed and was killed while attempting to take off. His aircraft smashed into an aviation fuel dump and he was burned alive – the first fatality at Calvi airfield.

In spite of the accident, the 4th FS sortied two flights of six aircraft on a sweep over France. When the first flight returned from the mission Lt. McCauley's aircraft hit a soft spot in the runway while landing, and his aircraft was destroyed. Things were worse for the second flight. Only three of the Spitfires returned and they had to land at Borgo and three others were reported as misssing. The three who landed at Borgo returned the next day after getting fuel. The unit diarist explained that the leader had flown: "*...too far north into Italy, while flying over the clouds. In attempting to fly back to the coast, he flew east into the Po river valley and by the time he found out where he was, his gas supply was too low to carry him back to Calvi. The pilots got back to Borgo with 2, 3 and 10 gallons of gas respectively. Three others stayed in the valley and either crash-landed or bailed out.*"

The weather again cooperated on 20 December and the 5th FS flew a secret reconnaissance mission south of Elba. One day later the 2nd FS diarist recorded that the Squadron: "*...suffered its first casualty in some time. 2nd Lt. Norman E. English failed to return from a shipping recco mission with Lt. Bruce Kellam. They spotted two tugboats off the Italian coast. He* [English] *was flying too low, hit the water, skipped about 50 yards, went up to 400 feet and dove into the sea. His loss was the first since North Africa.*"

There was some excitement at Calvi during the morning when a Ju 88 flew over the field. Two 4th FS Spitfires took off after it but, as the disappointed squadron diarist noted: "*We on the ground expected to see a wonderful show, but the pilots were unable to see the e/a after they had taken off.*"

On 22 December, the 5th FS flew six recce missions and Capt. Kelly, 4th FS, attacked a German E-Boat near the coast of France and left it burning in the water. It was not a one-sided skirmish, however, and Kelly returned to base with several Flak holes in his Spitfire. A 5th FS pilot also had a close brush with death when involved in a serious landing accident upon his return from the mission. The engine of Lt. Louis Weynandt's Spitfire quit at 25,000 feet and he belly-landed at the tip of Corsica. The diarist commented "*...how Weynandt got out is a miracle.*" Lt. Cowan remembered Weynandt "*...landed on terraced ground, went under high tension wires, hit one terrace and knocked off his left wing, dipped his nose and flipped over on his back, up one terrace four feet higher. He slid about 15 feet on his back and somehow tore the empennage clean off. It was soft mud and his head was way down in the mud but his oxygen mask gave him breath until a British guy from a control station right near, cut his straps and dug him out.*" If Weynandt's oxygen mask had been ripped from his face he might have suffocated.

Even though the weather was dreary and rainy, a fine Christmas dinner was enjoyed by the officers and men of the 52nd. There was no activity the day after that, because the wet and muddy condition of the field confined the Group to emergency operations. The Group also stood

It would appear that Lt. John Bishop of the 4th Fighter Squadron, was dreaming about a future pork dinner more than flying an alert mission in nearby WD-ZZ! (Credit: John Blythe)

down on 26 and 27 December because of the weather and condition of the flying field. The time was not wasted however and the 4th FS diary reported: *"The airplanes are now fitted with bomb racks and a shipment of bombs has arrived. We are all wondering just how a Spitfire is going to take off with a 250 lb. bomb under each wing."*

All the wondering ended on 28 December when Maj. Bob Levine and Lt. Edwin Fuller flew the first dive-bombing mission in an attempt to destroy a convoy of four river barges off San Vincenzo, Italy. The 52nd FG had learned dive-bombing techniques from the British who, on the island of Malta, had run tests of the Spitfire as a dive-bomber. For the first mission, armament men painted the names '*Adolph*' and '*Sally*' (Mistress of Ceremonies of German radio program for Allied Forces) on the bombs. As things transpired the mission was not an auspicious beginning of the Group's dive-bombing missions and all four boats escaped damage.

The pilot of WD-H walks away, apparently uninjured, after a crash-landing that left his Spitfire a somewhat damaged. (Credit: Paul Ludwig via Turk)

The day became worse when Lt. Dale F. Anderson, 4th FS took off on a mission. He had flown to about one mile west of Calvi, when his engine failed. Anderson pulled up to gain altitude to bail out, but the aircraft then dove straight into the sea. His body was recovered and a burial was held in the squadron cemetery: at Bastia. The diary solemnly stated: *"Lt. Anderson was very well liked and his death was a blow to all of us."* The day did end on a positive note, however, when Lt. Terrell Yon, 5th FS, shot down a Me 410 reconnaissance aircraft between Elba and the Italian mainland.

Four days after Christmas the tempo of dive-bombing picked up and pilots enjoyed flying different types of missions. The 2nd FS flew 32 sorties, the most it had flown in quite a while. The 4th FS diarist reported no activity but *"...we are expecting some new aircraft in soon and until they get here the squadron is limited to the number of missions it can fly."* The 5th FS flew a B-26 escort mission and two recce missions. On one of the recce flights, Lts. Robert W. Hine and Lt. Irwin Gottlieb were to check on shipping in the vicinity of Levanto and then to fly south along the coast to Piombino. Sector Operations picked up the call: *"Hello Irv, I think I'll have to bail out."* Both pilots failed to come back. The 5th FS diary wrote: *"It is surmised that they ran into a Flak bed in the form of harbor installations or an opportune target."*

Both pilots were lost in the vicinity of Leghorn (Livorno), Italy. An airborne search flown for the missing men proved unsuccessful..

The last two days of 1943 were pretty much a washout for flying, except for chasing a Ju 88 out of the area and shooting it down on 30 December. Lts. Chandler R. Brown and John L. Bishop, 4th FS, chased the enemy aircraft from Corsica almost to France before it was shot down. The 2nd FS closed out the year by moving the operations, intelligence and engineering sections into a new, one-story, 60 feet by 20 feet building divided into three rooms. The diarist noted: *"This is the best set-up we have had on the line since leaving Selfridge Field."*

The last day of 1943 on Corsica was a meteorological nightmare. According to the 5th FS diary: *"The year 1943 went out like an MGM roaring lion. Rain and wind of 40 MPH began immediately at dawn and continued most of the day. The bad weather and the resulting non-operational day afforded both officers and men an opportunity to start the New Year's Eve celebrations in the early afternoon and reached their respective climaxes just short of midnight. Editor's note: No casualties excepting one cut finger and the usual hangovers."*

The inclement weather continued during the first two days of the New Year, but on 3 January the skies had cleared and dive-bombing training resumed. Reviews of the day's training were mixed. The 4th Squadron diary recorded: *"The first attempts at bombing were not very successful although Capt. Kelly came close."* Yet the Group HQ diarist contradicted the 4th FS diarist stating: *"...the progress of our pilots in dive-bombing is quite remarkable."*

The Group returned to combat operations on 5 January and the 5th FS flew 11 dive-bombing sorties, two scrambles and one recce to Port Ercole. The dive-bombing mission to Piombino was its first and was only partially successful as

Spitfire Mk Vc VF-B of the 5th Fighter Squadron with 19 bombing missions to its credit, awaits its next call to duty. (Credit: George Hahn)

This photograph of WD-L, taken in early 1944, still wearing 1942 style markings illustrates that keeping the US national insignia up to date was not a priority with the ground crews. (Credit: Toppen)

Capt. 'Steiny' Steinbrenner being the only one to score a direct hit on one of the E-Boats that had been targeted. The 2nd FS also flew two dive-bombing missions on this date, but with less than positive results.

The weather continued to improve and 6 January was an even busier day for the 52nd FG. The 5th FS flew 22 dive-bombing sorties and lost a pilot to Flak. Lt. Lawrence H. Kruse had just released his bombs when his Spitfire was hit by Flak that ripped off a large chunk of his wing. He went in without recovering control of his aircraft.

Group HQ noted the Group's improvement in its dive-bombing skills after this mission and reported that *"...our pilots are rapidly becoming a thorn in the enemy's side."* Also noted was a new enemy anti-aircraft defense weapon encountered by the Group's pilots: *"One of the most unusual weapons we have encountered so far were projectiles coming up towards pilots trailing large cables which were anchored at the guns. None of our ships ran into the cables."*

The 2nd FS also flew some dive-bombing missions during the day and destroyed its first enemy aircraft of the New Year when Lt. Elmer Boney shot down a Ju 88 10 miles southwest of Ajaccio.

On 7 January the weather was so good that dive-bombing missions were flown continuously during the day and the diary recorded that: *"...the pilots were so eager that they asked the Colonel if they could fly moonlight missions."* Capt. Trowbridge, 4th FS, had an even more successful day when he pulled out of his dive and observed a He 115 twin-engine floatplane over Oneglia, Italy and promply shot it down. The 2nd and 5th FS flew a variety of missions during the day including scrambles, dive-bombing and a recce flown by Lt. James Bickford, 2nd FS, to Pianosa where he photographed roads, beaches and landing strips in the area.

The good weather continued on 8 January, and HQ went so far as to declare that: *"...apparently the rainy season has ended. We had two scrambles today. The shortage of 80 octane gasoline is still acute and the lack of it was tying down our motor vehicles."*

Lt. William L. Bryan, Jr., 2nd FS, damaged a Ju 88 on a scramble east of Pianosa Island. HQ praised *"...the engineering, radio and armament sections which were of great assistance in making it possible to fly 32 combat missions and as a result we are gradually becoming a little more accurate in dive-bombing."*

The 4th FS had an exceptionally busy day and the 5th FS flew 14 combat missions, five of which were dive-bombing and two recce missions. At the end of the day the diarist proudly noted: *"The dive-bombing is improving, due to many enemy shipping targets available for practice."*

Now that the 52nd FG was no longer operating over North African terrain, new regulations came down stating that the Group should repaint its aircraft in the European scheme for this area. On 9 January, HQ reported that *"...ten enlisted men and one officer of the 84th Engineering Battalion arrived at the field to change the camouflage on our planes. The desert coloring is far too conspicuous over the Mediterranean."*

The new paint requirement did not *"stop the war"*, however, and all three squadrons were in action. 2nd FS pilots flew two successful bombing missions and Lt. *"Dixie"* Alexander reported that he had scored a direct hit on an F-Boat and later sank a small gunboat. In doing so, his Spitfire took several hits from Flak. The 4th FS flew two recce missions and the 5th FS dispatched 29 sorties, mostly dive-bombing, to Pt. Ala Sparviero. Again, the after action reports noted the Group's improving dive-bombing accuracy.

On 10 January, the 2nd FS was inactive, but the 4th FS and 5th FS flew were quite busy and the dive-bombing attacks cost the 5th Squadron another pilot. Lt. Henry D. Crowe went missing in action off the coast of Clementino, Italy, while bombing F-Boats. He was forced to jump after his engine quit and was last seen in his dingy. When the air/sea rescue Walrus arrived on the scene, however, it was too dark to find him.

The 5th Fighter Squadron Officer's Mess Hall on Corsica. (Credit: Charles DeVoe)

On the following day, 4th FS pilots dive-bombed a freighter in Savona harbor and the 5th FS flew search missions for Lt. Crowe. The 2nd FS flew both recce and dive-bombing missions, and Lt. Bickford bombed and strafed an F-Boat off Castiglioncello.

Teletype service was established with Sector and Wing based in or near the great Foggia complex of airfields in Italy on 13 January, and high command began to integrate the 52nd FG into the mainstream of the battle for northern Italy. The 13th proved to be an unlucky day for the 2nd and 5th Squadron as each suffered casualties during the day's missions. The 5th FS lost a popular pilot, Lt. John Nangle. Nangle was still over Corsica when he went down in his Spitfire IX two miles from Borgo. Shortly after take off his prop ran away and he was forced to bail out. He landed in the sea but drowned before the Walrus rescue aircraft could get to him. His loss was a shock to the Squadron and the diarist said of him: *"Nangle was one of the best liked pilots the 5th Squadron ever had."*

The 2nd FS's loss took place as F/O John D. Myers and Lt. Armstrong were flying a reconnaissance mission. Myers' engine developed a coolant leak and he was forced to belly-land on Pianosa Island, which was occupied by German troops. After the war, John Myers related what happened: *"I pulled the emergency release for the canopy, but the ball simply came off in my hand. I could not ditch in the water with a closed canopy so I decided to put it down on Pianosa Island."*

He was unhurt, but was captured a few moments later by German soldiers who turned him over to the SS. Later the SS took their trophy prisoner to a cocktail party to show him off, but when Myers told them they *"...had already lost the war and didn't know it"* one SS man expressed the opinion that the American pilot should be shot!

A few days later as he was being escorted to a POW camp near Verona, an Italian soldier made himself known to Myers, saying he wanted to help him escape. Unfortunately, Germans found out that the Italian was a partisan and they hung him and made sure that Lt. Myers saw his body hanging from a tree.

On 15 January, the squadrons of the 52nd FG flew a variety of missions and although they scored some victories, they suffered more casualties. The 2nd FS escorted six B-25s that were attacking shipping along the Italian coast. The 4th FS was dive-bombing. After 1st Lt. William B. Canning and his flight dropped their bombs, Canning spotted a group of He 115 twin-engine floatplanes on the water. He shot up two He 115s and 2nd Lt. Norman C. Gross and 1st Lt. Raymond W. Storey shared one. All of the enemy aircraft were at rest on the water 10 miles southeast of Savona, Italy. The 5th FS few ten sorties and lost another popular pilot, Lt. Charles T. 'Chuck' O'Connor who was killed while escorting bombers. Witnesses said his engine quit and he bailed out ten miles south of Monte Cristo in the water. He was picked up by a Walrus crew, but the impact and exposure cost him his life. Lt. O'Connor had recently been discharged from the hospital following a bout of

Engine maintenance on a 5th Fighter Squadron Spitfire Mk V on Corsica. (Credit: Thomas Thacker)

"Dixie" Alexander's Spitfire Mk IX QP-A awaiting its next mission. (Credit: Robert C. Curtis)

Another view of a 4th Fighter Squadron Spitfire Mk IX still wearing 1942 style US markings in 1944. (Credit: Paul Ludwig)

Captain Edwin Fuller, 2nd Fighter Squadron, was photographed over Cape Bon during August 1943 in his Spitfire Mk Vc (QP)–V. (Credit: Marvin Haskins)

yellow jaundice, and his weakened condition may have contributed to his death in the water. The 5th FS diary noted: *"Lt. O'Connor was another of the 'better' boys of the 5th. He will be missed by all."*

Borgo's defenses against night raiders were improved on 16 January when two Beaufighters arrived and a new anti-aircraft unit set up at the base. All of the 5th Squadron's planes were grounded for a thorough check in view of the recent accidents, and to see if sabotage may have been involved. On the next day there was little activity in the 5th FS because, as the diarist noted: *"We are short of pilots and planes."*

The 2nd FS pulled off a very successful dive-bombing attack on 18 January. Lts. Bob Curtis, Richard *"Dixie"* Alexander, Mason Armstrong, Mike Encinias and Marv Haskins and others dive-bombed a 3,000 ton ship sitting in the water five miles from the Italian mainland and five miles north of Elba. The freighter was surrounded by Flak boats and heavy anti-aircraft fire greeted the dive-bombers when the first of three attacks began at 10.15 hrs. The third attack commenced at 15.00 hrs and when the Spitfires departed the ship was left burning and settling low in the water.

The following day, 18 Spitfires of the 5th FS escorted B-26s in an attack on Viterbo airdrome north of Rome. No enemy aircraft were encountered, but 5th FS pilots shot up one locomotive in northern Italy, and destroyed a second locomotive in a dive-bombing attack.

By 20 January the weather had greatly improved and Borgo had virtually dried out, making operations somewhat safer from there. The Group diary recorded: *"Continued excellent weather has made life very pleasant and the ground has been dry and solid – difficult to believe that a few short weeks ago we were living in a sea of mud. With the improved weather work on the new metal runway was also nearing completion."*

All three squadrons were in action on 21 January and the 2nd and 4th Squadrons were relatively busy. According to the diary, 2nd FS pilots *"...got in a few licks at ground targets, bombing locomotives and strafing several vehicles."*

The 4th FS, on the other hand, encountered the *Luftwaffe* during a mission to southern France, and Capt. Lee M. Trowbridge downed an Me 109 south-east of Toulon, France. In addition to Capt, Trowbridge's kill, Lt. Guy S. Cummins damaged one Me 109 and Lts. Lyle R. Kater and John C. Burchfield shared in damaging another Me 109 north of Perquerellas Island, France. The 5th FS closed out the day with two recce missions that were without incident.

The landings at Anzio began on 22 January and the Group's squadrons were put on alert. During the day, several missions were flown and during theirs, Lts. *"Dixie"* Alexander and Mike Encinias, 2nd FS, ran into some unexpected problems while strafing a convoy. Just as they attacked the last two trucks in the convoy, the remaining trucks entered a town and Alexander stopped firing to prevent hitting civilians. As he pulled out of his strafing run his Spitfire was hit just when he was doing a *"...couple of rolls to show off for the Italians."* Since he had not previously encountered Flak in this area Dixie was surprised and enraged when he felt the 20 mm shells hit his Spit. He then led Lt. Encinias on a strafing attack against

Spitfire Mk Vc WD-X and its crew. From left to right, Sgt. Richard Potter, Lt. William Canning and Sgt. Murray Parker. (Credit: Richard Potter)

Spitfire Mk Vb, serial number unknown, *Julie II*

**Lt. Robert C. Curtis,
2nd Fighter Squadron,
52nd Fighter Group,
Corsica, December 1943**

Bob Curtis recalled that his clipped wing Spitfire Mk Vb Julie II featured another non-standard upper surface camouflage, consisting of two shades of green, probably dark green and olive drab.

Lt. Robert C. Curtis' clipped-wing Spitfire Mk V "Julie II" on Corsica. Note that by this time, this Spitfire was painted in the British temperate color scheme. (Credit: Robert C. Curtis)

JULIE II

QP C

Captain Lee Trowbridge's Spitfire Mk Vc displays three Swastikas, indicating that this photograph was taken shortly after his victory of 21 January 1944. (Credit: Paul Ludwig)

Lt. Jim Bickford, 2nd Fighter Squadron, downed two He 111s on 23 January 1944. (Credit: Robert C. Curtis)

QP-Z and another 2nd Fighter Squadron Spitfire on their hard-stands. (Credit: Robert C. Curtis)

Lt. Bob Liebl, 2nd Fighter Squadron, shot down one Ju 88 during the air battle of 23 January 1944. (Credit: C. G. Jones)

the offending gun position and while doing so, fire from another Flak gun hit his aircraft. The hits sent the Spitfire's nose up and Alexander had to use full nose down trim and full force on the stick to get the plane flying level. When he asked Encinias to come alongside to give a damage report Alexander saw that his fellow airman's machine was also badly damaged and both men were forced to make a wheels up crash-landing upon their return to Borgo. Alexander's 'QP-A' was a complete write-off and Enclinias' Spitfire was heavily damaged, but repairable. The 4th FS flew one scramble and a recce and the 5th FS flew one recce mission and a four-plane bomber escort with the 2nd FS to the dock areas in Port Ferraio to close out the day's activities.

The 23rd of January turned out to be a magnificent day for the 52nd FG as a whole and the 2nd FS in particular. After nearly half of a year of covering ship movements, dive-bombing, dawn and dusk patrols and harbor patrols, four fighter pilots had a day they would remember the rest of their lives. The Group's diarist recorded: *"The successes of this day have justified all the losses and all the headaches the group has had or will have in Corsica."*

The action began on a limited scale at about 15.45 hrs when Lieutenants Terrell E. Yon and Frank Atkins probably destroyed a Ju 88 recce north of Pianosa. In this encounter, Terry Yon was wounded in the leg when his aircraft was hit by return fire from the Ju 88. The Junkers may have been on a pre-strike recce mission for the German bomber force encountered about an hour later by four pilots of the 2nd FS. Lts. Robert Liebl, James Bickford, Mike Encinias, and Arthur Johnson were on a dive-bombing mission when they sighted 50 to 60 German bombers heading for the Anzio beachhead. If the enemy bombers had got through to the invasion fleet and launched a successful attack, there could have been a disaster. The pilots reported the incoming bombers to the controller so that other units nearer Rome could be warned, then jettisoned their bombs and attacked. The enemy formation composed of He 111s, Ju 88s and Do 217s dropped aerial torpedoes and tried to escape when they saw the Spitfires boring in on their formation, but they were overtaken near Viareggio, Italy. Six enemy bombers fell from the sky. Lts. Bickford and Encinias got two each, and Lts Arthur G. Johnson, Jr., and Robert Liebl each destroyed one enemy aircraft.

Lt. Jim Bickford, one of the four 2nd FS pilots attacking 50 to 60 enemy bombers, recalled: *"It was a slow day – not much going on. I wanted to attack the E-boat pens at Marina di Pisa, so a few of us asked Bill Beard, the Operations Officer, to get an OK for such a mission. After getting permission, I led the flight and as we approached Marina di Pisa the pilots spotted the huge formation of enemy bombers heading south just off the coast and very low over the water."*

Bickford ordered his flight to jettison bombs and attack. He shot down two He 111s and *"...the return fire was heavy but everyone survived it. After we ran out of ammunition – the Spitfire didn't carry much, and certainly not what was needed in this situation –*

we headed back to base. We split up the enemy bomber formation a little, but they closed up and continued south to Anzio. I reported to control the number and type of aircraft and their direction of flight, so I assume that our forces were alerted."

Lt. Mike Encinias remembered: *"When I saw all those bombers flying past us, I thought they were friendly. Don't ask why; I just couldn't believe that we would have the luck to run into so many enemy aircraft. When our other planes started peeling off, it dawned on me and I started looking for markings, etc. There were so many of them that I didn't need to maneuver; I simply sat behind them and traded fire until they fell. I could tell that one was a Heinkel 111 from the shape of the tail. The other one looked so different, so I assumed that it was a Ju 88, but I can't swear to it. I stopped my attack when I ran out of ammunition."*

Lt. Art Johnson reported: *"As our flight approached the coast of Italy near Viareggio, we sighted more than fifty bombers and two He 177s below us, headed for the Anzio-Nettuno beachhead. We jettisoned our bombs over the water and went after the He 111s. At this point the two He 177s headed inland. I maneuvered onto the tail of an He 111. After I fired several bursts it blew up and I flew through the debris. I then got on the tail of another He 111 and gave it a couple of bursts, hitting the right engine. At this time I looked up and saw a flight of Me 210s above, so I broke off and headed for home."*

Lt. Bob Liebl recalled: *"Our flight of four aircraft left Borgo late in the afternoon and headed toward Italy. At near dusk we encountered 70 to 80 German bombers, headed south along the Italian coast and just above the water. In the formations were Ju 88s, He 111s, possibly some Do 217s and a few large single-engine planes carrying torpedoes. We attacked and the Jerries broke in all directions and many of them jettisoned their torpedoes. I picked a He 111 which immediately jettisoned its torpedo and headed inland, on the deck. I was being fired upon by the tail gunner and I fired four or five bursts at the bomber from nearly directly astern and scored enough hits to see chunks of the left wing and the left engine nacelle fly off. Shortly thereafter the bomber crash-landed but did not burn. I rejoined the flight and we all flew back to base intact."*

In other action, Lt. LaBarge, 4th FS had to bail out over the sea, about five miles off Calvi harbor. Liebl recalled: *"His plane had a glycol leak and he was only about 300 feet above the water when he attempted his bail-out. It's a miracle he lived through it."*

He was seen to enter the water and was rescued immediately.

On that same successful day, Beaufighters stationed on Borgo were scrambled on an alert at about 19.30 hrs when two German bombers came near, and both were shot down. One came down in flames north of the field in clear view of 52nd FG personnel.

It had been a great day for the 52nd FG and the results proved to Brigadier Gen. Morris, Commanding General of XII FC and Col. Graves, Commanding Officer of the 62nd Fighter Wing, that these courageous and successful fighter pilots were being wasted by being kept so far from the action over Italy proper. In fact, the success of 23 January may have helped senior officers to decide to give the 52nd FG a greater mission in the near future. The next day, the BBC reported that: *"...the bomber fleet turned back without attacking our invasion forces. Once again enemy planes headed for the invasion forces south of Rome were intercepted."*

The battle on the beach at Anzio and the anchored Allied ships there drew more enemy aircraft on 24 January, but on a much smaller scale. Six Do 217s were spotted a by flight composed of four 2nd FS and two 5th FS Spitfires and a running battle ensued. Two of the German raiders were shot down and another was damaged, but their return fire managed to shoot down two of the Spitfires. Lt. Arthur Johnson, Jr., and Lt. Clyde S. Cleveland each shot down a Do 217. Cleveland's claim was made north-west of Pisa, but he was hit by return fire and was forced to bail out and was last seen in his dinghy. Air/sea rescue Walrus did not reach the area until it was too dark to find him and Cleveland was reported missing in action. Lt. Harvey E. Scheu damaged a Do 217, two miles southeast of Pisa, Italy and Lt. Harry O. Schellhase was reported killed after his aircraft was seen to hit the ground and explode, probably after being hit by return fire.

Lt. Art Johnson was: *"...on this mission flying wing to Schellhase in a flight of six Spitfires when we encountered six low-flying Do 217s overland near Viareggio. We attacked while some of the others remained above as cover. I followed Schellhase as he attacked a bomber from the rear. As we neared the bomber Schellhase peeled up and to the right. That was the last I saw of him, but heard later that he crashed. We were only a few hundred feet off the ground. I continued toward the bomber and began firing. The left cannon was not working, so every time I fired a burst, my plane would yaw to the right. I then began aiming at the left engine and would fire until the yawing brought the strikes along the bomber to its right engine. After about three of these exercises the bomber plowed into the ground. Probably the yawing of my plane due to the jammed cannon saved me from being hit by return fire."*

Lieutenants Bob Curtis and Barry Lawler flew

From left to right, four pilots of the 4th Fighter Squadron: Lts. William LaBarge, Frank Tribbett, Fred Bullock, and Norman Gross. (Credit: Fred Bullock)

John Fawcett, 2nd Fighter Squadron, and a heavily weathered Spitfire Mk IX on Corsica. (Credit: John Fawcett)

Sgt Robert Klug of the 4th Fighter Squadron posing with a clipped-wing Spitfire Mk IX on Corsica. Note this Spitfire is painted in the RAF temperate scheme. (Credit: R. Klug)

a recce mission that same day and Lawler destroyed a Ju 88 on the ground. Curtis noted that the location was an airfield near Pisa and that he damaged a Ju 88, hitting it in the right wing and engine.

One other pilot was lost on 24 January when Lt. Thomas Watts, 4th FS, was killed while on a test flight. He parachuted from a very low altitude and was probably knocked unconscious when he landed and the waves lashed him against the rocks. A rescue party saw him from a distance, but when they got close to him his body had gone under and was never recovered.

Worsening weather limited missions on 25 January and shut down flying on 26 January. The ground crews did make good use of the time repairing and repainting the Spitfires in the northern European camouflage scheme. 27 January was unusually cold but clear and the wind subsided and missions resumed. Eight Spitfires, led by Maj. Houston, Commanding Officer of the 4th FS, flew an ill-fated recce mission to France. As the formation approached the German airfield at Grande Bastide, Lt. Ottoway Cornwell's flight observed Me 109s taking off, and he and Lt. Harold Beetle dove to attack them. On their first pass they used their combined firepower to shoot down one of the Me 109s, but failed, until too late, to see more Messerschmitts closing in on their tails. Cornwell and Beedle had left two Spitfires up high as top cover, and then dove to attack six Me 109s which were taking off. However, the attacking German fighters struck so quickly the top cover could not react. The Me 109s hit both Spitfires with fatal bursts and both of them were seen to hit the side of a nearby mountain and explode. As this took place three other Me 109s bounced the two Spitfires flown by Lts. Kater and Lt. Burchfield and Kater's Spitfire was shot down and crashed in the water south of Grand Bastide. Burchfield returned home safely.

The 2nd and 5th Squadrons had a better day. The 5th flew 28 sorties and successfully dive-bombed radar installations on Giglio. The 2nd FS flew an unsuccessful fighter sweep and a dive-bombing mission against F-boats. The F-Boats escaped damage as the attack was somewhat disrupted by intense and accurate Flak. The day was not a complete failure, however, as *"Junior"* Adams, while flying a recce mission, managed to catch a German Do 24 flying boat as it was landing. His report read: *"Got a squirt at a Do 24 at Spezia. This flying boat was on its final approach to the harbor when I jumped it, line astern. I was too close and fishtailed to bracket it with my fire. Saw some hits but it landed and groundlooped (waterlooped?!). Had to leave in a hurry as some people on the ground were very unfriendly."*

On 28 January, the 2nd FS diary reported that the squadron was suffering an acute shortage of aircraft and pilots, and sent four pilots to pick up aircraft from Setif, Algeria. To add insult to injury the diary also reported that PX rations were discontinued because Corsica was not considered in a 'combat' zone. In spite of these aggravations and with only 16 pilots available, the 2nd FS still managed to put up 32 sorties during the day. The 5th FS flew three bomber escort missions and witnessed the B-25s they were escorting make a very deadly strike on a flotilla of six F-Boats. Two of the F-Boats were sunk and two others were damaged. On another mission the Squadron's Spitfires dive-bombed and damaged the road bridge at Cecina.

Although bad weather curtailed most operations, the Group did dispatch a mixed formation of 2nd and 5th FS Spitfires on a sweep to Italy to check on some newly occupied German airfields in the area between Rome and Florence. As the formation passed over the Italian coastline it received light Flak and small arms fire, and Lt. Marvin R. *"Pappy"* Haskins' Spitfire took a hit in the glycol tank. After the war he recalled the day as follows: *"I was summoned to the field for a briefing and a mission. I was to lead a six-plane flight, with high cover by a six-plane flight from the 5th Squadron. We flew over on the deck, hit the coast of Italy and climbed to 6,000 feet, with the 5th Squadron flight going to 12,000 feet. We got some small arms fire as we crossed the coast but all went well, or so I thought."*

As Haskins continued on into Italy his engine temperature indicator needle *"hit the peg"* and he called *"Dixie"* Alexander and told him that he would have to bail out. Haskins headed for Corsica. When *"...the smell of hot metal became overpowering"*, Haskins said his goodbyes and *"...was called by sundry Beagles who wished me luck and requested that I 'will' them some of my items of value, such as my beautiful all-leather flying boots, my air mattresss, and so on. I promptly acceded to these requests, in the good form dictated by tradition."*

Haskins trimmed the plane nose down, unbuckled, rose high in his seat and kicked the

From left to right, 5th Fighter Squadron personnel, Lts. Frank Sherman, Thompson, Louis Weynandt, and Joe Blackburn. (Credit: Charles DeVoe)

The 4th Fighter Squadron's Spitfire Mk IX WD-M on Corsica sporting a rather clean and fresh paint job. (Credit: Paul Ludwig collection)

control stick. The *"bunt out"* procedure worked and he was out, counted five and pulled the ripcord. He was half a mile to the north of the island of Elba when he entered the water and struggled for *"...an hour and a half to free that damn dinghy pack with its jammed snap fasteners."* The CO2 bottles needed to inflate his Mae West were empty and he inflated it manually, but he lost feeling in his arms and legs and could not swim. Two Germans from an anti-aircraft shore battery swam out to him and towed him to shore. Once safely on terra firma one of the Germans, who spoke English, offered him some cognac. After Haskins had a few sips and felt revived, he and his German rescuers climbed the cliff and traveled to the German installation where he was given warm clothing and taken to a building where he slept through the night. Shortly afterwards Haskins was transferred to *Stalag Luft* III and remained there until the Russians liberated the camp. Many months after the war, Haskins received a letter from the Office of the Military Governor in Bremen enquiring about a German citizen looking for work in Germany. The German said he knew Haskins and he was hoping Haskins would give him a recommendation. The man was the English-speaking German who rescued Haskins from the water and he had sent a photograph of himself and the building where Haskins had spent his first night in captivity. Haskins gave the man a recommendation.

On the last day of January the weather limited operations, but the 2nd and 5th Squadrons did go up. The 2nd flew an escort mission, a fighter sweep and a shipping patrol. On the escort mission Lts. James Bickford, Barry Lawler, Bob Curtis and Daniel Zoerb shepherded B-25Gs fitted with 75 mm cannon in the noses for anti-shipping work. According to Bob Curtis the experiment did not meet with much success. He noted that the cannon fire was not very accurate and also in using it, the B-25s opened themselves up as juicy targets for Flak. On the sweep, Spitfire pilots strafed locomotives, and knocked out one

Lt. Marv Haskins, 2nd Fighter Squadron, in the cockpit of his Spitfire Mk V. (Credit: Marvin Haskins)

Lt. Richard L. "Dixie" Alexander, 2nd Fighter Squadron, who drew a bit of 'friendly flak' from his buddies after downing a Fi 156 Storch on 6 February 1944. "Dixie" countered their teasing by exclaiming: "Who knows? He might have grown up to be a 109 pilot!"

Lt. William "Bev" Canning's Spitfire Vc proudly displays the 4th Fighter Squadron emblem under the windscreen. (Credit: Richard Potter)

F/O Robert A. "Bob" Hoover, 4th Fighter Squadron, was shot down on 9 February 1944 and became a POW. (Credit: R. Klug)

steam and one electric locomotive. The 5th FS flew a fighter sweep over the Italian mainland and located a new German airfield for later attention by the bombers.

On 1 February the 5th FS flew a recce mission, a bomber escort and a fighter sweep and a Do 24 was destroyed by 1st Lt. William J. Roberts near the mouth of the Gulf of Spezia during the escort mission.

During the next few days inclement weather and inactivity by the Germans limited the Group's activities. The main activity during this period occurred on 3 February when the 5th FS flew 17 combat sorties, all uneventful. High winds the next day curtailed all flying. There was more high wind on the 5th.

The lull ended on 6 February when 2nd and 5th Squadron Spitfires encountered a flight of slow-flying liason enemy aircraft over Malignano airdrome in Italy and worked it over. The German formation consisted of Hs 123s, Hs 126s and Fi 156s and was *"meat on the table"* for the Spitfire pilots. Moments later two Hs 123s, one Hs 126 and one Fi 156 lay as smoldering wreckage around Malignano airdrome. In a short and one-sided battle Lts. Harold A. Taff, 5th FS, Jack R. Schneider, *"Dixie"* Alexander and F/O Albert R. McGraw, 2nd FS, each downed one enemy aircraft. McCraw and Taff each shot down a Hs 123, Schneider a Hs 126 and Alexander a Fi 156 *Storch*. Back at the base Dixie took a little *"friendly Flak"* from his fellow pilots who teased him about shooting down a Fiesler *Storch*, but Dixie fought back with this argument: *"Who knows? He might have grown up to be a Me 109 pilot!"*

The destruction of slow-flying enemy aircraft continued on 7 February when pilots of the 4th FS met a flight of Hs 126s towing DFS 230 gliders and downed four of them. Lieutenants John L. Bishop, Robert L. Burnett, III, Robert H. McCampbell and William B. Canning each were credited with one Hs 126. Burnett and Canning also claimed kills for glider victories, but did not receive official credit for them. The 4th also lost a man as a result of this air battle when Lt. *"Bev"* Canning was forced to parachute from his Spitfire after its engine stopped. He was taken POW. He later commented: *"To this day I didn't know if I was hit or I just had engine failure."*

The Group's fifth victory of the day was scored about an hour and a half later when *"Junior"* Adams, 2nd FS, downed an Me 410 during a scramble off the west coast of Corsica near Point Palazzo. The 5th FS flew 24 combat sorties including bomber escorts and fighter sweeps, and one of its pilots, while landing, shook up the base by accidentally touching his trigger and sending a stream of gunfire down the runway.

The HQ diarist noted that 8 February: "*...was a big day for the bombing of north central Italy. Heavies, mediums and dive-bombers took part in the show.*"The 2nd FS Spitfires escorted 32 B-26s but weather prevented dropping bombs. The 2nd FS diary noted that several B-24s made emergency landings at Borgo during the day, and that Brigadier General Graves, Commanding Officer of the 63rd Fighter Wing, was lost when his B-25 went down off shore near San Stefano. The 4th FS morning recce showed nothing of importance. The 5th FS flew 26 combat sorties including escort to a Walrus search for General Graves.

The 9th of February 1944 turned out to be bad day for the 4th FS as a dive-bombing mission resulted in the loss of three pilots. The first air battle took place over the harbor at Nice in France when the flight of four Spitfires led by Lt. Henry Montgomery was jumped by Fw 190s as they were pulling up from their dive-bombing

Captain Stanley Rollag of the 5th Fighter Squadron and his Spitfire Mk IX. Rollag would later score four aerial victories after the Group converted to Mustangs. (Credit: Stanley Rollag)

attacks. Widely separated and under attack at all times, the Spitfire pilots were unable to aid each other. First to fall was F/O James H. Montgomery, Jr. whose aircraft was last seen going down in flames. He would become a POW. Next, F/O Bob Hoover's Spitfire was hit and he bailed out and went in the water three miles off Nice harbor. Two enemy speed boats were observed to go out after him. The Germans then turned and pursued the other two Spitfires, but Henry Montgomery and Bradley Smith managed to elude the Fw 190s after desperately maneuvering for 25 minutes.

Later that day, Maj. William M. Houston led a section to search for the two downed pilots and Houston's flight was attacked by Fw 190s. Lt. John L. Bishop was shot down six miles southeast of Cannes, France and became a POW, and Lt. Stanley Pell suffered a hole through his left wing. Houston and Lt. Robert L. Burnett, III, managed to escape the bounce and claimed they probably destroyed a Fw 190 near Nice. Their claim was never given official credit.

During the next few days a number of escort, recoonnaissance and dive-bombing missions were flown by all three squadrons while conflicting rumors ran around the base. One rumor reported in the 2nd FS diary, was that the squadron would no longer participate in morning dive-bombing missions and would instead, fly weather recce missions. The 2nd FS diary recorded: *"...that the pilots took a dim view of this."* On the other hand, the receipt of 90-gallon drop tanks meant that the Group would soon begin flying long-range escort missions to Italy and France.

According the 4th FS diary, Lt. Goettelmann *"...provided a thrill on 11 February when he was taking off on a scramble and his engine refused to function properly. He dropped his wheels in an effort to land and couldn't quite make the final turn. He headed toward operations. Men scattered, feeling helpless, for you never know where an a/c will hit when it is seemingly out of control. Lt. Goettelmann showed a fine display of courage – coaxing his engine into operating, so he could go on and clear us all. He finally landed safely."*

The next two days found the squadrons of the 52nd escorting B-25s to various targets in the area. To better support the bomber escort missions the 52nd sent 19 men to Ghisonaccia, Corsica to service the Group's aircraft operating out of there daily as escort for B-25s.

Lt. James Bickford, 2nd FS, started something new on missions, taking *"recon"* photos with a hand-held camera. The squadron diarist noted that, on 14 February, he borrowed a *"projector to examine the pictures from his latest recce."* Within a short time, the OSS took notice and Bickford was ordered to photograph certain enemy targets. On another fighter sweep during the day F/O Robert Confer, 2nd FS, shot down a Fw 190 southeast of Sienna. The 5th FS flew 26 combat sorties including a sweep and a dive-bombing mission on a large freighter. Near misses, which damaged the ship, were scored by Capt. Steinbrenner, Lts. Boyd and Stanley Rollag, and F/O Tresvik.

On 15 February the 2nd Squadron escorted B-26s on a mission to central Italy and encountered nothing but terrible weather. Belly tank-equipped 5th FS Spitfires, on the other hand, flew a sweep over central Italy that day and encountered a formation of Me 109s and Fw 190s and attacked them. The 5th FS diary reported: *"Results: :two Me 109s destroyed by Lt. John Anderson, one Fw 190 and one Italian biplane destroyed by Capt. Eugene Steinbrenner, one Fw 190 destroyed by Lt. Arthur R. Tower, one Me 109 probably destroyed by Lt. Frank Atkins and a Fw 190 damaged by Lt. William D. Gahagen. 1st Lt. Arthur R. 'Dusty' Tower was shot down by Flak southwest of the town of Viterbo shortly after he saw his Fw 190 crash in flames. No one saw him go down. His last words over the radio were 'Good luck and good hunting.' The enemy plane led Lt. Tower in low over a strong Flak position and the Germans led him enough to hit his cooling system causing a glycol leak."*

Belly tanks caused problems because Spitfires did not have a reliable drop tank release mechanism. Later, on the ground, pilots and mechanics discussed what to do. The Squadron diarist reported: *"Lt. Anderson secured his victories with the tank still on. It fell off into the sea on the way home. Lt. Gahagen's tank came off as he landed. Over Viterbo airdrome when Capt. Eugene C. Steinbrenner tried to drop his belly tank, his plane went out of control and he did three snap rolls down and away from the flight. When he recovered he saw three Fw 190's ahead. He immediately opened fire on the leader on a 90 degree angle shot from the left, and to his amazement the plane on the leader's right burst into flames and went to crash near the field. Capt. Steinbrenner then pursued one of the Fw 190s down to the deck with the remaining one on his tail. As they roared over the field, an Italian biplane either landing or trying to land after take-off was seen to crash and burn."*

The 2nd FS flew a fighter sweep on the 16th and engaged a mixed formation of Me 109s and Fw 190s. One of the Messerschmitts was shot

Two views of Lt. John Anderson's Spitfire Mk Vc and its non-standard camouflage scheme. The photograph to left must have been taken shortly after his two victories on 15 February 1944. At least two of the 5th Fighter Squadron's Spitfires carried this non standard scheme. (Credit: James Empey)

Spitfire Mk Vb, VF-K, serial number unknown

**Assigned pilot unknown,
5th Fighter Squadron,
52nd Fighter Group,
fall 1943, Corsica.**

This Spitfire featured a non-standard three tone upper surface camouflage. At least one other similarly painted aircraft, VF-R, is known to have been flown by Lt. John Anderson, in the 5th FS

Spitfire Mk Vc VF-K of the 5th Fighter Squadron also wears the non-standard three-toned color scheme. (Credit: Ed Martin)

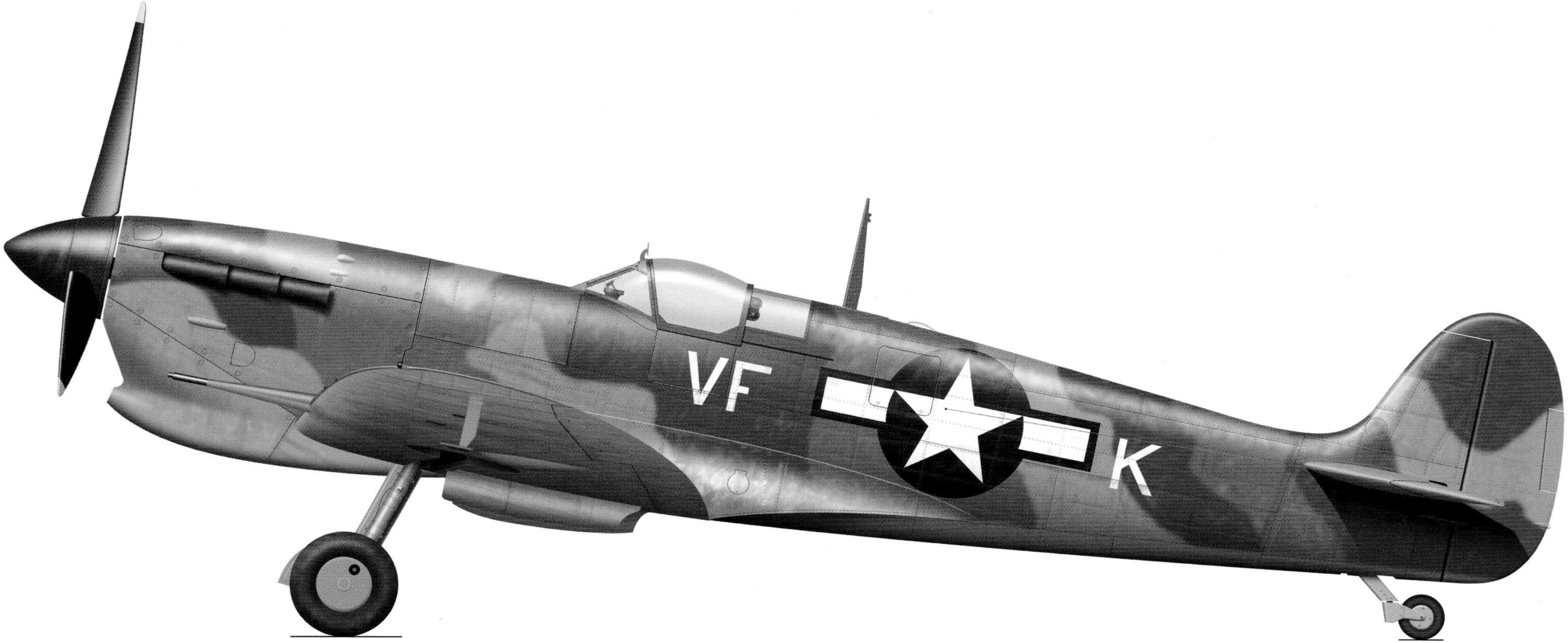

The second of the two known 'sharkmouth' Spitfires belonged to the 5th Fighter Squadron. It is assumed that Lt. Fred Jones, seen in the photograph, was its assigned pilot. (Credit: James Empey)

Lt. Bob Curtis, 2nd Fighter Squadron, who scored his first aerial victory on 19 February 1944 by downing Oblt. Rolf Klippgen, Staffelkapitän of 7./JG 53, in an air battle near San Lorenzo Nuovo, Italy. (Credit: Paul Ludwig)

down by F/O Robert L. Confer and Lt. Mike Encinias west of Lake Bracciano, Italy in the Viterbo area. Lt. Curtis recalled: *"About twelve Me 109s were encountered by about the same number of Spitfires. Suddenly Bob Confer, who was flying my wing, took off after them without saying a word."*

Encinias also broke formation. *"This action startled me since I was the element leader and Confer was supposed to stay with me. But I quickly recovered and called Confer on the radio saying I was following him."*

One of the Me 109s dived toward Confer and Curtis attempted to shoot it down. Confer pressed his attack on the Messerschmitt. His firepower damaged the enemy aircraft but he had to break off because his windshield was covered in oil from the seriously damaged German aircraft.

Lt. Mike Encinias reported that Confer: *"kept firing at it but could not knock it down. I called him several times saying that I was covering his tail. He finally told me that he couldn't see the Me 109 because his windshield was covered with oil. I then pulled ahead of Confer and closed to about a hundred feet and fired a long burst at the 109. It exploded and the pilot apparently was blown out because he went right by me with a trailing parachute. Since we were almost right on the deck, he hit the ground with his parachute not fully opened."*

The German pilot was Lt. Hans-Dieter Heinecke of *Stab* III./JG 53.

Bob Curtis later commented that he knew *"...Confer's action showed a lack of discipline but it also showed an unwillingness to wait forever for a leader to make a decision. I was completely in favor of Confer's action, namely, attack them, and let them respond to our attack, rather than wait for their attack."*

In other action during the day the 5th FS flew 34 combat sorties including escort for 72 B-26s headed to Piombino.

The 17th of February was a day set aside for maintnance and only a few missions were flown during the morning. The 4th FS escorted B-25's from Ghisonaccia while the 5th FS flew a recce and a dive-bombing attack upon F-Boats in Port Ercole.

On the next day, HQ 52nd FG reported: *"Bad weather at Viterbo prevented a sweep, where so many enemy fighter planes are based. The 4th Squadron is now doing all the escort work our group does for the B-25s, assisted by French Spitfires from Ajaccio."*

The 5th FS flew a recce in the area of Florence, Italy, and Lieutenants Yon, Tierney and F/Os Weynandt and Moore strafed a locomotive and left it burning and stopped.

The 2nd and 5th Squadrons attempted another sweep of the Viterbo area on 19 February and this time a major encounter ensued. Twenty-four Spitfires of the 2nd and 5th Squadrons fought 15 Me 109s and Fw 190s. The dogfight was costly to both sides. The first engagement took place at 13.10 hrs when Bill Bryan, 2nd FS, downed an Me 109 and 20 minutes later Lt. Bickford, 2nd FS, shot down another Me 109. Shortly after this kill, the conflict grew and both the 2nd and 5th Squadrons took on the enemy fighters. *"Dixie"* Alexander and Bob Curtis each got one Me 109 and raised the 2nd Squadron's total for the day to four.

Lt. Alexander's encounter report stated: *"Then*

Spitfire Mk Vc, serial number unknown

Lt. Richard "Dixie" Alexander,
2nd Fighter Squadron,
52nd Fighter Group,
Corsica, 1944.

Richard Alexander's sharkmouth Spitfire also displayed artwork under the left windscreen in the form of a bloody knife blade stabbing into two and a half Swastikas, and the emblem of the "American Beagle Squadron" painted on the left side of the cowling.

At least two of the 52nd Fighter Group's Spitfires wore 'sharkmouth' nose art. This one named "Chappie" and "Dixie Mk VI" was assigned to "Dixie" Alexander of the 2nd Fighter Squadron and was coded QP-A. (Credit: Air Force Museum)

Two views of the battle damage received by the 5th Fighter Squadron's Spitfire Mk Vc VF-R during a skirmish over Italy. (Credit: Paul Ludwig)

I looked up and saw only two enemy aircraft. They were about a mile north of me at about 8000 feet. They separated, one heading northeast and one heading southeast, both losing altitude rapidly. I went after the one going northeast, pushing everything forward and going into a shallow dive, reaching 400 mph by the time I leveled out on the deck. I was about 1000 yards behind the enemy aircraft at this time and closing on him rapidly. I estimate that his speed was not much over 300 mph. I had to throttle back to keep from overshooting him. When I had closed to about 200 yards, I fired a half-second burst, but saw no strikes. Then at about 100 yards I gave him another short burst, closing to 50 yards, but, again so no strikes. I noticed that my port cannon was not firing and I gave him a final burst of about one-second from about 50 yards dead astern and slightly above. I saw cannon strikes on the tail and the top of the fuselage. He was about 20 feet above the ground and I was about 50 feet. The enemy aircraft nosed down and crashed into the trees, at about 240 mph."

Lt. Bob Curtis saw enemy aircraft milling around and reported: *"Other Spits attacked and as one German fighter leveled out in front of me about 1,000 yards away. I closed to about 200 yards, directly behind and slightly below it and fired about a one-second burst of cannon and machine gun fire but observed no strikes. I had no gun-sight because the light bulb had burned out. We were both at about 6,000 feet and as I fired the burst the enemy aircraft flicked over and headed straight down. I rolled over and followed it."*

The Me 109 made corkscrew evasive actions and diving turns, but Curtis kept close, and soon the two were near the ground. A Spitfire could make tighter turns than an Me 109 and the German fighter had been hit and damaged and it was not flying fast. Curtis: *"As it started a medium turn to the left I fired another two-second burst from about 200 yards behind and slightly above it. I saw strikes all over the fuselage and wings of the enemy aircraft. About 500 feet off the ground it flipped onto its back, flew on into the ground on the side of a hill, and broke up about five miles west of San Lorenzo Nuovo. During this engagement I never had to use full throttle."*

Curtis' victim in this engagement was *Oblt.* Rolf Klippgen, the newly appointed *Staffelkapitän* of 7./JG 53.

As the air battle was taking place above them the 2nd Squadron's low flight began a strafing run on Viterbo airfield which was packed with enemy aircraft. Lt. Bob Liebl later recalled the strafing run: *"We started our strafing run about 13.30 hours, flying line abreast. We shot up and damaged or destroyed several enemy aircraft on the ground as well as damaging hangars and other buildings."*

As the strafers pulled up from the strafing run, the flight was bounced by enemy aircraft and Lt. Liebl was shot down. Moments later Mike Encinias suffered the same fate and both men spent the remainder of the war as POWs.

Lt. Miguel *"Mike"* Encinias described after the war how he was shot down: *"A 20 mm projectile from an Me 109 came through the canopy and went through the instrument panel and into the gas tank in front of the cockpit and on into the engine where it started a fire. I was drenched by gasoline and very much afraid that the fire would reach me."*

Encinias struggled to release the canopy, which at first would not break free because it had been damaged by gunfire. Finally Encinias managed to force it off and dived out of the cockpit. Captured, he was taken to the airfield at Viterbo where he talked to the *Luftwaffe* Sergeant Pilot who had shot him down.

Meanwhile the battle was in full swing and the 5th Squadron managed to destroy eight more enemy aircraft but paid a heavy price for its victories. Lt. Franklin A. Everett and F/O James H. Johnson claimed two Me 109s each, while 1st Lt. William D. Gahagen and F/O Billie E. Quisenberry each accounted for one. Before he was shot down, 2nd Lt. Sheldon H. Cooper, 5th FS, claimed he destroyed a Me 109. 1st Lt. William J. Roberts claimed one Me 109 destroyed and he may have claimed another Me 109 before he was shot down. In addition to the kills, Capt. Omer McDuff, Lt. Harold A. Taff, F/O James H. Johnson and Lt. Edward O. Tierney each damaged Me 109s. The 5th Squadron, however paid dearly for its victory. Lieutenants Roberts, Gahagen and Cooper lost their lives during the dogfight, and Lt. Everest was shot down, evaded capture and returned to the Squadron in June. The 5th Squadron diary

"Malarkie" was assigned to future 5th Fighter Squadron Ace, Lt. Calvin D. Allen. (Credit: James Empey)

stated, commented on the losses: *"All of these pilots have been with the squadron since the close of the Tunisian campaign. This is the highest number of casualties we have had since the beginning of the war in one day."*

In mid-June, 1944, Lt. Franklin A. Everett was back in American hands after being shot down during the mission of 19 February and wrote an encounter report describing his participation in the air battle. On that date 12 Spitfires took off from Borgo headed for Viterbo A/D #2. The formation consisted of two flights, Black Flight and White Flight, with White Flight in the lead. Three miles south of Tuscania, Italy Lt. Johnson of Black Flight spotted two enemy aircraft on the deck and he and Lt. Roberts headed down to attack them, leaving the remaining four aircraft of Black Flight at altitude to cover them. Seconds later Lt. Everett spotted six Me 109s diving toward Roberts and Johnson, and described the action as follows: *"The four of us started down, but we were soon bounced by two Me 109s from above at five o'clock. Lt. Cooper and myself broke while Lts. Gahagan and Winnard kept right on going toward the e/a below. The two Me 109s made a pass and kept on diving so we did a 360 degree turn and followed them. This was the last time I saw Lts. Gahagan and Winnard."*

"As we went down in the chase I saw an Me 109 with a Spitfire on its tail. I saw a Me 109 cross my path so I turned after him and Lt. Cooper came up line abreast with me on the left. I fired but saw no hits. Lt. Cooper and I broke left and I cut across his tail as an Me 109 bounced him from the rear. In an instant we ended up in a Lufberry Circle with five Me 109s. Lt. Cooper fired on one Me 109. When I last saw the e/a, it was going down in an apparent glide at about 100 miles per hour. Heavy black smoke from the engine was obscuring the cockpit. At this point someone transmitted 'Let's go home, there are too many of them'. Lt. Cooper broke out of the circle and I started to follow. I cleared his tail once and then I was fired on. I broke and ended up in another Lufberry. At this [illegible] my radio went out and I heard no more R/T. When I last saw Lt. Cooper his ship was in a dive and I thought he would easily make it home. Right after this an Me 109 broke out of the circle. I followed him, closed and fired from directly behind. He hit the ground and exploded at 4225N-1143E at approximately 1350 hours. I turned toward home but had to break into Me 109s that were on my tail. I could just turn with them due to my belly tank. This ended up in a Lufberry in which I fired several bursts at an Me 109 directly ahead of me. He left the Lufberry in a very gentle turn. This gave me an opportunity to fire from directly astern and close the range to 75 yards and finally down to 50 yards. I saw him release his canopy and start to climb out. He was 3/4 out of the cockpit and his right leg was over the side when I had to break right due to an enemy aircraft firing at me. I did not see what happened to him after this. We were at 3000 feet and the time was about 13.55 hrs. His ship went down very near the first one I got."

After his second victory Lt. Everett, now out of ammunition, broke away and headed for home with five Me 109s on his tail. Alone and under fire, he went into another Lufberry and this time he was the victim. One of the Me 109s put some well placed 20 mm shells into his engine and

F/O James Johnson's Spitfire "Hazel" undergoing engine maintenance in March 1944. Note the two German crosses under the windscreen signifying his two victories of 19 February 1944. (Credit: Thomas Thacker)

Everett was forced to jump. As he was descending in his chute he thought he was going to be strafed when two enemy aircraft turned and came at him, but much to his relief the Germans just waved and flew on by. He landed safely, evaded capture for four months and returned to his unit in June 1944.

F/O James Johnson was the number 2 man behind Lt. Roberts, leader of Black Section: *"We were in a six-ship box, three Spitfires line abreast with White Section 2 miles ahead and at 5,000 feet. We were headed SW, three miles E of Tuscania when Lt. Sherman of White Section called out at 13.40 hrs an enemy aircraft on the deck."*

Five minutes later Johnson saw two enemy aircraft and he and Roberts dived on the Me 109s. At 250 yards Johnson gave one a 3-second burst on 20 degrees deflection with his cannon and the Messerschmitt *"...started to disintegrate hit the ground on the perimeter of the Viterbo No. 2 A/D."*

Roberts had shot down the other Me 109. Johnson and Roberts lost sight of each other and when more enemy aircraft appeared, Johnson picked out an Fw 190 and attacked it. However his approach was too fast and when he began to overrun it, Johnson gave it a three second burst, damaging it. He turned his attention to an Me 109 and in a head-on pass, kept firing down to a 50-yard distance: *"I had tried to drop my belly tank during the first encounter without success. We both made about five tight circles to the right with the e/a gaining on me. The belly tank fell off at this point and I was able to turn much tighter giving me the advantage. I got within 50 yards and shot him down."*

The 20th of February was set aside for maintenance and some 4th FS Spitfire Vcs escorted B-25s from Ghisonaccia to Leghorn harbor, while the 5th FS flew two morning recces and a dusk patrol. On the following day at Borgo, bad weather and a temporary shortage of aircraft forced the cancellation of a bomber escort mission. The weather at Calvi was better, but the 4th FS flew only one late patrol. The 5th FS flew one recce over the Italian coast.

Weather continued to be a factor on the 22nd. All three of the Group's squadrons saw their respective escort missions aborted because of bad weather over the targets and the 5th Squadron's dawn and dusk patrols turned out to be the only successful missions of the day.

Col. Robert Levine took command of the 52nd FG on 23 February and Col. McNickle moved up to the 63rd Fighter Wing. Capt. Trowbridge became Commanding Officer of the 4th FS and Maj. Houston became Group Exec. The only air activity was a 5th FS recce to Piombino. It rained so hard on the 24th that the 4th FS diarist wrote: *"The Gods of weather released their fury on this poor little spot."*

Despite the rain the 5th FS sent six Spitfires on a weather recce over the Italian coast. It was raining the next day when twelve replacement Spitfires were flown in, six Mark Vs and six Mark IXs. Down at Calvi, the 4th FS stood on alert and the 5th FS flew a morning weather recce and escorted B-25s temporarily based at Borgo to attack F-Boats in Talamone harbor. The sky cleared the next day when the 2nd FS escorted B-26s to bomb Viterbo. No fighter opposition was encountered but Flak downed two bombers. On the 29 February, the sky was clear again and the 5th FS escorted 80-plus B-26s sent to bomb Viterbo airdrome.

The weather was bad on 1 March, hampering

Colonel Robert Levine, who took command of the 52nd Fighter Group on 23 February 1944, replacing Colonel McNickle. (Credit: John Blythe)

5th Fighter Squadron pilots and VF-AA. Standing: Lt. Richard Monson. Left to right on Spitfire: Lts. Robert G. Anderson; Irwin Franklin; Alexander Watkins; Charles Denham and Henry Woods. (Credit: Paul Ludwig collection)

A Walrus Mk 1 flying boat similar to those that plucked a number of 52nd Fighter Group pilots out of the waters of the Mediterranean. (Credit: C. G. Jones)

flying, except for a dawn patrol by the 4th FS. During the night, 40 enemy bombers circled Corsica trying to locate the base at Borgo. The enemy aircraft dropped flares at 01.30 hrs but when Allied anti-aircraft guns fired on them, the enemy departed without causing damage. The weather on 2 March was better and the 2nd flew a morning recce and then joined with the 5th Squadron and 253 Squadron to escort B-26s, while the 4th FS escorted B-25s.

On the next day the 2nd FS and 5th FS escorted B-26s to the marshalling yards south of Rome. The mission was without incident, but on the trip back to base Lt. *"Junior"* Adams, 2nd FS, lost his engine at 5,000 feet and he bailed out and landed in the water 20 miles south-west of Marinello. His Mae West inflated only on one side and when he tried to inflate his dingy it exploded. Lt. Chuck Fuller, orbiting Adams, saw what happened and Fuller separated his own dinghy, and threw it down to Adams who was unable to retrieve it. After an hour-and-a- half in the water, Adams was picked up by an air-sea rescue Walrus and returned to Borgo.

On 4 March all three squadrons were busy for part of the day. The 2nd FS strafed a train south-west of Viareggio and left the locomotive stopped and belching steam. The 4th FS flew two scrambles and two sections escorted bombers from Ghisonaccia, both of them raining havoc on P. San Stefano which was reputed to be an F-Boat base. The 5th FS flew recces from Piombino to Civitavecchia.

It rained, snowed and sleeted all day on 5 March without a halt and there was no flying at all. Bad weather carried over into 6 March and all airfields were unusable except for emergency flying.

The 4th Squadron diarist reported on 7 March that a flight of its Spitfires was sent out to investigate a large mine five miles south of Pianosa. During the mission Lt. H.E. Montgomery, for unknown reasons, bailed out 20 miles north-west of Giglio Island. He was in the water a long time and after the Walrus rescued him, it and escorting Spitfires landed by moonlight, which was an unusual experience for day fighters and Walruses. 5th FS Spitfires escorted B-26s to the marshalling yards south of Rome and there was no Flak or fighter opposition.

There was a surprise when a Merlin engine expert lectured mechanics of the 4th FS on 8 March and the diarist said it was *"... hard to understand"* why the lecturer talked about Spitfires *"... seeing we'll soon have Mustangs."*

The big event of the day was the rescue of a pilot from 253 Squadron RAF who was shot down into the water eight miles north of the island of Elba. An air-sea rescue Walrus was escorted by the Group's Spitfires, and as the Walrus made a water landing it came under heavy fire from a German coastal battery on Elba. Capt. James Bickford, 2nd FS, in an effort to defend the Walrus, strafed the battery, but not before the Walrus was sunk. A High Speed Launch retrieved its crew.

Lt. Benjamin Jones, 4th FS, had been with the Squadron for only three days when he flew his first mission on 9 March 1944, a sweep over France. During the course of the mission, the Squadron encountered a flight of Fw 190s and Jones shot one of them down but he was killed while chasing another Fw 190. According to 4th FS witnesses, Jones was chasing another Fw 190 and while he was in a very tight turn, his aircraft

Spitfire Mk Vc, JK180 *Betty* I

Lt. Richard Lampe,
2nd Fighter Squadron,
52nd Fighter Group,
January 1944, Corsica

Richard Lampe's aircraft carried a non-standard one shade of brown scheme on the upper surfaces on Corsica, replacing its earlier desert scheme. Lt. Lampe became an Ace scoring 5.5 victories after the Squadron converted to Mustangs. His assigned P-51B was named Betty II/They are Loaded. Above the They are Loaded was a pair of dice.

Two views of Lt. Richard Lampe's Spitfire Mk Vc named "Betty I". C. J. Jones, in the photograph of the tail section, obviously approves of the artwork by Bill Borosky. (Credit: Carlton Hogue)

Lt. Charles Botvidson, 2nd Fighter Squadron, and his Spitfire Mk Vc, which displays the "American Beagle Squadron" emblem. (Credit: Robert C. Curtis)

spun into the sea 50 miles off the west coast of Corsica.

Meanwhile, the Office of Strategic Services (OSS) had found the photographs that Capt. Bickford took with a hand-held camera very useful, and in March it sent an agent and a large camera to the 2nd FS and requested photographs taken of certain areas of Italy. Bickford asked a crew chief to mount it on the radio rack so it could be operated from the cockpit by cable. Bickford took aerial photos of strategic points on the Italian coast for the US and Allied ground forces sent in by OSS on 9 March.

Next day, the 2nd and 5th Squadrons from Borgo dive-bombed a highway and a railroad bridge northwest of Pisa and scored two hits on the center of the bridge. The usual B-26 escort was flown, to the Paschi railroad bridge. The 4th FS flew one escort from Ghisonaccia and a dusk patrol, while the 5th flew a B-26 escort to the Orvieto railroad bridge and cover for a High Speed Launch rescuing a French pilot in the Pianosa area.

All 2nd FS aircraft were grounded on 11 March for inspection because of a report from higher headquarters concerning possible sabotage. After the inspection was completed, the 2nd and 5th Squadrons flew dive-bombing and escort missions. The 2nd FS dive-bombed a railway switch house on a siding near Cosina and the 5th FS strafed and destroyed a locomotive. Lt. Charles Mann, 2nd FS, suffered engine failure during the mission and bailed out five miles east of base and was picked up by a PT boat.

On 12 March, high command changed the 2nd FS's usual dawn recce to a weather, shipping and armed recce, and when the 2nd FS flew its mission over Leghorn harbor, Lt. Edwin W. Fuller, 2nd FS, downed a Ju 88, 10 miles west of the city. He and Lt. Charles C. Botvidson had chased the Ju 88, but Botvidson was flying a Sptifire Mark V and Fuller a Mark IX, and Fuller passed Botvidson and waved to him commenting: *"Tough shit old man, won't that ship go any faster?"*

The 5th FS sat on alert and flew a recce strike and a scramble and dawn and dusk patrols.

On 13 March the 2nd FS flew 46 sorties and hit a railway bridge four miles north of Pisa as well as factories at Viareggio. Pilots of the 4th FS flew to Ghisonaccia to escort B-25s on two missions. The 5th FS flew two dive-bombing and one B-26 escort mission to the rail yards at Montalto di Castro.

The 4th FS escorted B-25s raiding a seaplane factory at Marina di Pisa, and the 5th FS escorted B-26s to Rome and flew a dive-bombing mission to the Montalto marshalling yards on 14 March. During the dive-bombing mission the Squadron's Spitfires destroyed a building, cut the tracks and strafed tank cars.

On 15 March, Staff was able to declare that *"...our dive-bombing continues with increased accuracy" because Lieutenants Taff, Devoe, Anderson and Winnard, all from the 5th FS, made direct hits on anchored boats and ship repair buildings on the docks at Viareggio. During the afternoon mission Lt. Robert M. Moore, 5th FS, died in a bizarre accident. Moore was on a recce over the Italian coast when he, or his leader, spotted a minelayer south-west of Elba, and orders were given to drop tanks and strafe the vessel. When Moore jettisoned his belly tank it hit the underside of the tail of his Spitfire and knocked the entire tail section off. Moore's death resulted in the 5th FS designing a device to make jettisoning a belly tank foolproof. The device rested on top of the tank and its shaft came up through the cockpit floor beside the heel of the pilot who would pull "...the release knob and kick hell out of the shaft until the tank released."* There is no doubt that the 2nd and 4th Squadrons copied the device.

On 16 March, Capt. Sanborn led the 2nd FS on a six-plane dive-bombing mission to Sestri Levanti. Sanborn achieved a near miss on a destroyer near Spezia, and a direct hit was scored by Lt. William L. Bryan, Jr. The 4th FS diarist observed that this was *"...the first real spring day of the year"* and pilots flew dive-bombing missions to Viareggio harbor. On the following day, dive-bombing became an art, as the diarist put it, when the 2nd FS put *"two direct hits on a power plant at Sestri Levanti and Lt's. Daniel Zoerb and Adams made near misses on a 200 foot tanker, sinking same, and destroyed two 50 foot tugs off Marina D'Avenza."*

The 5th FS at Borgo flew a recce, a B-26 escort mission to an RR bridge at Cecina and a dive-bombing mission on 17 March. On the recce, pilots strafed trains and trucks, but an Fw 190 attacked Lt. Richard A. Ritchings' Spitfire, holing his glycol system, forcing him to bail out north of Talamone, Italy. It was believed that the Italian underground rescued him. Lt. Louis Weynandt chased the offending Fw 190 for several miles but was unable to get in position for an attack.

As the 2nd FS escorted B-26s heading for the Poggibonsi and Orvieto railroad bridges on 18 March, its Spitfires strafed an ammunition dump five miles northeast of Cocina and set off a violent explosion. The massive explosion occurred after a Spitfire strafed two buildings, which burst into

Future Ace Daniel Zoerb, 2nd Fighter Squadron, seems to be enjoying his "hand holding" with the naked lady adorning F/O Al McCraw's Spitfire, "Fascinating Bitchy" (Credit: Daniel Zoerb via Jeff Ethell)

Sgt. Robert Klug poses with Lt. Cummins' bombed-up Spitfire "Franny Lou II" as it awaits its next dive-bombing mission. (Credit: Robert Klug)

sheets of flame, and Lt. Curtis strafed a third building that exploded and set two others on fire. The blast damaged Curtis' Spitfire severely enough that he had to bail out. He landed in the water near Cecina Marina and was rescured by a Walrus while 5th FS Spitfires circled overhead providing air cover. The 2nd FS diarist commented that *"The pilots said it felt like someone had kicked them in the pants."* Once the Walrus returned him to base, the diarist noted that: *"practically the entire squadron was at the field around 1945 hours when the Walrus landed after dark by Jeep headlights."*

The 52nd Fighter Group received some exciting news on the 19th when Brig. Gen. Laurence Craigie, Commanding General of the 63rd Fighter Wing, announced that the Group would be equipped with P-51Bs within six weeks. This good news, however, was overshadowed by the death of Capt. Eugene Steinbrenner, 5th FS, who was shot down and killed. Steinbrenner and others were on a six-ship recce strike when a Ju 88 was sighted and Lt. Robert C. Boyd and Lt. Billie E. Quisenberry went down after it while the other four Spitfires covered them. Boyd and Quisenberry damaged the Ju88, but return fire hit Boyd's Spitfire causing a glycol leak and Boyd headed for the coast where he bailed out a half mile off shore from Civitavecchia. He was taken POW.

When the 5th Squadron heard one of its pilots was down in the water, it sent a four-ship flight led by Steinbrenner to cover Boyd until a Walrus picked him up. When two Me 109 decoys were seen over Boyd's dinghy, Steinbrenner, Lt's. Winnard, Weynandt and Charles E. Devoe dove onto the German fighters, and they, in turn, were bounced by 12 Fw 190s. The Fw 190s opened fired and Capt. Steinbrenner was quickly shot down into the sea, a few miles north of Civitavecchia. Lt. Devoe's plane was damaged in the same attack, but Winnard and Weynandt escaped the enemy fire and turned on their attackers. Winnard downed an Fw 190 and Weynandt damaged a Me 109, 3 miles south of Montalto di Castro, Italy.

The loss of Capt. Steinbrenner was devastating to the 5th Squadron as evidenced by the diary entry for the day which stated: *"To say that Capt. Steinbrenner was well liked would be a gross understatement. He was, without a doubt, the most popular and most friendly to enlisted men and officers alike of any of the pilots the 5th Squadron has had. He will indeed, be missed by everybody."*

Lt. Devoe later recalled that he saw Fw 190s diving out of the sun onto Steinbrenner and he *"...swerved to meet them. I climbed for altitude, losing sight of Weynandt. As I reached the top of my climb, I heard someone say 'Spit, break right!' Next thing I knew something slammed into the left side of my head above my ear and something struck my right eye. I remember saying 'I can't see.' I dove for the sea, headed in what I thought was the correct direction." He radioed for directions to Borgo, got back to the field, landed without flaps or brakes and nosed up at the end of the runway."*

DeVoe had suffered several wounds, but the most serious was the damage to his right eye which was so severe that he was returned to the US for treatment. However the eye could not be saved and he would never fly again.

As a result of these latest losses Brig. Gen. Craigie issued orders to the effect that *"...all armed recces to stop and hereafter we shall confine our activities to escort and alert until we have received more pilots and a/c."*

On 20 March, the 4th FS flew dawn and dusk patrols and an escort for Beaufighters while the 5th FS diarist noted: *"Due to a shortage of pilots and aircraft we flew only 2 combat sorties, a B-26 escort."*

The 2nd FS flew more B-26 escort missions to the Arezzo viaduct the next day. The 5th FS flew two more B-26 escort missions on 22 March and B-26's pounded the Arezzo and Poggibonsi railway bridges. Spitfires of the 4th FS from Calvi escorted B-25s to an undisclosed target, and the 5th FS escorted B-26s to the Florence marshalling yards. On another mission, the 4th FS escorted the 2nd FS on a dive-bombing mission.

5th Squadron again escorted B-26s on the 24th to the Orvieto railway bridge, and flew a dive-bombing raid on E-boats in Leghorn harbor, probably escorted by Spitfires from another squadron, since dive-bombing put dive-bombers into a vulnerable position at low altitude. The next day the 5th Squadron escorted 48 B-26s heading for Poggibonsi, reaching the Italian coast where the weather turned bad. The afternoon escort to the Rignano RR bridge was obscured by cloud. The 2nd FS escorted B-25s and strafed locomotives. The bridge at Arezzo received another attack on 26 March. New pilots practiced formation flying and *"rat racing"*, a form of free-for-all flying.

On 27 March, the 52nd FG escorted convoys and flew an armed recce mission. The 5th FS flew a B-26 escort to the Poggibonsi bridge and a convoy patrol, while 4th FS Spitfires flew a recce for the first time in weeks, over the coast of France but saw nothing. Twelve 4th FS Spitfires flew to Ghisonaccia to escort B-25s. One day later the 5th Squadron took the lead in activity, dive-bombing a target in Marina D'Avenza and escorting B-26 missions to Florence and Certaldo. 4th Squadron's new pilots practiced formation flying.

On the last day of the month, one of the new pilots, Lt. Richard L. Monson, 5th FS, was killed when his aircraft crashed into the sea. He was in a flight of four aircraft sent to dive-bomb trucks 10 miles north of Leghorn, but due to bad weather, the Spitfires jettisoned their bombs in the sea and prepared to strafe along the coast. The diarist noted that as Monson dived he *"...had trouble with his plane and did not fully recover from his dive. He went into the water one half mile off shore and 3 miles north-northwest of Leghorn. He seemed like a good fellow."*

Captain Eugene Steinbrenner, a very popular member of the 5th Fighter Squadron, was shot down and killed on 19 March 1944. (Credit: Thomas Thacker)

Spitfires of the 5th FS began the month of April, 1944 with two B-26 escorts and on the following day, the 2nd, 5th Squadron and 253 Squadron RAF, sent Spitfires to escort B-26s to the Arezzo bridge, in what was becoming *"a real milk run."*There was no mention of Flak or fighter opposition. Bombers also hit the Ficulle railroad bridges and the 2nd FS blew up a train, strafed a staff car and a radar station and shot up a locomotive. The 2nd FS was on alert all day and flew a single scramble. The 4th FS escorted B-25s to Poggibonsi, another milk run.

On 4 April, the 2nd FS escorted B-26s to a target obscured by weather and 12 Me 109s made what the diarist noted was *"a very aggressive attack on the flight"*, yet only one enemy aircraft came within firing range of the bombers and there were no victories or losses. The 5th FS also escorted B-26s to an undisclosed target. The major news of the day appeared in the 52nd FG HQ report which stated: *"That with the re-equipping of the group with P-51s we are to leave the Coastal Command after almost a year of service with it and go under the Fifteenth Air Force... The 52nd FG was now in daily contact with our future headquarters, the 306th Fighter Wing at the Foggia, Italy airfield complex."*

On 6 April, when 2nd and 5th Squadron Spitfires escorted B-26s to bomb the Ficulle railroad bridge, four Spitfire IXs of the 5th FS flying top cover were attacked by six Me 109s and Lt. Joe H. Blackburn shot down two. Another was probably destroyed by Capt. Terrell Yon. In fact, these were the last Spitfire victories of the war for 52nd FG. The 2nd FS dive-bombed a railway bridge north-east of Follonica and the 4th FS escorted B-25s to Cecina Marina. More railway bridges were bombed on 7 April, the 2nd FS attacking at Incisa, the 4th FS and B-25's attacking at Certaldo, and the 5th FS dive-bombing other targets.

The 52nd FG diarist noted: *"Word has been received that our first P-51s are available, twenty at Casablanca, Morocco and five at Sidi Ahmed near Bizerte."*

Thus alerted, a PBY was provided the next day to fly pilots to Casablanca to pick up P-51s. Additionally, Lt. White, 5th FS, and M/Sgt. MacBeth left for Sidi Ahmed along with pilots and Crew Chiefs to learn the intricasies of the new P-51, while S/Sgts. Hopkins and Meade left for Ajaccio to teach a French Spitfire squadron how to install bomb racks on their Spitfires. The PBY took off on 9 April with a full load of pilots to ferry Mustangs back to Corsica, and the B-25 belonging to the 52nd FG ferried pilots to North Africa for other P-51s. The diarist recorded that bad weather prevented combat operations. By that date, Maj. Sanborn had flown his 130th combat sortie which surpassed Capt. Norman McDonald's 129 for a new Group record.

The 52nd FG did not have many pilots available for missions on 10 April because a number of its pilots were ferrying Mustangs, while replacement pilots for those lost in combat had not yet arrived. In spite of the pilot shortage, the 2nd and 5th Squadrons flew escort and dive-bombing missions to Arezzo, Marina di Pisa and a factory at the mouth of the Arno River in Italy. On the dive-bombing mission, Lt. Denham, 5th FS, scored a direct hit on an railway track.

On 11 April, 34 of the 52nd FG's Spitfires escorted bombers heading for the Sienna marshalling yards. As the formation approached Piombino while enroute to the target, it flew into a tremendous Flak barrage and Maj. Bert Sanborn's aircraft took an explosive round just ahead of the firewall. Realizing that he was in trouble Sanborn turned, flew out to sea and bailed out. Lt. Frank Grey strafed the Flak guns and then flew cover for Sanborn until after the Walrus arrived. After Sanborn was back at Borgo, he was very angry and was about to jump into a Spitfire to strafe those who shot him down, but Col. Levine caught him getting into an aircraft, grounded him and sent him to rest camp. The 4th FS escorted B-25s to Montalto di Castro.

A change of targets from northern Italy to southern France marked the missions of 12 April. The 2nd FS flew an armed recce, dive-bombed and escorted B-26s; the 4th FS escorted B-25s to the Cecina railway bridge; and the 5th FS escorted B-26s to Nice.

Two days later, At 12.30 hrs, six P-51s arrived on Corsica for the 52nd FG, and roared over the Operations Building at an altitude of about 50 feet. The 2nd FS flew a B-26 escort, dive-bombed, and escorted Maj. Gen. Ira Eaker, commanding MAAF and Gen. Jacob Devers, commanding the US Army in the ETO in Eaker's C-53 transport to Bastia and then to Sardinia.

High winds the next day caused cancellation of the B-26 escort, and that gave everyone a chance to crowd around the new Mustangs. On 16 April the weather turned bad and the only flying done was a harbor patrol by the 2nd FS.

Starting on 17 April, the three squadrons began going off operations to transition to the P-51 and more pilots departed for Casablanca to ferry P-51s back. Three days after receiving Mustangs, one of the pilots ruined a Mustang which was *"disenbowled"* to provide spare parts for future use. A report of an unidentified boat in the vicinity of Populonia prompted the CO to allow Lt. Dan Zoerb to fly a Mustang to search for it, leading to speculation that this was the first P-51 mission in the 52nd FG, but this was not the case. There was

The ground crew of Spitfire Mk IX WD-U is checking the aircraft's cannon to determine what caused them to malfunction after firing only one round. (Credit: Toppen)

Lt. Daniel Zoerb, 2nd Fighter Squadron, taxies down the runway in his new P-51B after turning in his Spitfire which would be overhauled and sent to the French Air Force. (Credit: Daniel Zoerb via Jeff Ethell)

Ground crew inspect a pair of the 52nd Fighter Group's newly arrived Mustangs, 19 April 1944. (Credit: Thomas Thacker)

a big scare when two Ju 88s flew overhead and possibly photographed the new aircraft on the field, An air raid was expected that night, and at 01.00 hrs, Bastia was targeted by the enemy.

Pilots and ground crew had grown to love their Spitfires and it must have been a shock on the 21st when French pilots from Ajaccio arrived to select those Spitfires that they desired to use. On 22 April, intensive flight training filled the sky with P-51s. Col. Levine, Capt. Morgan and the Squadron Commanders left by staff car on 23 April for the new base of the 52nd FG at Aghione, 40 miles south of Borgo, near Ghisonaccia. 24 April was a day of breaking camp at Borgo and Calvi. Men who had lived on Corsica for five months had to tear down their tents and pack them for shipment. Taking down a tent might be thought to be simple, but the HQ diarist recorded *"...every tent is a masterpiece"* and the things that men added to their tents made taking them down *"a headache."* After all the tents were down, the camp site resembled a jumble of boards, wire and cans. The first trucks full of men and tents arrived at Aghione airfield by 17.30 hrs. From the 24th through to the end of April, the transfer from Calvi and Borgo to Aghione took up all the time and no missions were flown. The need for encrypted communications required a cryptologist and Lt. Hodges arrived at Aghione to set up his code room. Soon there was a maze of aerials and radio equipment pointing into the sky at Aghione.

By 30 April the conversion to Mustangs had progressed to the point that the 306th Fighter Wing, based in Italy, required the 52nd FG to hold a practice mission briefing as if it were going to fly a combat mission alongside other fighter groups already based in Italy. The 52nd FG was told that it was to receive the necessary information from the Wing and to make preparations for an early morning briefing just as if it was included in the operational order. The next morning, the 52nd FG held its first practice briefing for the day's mission. Things did not go as well as hoped and the 52nd FG's diarist noted on 1 May *"...that the inability to get the operational and intelligence data by radio in time to prepare a briefing prior to takeoff time might force a move from Corsica."* The diarist was correct, but still there was no indication of another move to any place.

Mustang flight training continued on 2 May when pilots flew a practice mission around Corsica to simulate a rendezvous with bombers, and the order for the 52nd FG's transfer to Italy was issued. The HQ diary reported: *"...the first echelon will leave for Italy on the fifteenth of the month."* In the 5th Squadron's area, a British pilot taking off in a Spitfire ran off the side of the runway and hit one of the P-51s. Two new Mustangs had been ruined within days.

On 7 May pilots flew a long practice mission around Sardinia and a sweep over France was scheduled for 9 May. It was canceled due to weather over France, but the weather over Corsica was good enough to practice flying Mustangs, and on take-off, two cows ran across the runway in the path of a P-51 taking off killing the cows and ruining the third Mustang. This unfortunate incident ended the Mustang training period and on 10 May the Group was to become operational on the P-51.

Some of the 52nd Fighter Group's new Mustangs lined up at the Group's new airfield at Aghione, Corsica. (Credit: Paul Ludwig collection)

Chapter Seven

"This little corner of Italy"

The Mustang Era begins

May–June 1944

With the conversion to P-51 Mustangs now complete, the 52nd Fighter Group was ready to carry out its new assignment. The conversion was not merely a change of aircraft, it represented a major change of mission for the Group. After nearly a year of flying coastal command and tactical missions in Spitfires the Group would now, as a part of the 15th Air Force, begin flying long-range escort missions into Germany and other Axis countries. The Fifteenth Air Force was activated in November 1943 as a strategic air force to assist in carrying out the Combined Bomber Offensive against the *Luftwaffe* and German industry from the south. Up to this time it had been the responsibility of the US Eighth Air Force and the RAF Bomber Command to carry out this important and difficult task. These organizations had suffered severe losses to date, and with the addition of the Fifteenth Air Force, it was hoped that the *Luftwaffe* would be spread thin in its attempt to defend the Reich against forces attacking from two directions.

Upon activation of the Fifteenth Air Force, all heavy bomber groups and four fighter groups were taken from the Twelfth Air Force and assigned to the Fifteenth. The Twelfth Air Force, now equipped with light and medium bombers, and fighters would become a tactical air force, supporting the ground campaign in Italy. When new bomber groups began arriving in Italy during the early months of 1944, the Fifteenth Air Force's need for more escort fighters was realized and two more fighter groups, the 31st and 52nd Fighter Groups, were transferred to the 15th in April 1944. In May 1944 the 332nd Fighter Group was added to the fold. The role of the Fifteenth Air Force in Allied planning was: to destroy the German Air Force and the air forces of its Axis partners in the air or on the ground, where ever they could be found within the Fifteenth Air Force's zone of operation; to participate in Operation Pointblank, the Combined Bomber Offensive which called for the destruction of Germany's industrial might i.e., to strike communications and traffic systems in support of the Italian campaign and to disrupt and weaken the German hold in the Balkan countries.

For the pilots of the 52nd FG this transfer and mission change was very welcome since it would allow them, for the first time in quite a while, to search out and destroy enemy aircraft in aerial combat. The morale slump that began when the 52nd FG was relegated to Coastal Command at the end of the North African campaign was now over.

The 52nd Fighter Group's first Mustang mission occurred on 10 May 1944 when it escorted B-17s to Nice, France for an attack on the bridge over the Var River. The opening round, however, was less than memorable since the B-17s were unable to bomb as clouds totally obscured the target. The next four missions from Aghione, three bomber escorts to targets in Italy, and a fighter sweep into southern France were also uneventful.

On the ground, however, this time frame was anything but uneventful for the 52nd. On 12 May several of the 2nd FS's personnel who were in Bastia to pick up rations were subjected to two air raids by the *Luftwaffe* during the evening, and these raids were followed during the early morning hours of 13 May on a nearby airfield. The second attack struck the 340th Bomb Group's airstrip in the Aleria/Ghisonaccia area and heavily damaged the 340th. Many of its B-25s were destroyed and others damaged. The Group diary described the attack: *"The raid was a heavy one and only a few miles from our field. Everyone was watching the fearful spectacle and at the same time ready to dive for a shelter if the bombers came to our field."*

Even as these events were taking place the 52nd began its move to its new base at Madna, Italy. The advanced sections were flown there between 13-16 May, 1944, and the remaining ground personnel followed on 20 May, via LSTs to Naples and by motor convoys to Madna.

The pilots departed Aghione for Madna on 16 May, and the day was not without incident. As the Mustangs were taxying in preparation for take-off, Lts. Bofinger and Burnett of the 4th FS collided in the thick dust, damaging both aircraft. Only the wingtip of Burnett's Mustang was damaged, but Lt. Bofinger's P-51 required a wing change before it could make the trip to Madna. The 2nd FS's problems turned out to be far more costly. Lts. Mann and Boney were delayed due to Mann's Mustang needing some work and had to make the trip as a two-aircraft flight. As they

One of the 4th Fighter Squadron's new P-51C Mustangs. It displays the first generation of 52nd Fighter Group unit markings, in this case a narrow yellow band on the rear of the fuselage. It is also painted with the MTO red spinner and (barely visible in this photograph) yellow mid-wing stripes. (Credit: Richard Potter)

WD-C of the 4th Fighter Squadron departs Aghione enroute to the Group's new base at Madna, Italy. (Credit: Paul Ludwig collection)

The newly appointed Commanding Officer of the 2nd Fighter Squadron, Lt. Robert C. Curtis (Credit: Robert C. Curtis)

headed toward Madna the section got off course and overflew enemy territory. As they approached Gaeta they were met by a Flak barrage, and Boney's Mustang was hit, forcing him to bail out. Unfortunately, his chute got hung up on the tail of his P-51 and Boney was dragged earthward to his death.

As the 52nd started settling in at its new home, escort missions in support of 15th Air Force bombers resumed. The first mission from Madna was to Ploesti, Rumania, and although uneventful, it was an indicator of the long-range missions the Group would now be flying as escort fighters. This mission, lasting five hours and fifteen minutes, was a far cry from the 52nd's Spitfire missions which normally lasted from one to two hours. The 2nd FS diary entry did lament the fact that its pilots did not get the opportunity to engage the *Luftwaffe* on a day that a total of 16 enemy aircraft were claimed by other Fifteenth Air Force fighters.

This mission was followed by another uneventful mission on 19 May, but the flight was not without incident. The tragic story was noted in the Group diary:*"Today's mission was to Spezia. Lt. B. J. Harris (4th FS) had to bail out over the Corsican coast when he had motor trouble. He was seen to parachute successfully but an intensive air/sea search until dark failed to locate him. Eight planes landed in Corsica, some due to mechanical difficulties and others to do their part in the search for Lt. Harris. No enemy aircraft were encountered during the mission."*

No missions were flown during the next two days, but activities continued at the base. The 4th FS had to move its bivouac area for the third time since its arrival at Madna, and in the 2nd FS a change of command was taking place. Maj. Bert Sanborn, after serving two years and five months in the Squadron (10 months as Commanding Officer), was going home. Replacing him was 1/Lt. Robert C. Curtis. The Group also received 18 new pilots who were assigned to the 2nd and 5th Fighter Squadrons. The diary also mentioned improved morale: *"Mess conditions are considerably better here with fresh meat and butter at least once a day."*

After two more uneventful missions on 22 and 23 May, the Group's luck took a positive turn. On 24 May the Group flew to Vienna and claimed its first victories in the Mustang, all of them by the 2nd FS. The Group's mission was to escort four Groups of B-17s from the 5th Bomb Wing, providing close support during the penetration, over the target, and the withdrawal. The target was an aircraft factory located on the south edge of Vienna. Lt. Bob Curtis, Commanding Officer of the 2nd FS, led the Group on the mission, and made rendezvous with the bombers over Blieburg. As the attacking force passed over the target area, enemy fighters were sighted making passes at the Fortresses. Curtis picked out his target and radioed his flight to follow him down. They bounced a flight of Fw 190s and Lt. Curtis scored a number of hits on one of the German fighters before losing it the clouds. Lt. Jack Schneider then led his flight into the melee and he and Dan Zoerb destroyed an Fw 190 with their combined firepower. The Fw 190 exploded in mid-air and crashed to the ground about 20 miles south-east of the target. Lt. William L. Bryan managed to damage another Fw 190, but had to break off his attack because his guns were jammed.

The next encounters took place when Lts. *"Dixie"* Alexander and Dick Lampe chased two more Fw 190s to the deck. Alexander's victim crashed in flames on the outskirts of Vienna, and Lampe claimed a probable as his target was smoking heavily as he pulled away. With this victory Lt. Alexander raised his total to four confirmed victories and one probable.

During these initial encounters, some of the pilots were separated from their flights and formed up with other flights. Such was the case of

Lt. Bill Bryan, 2nd Fighter Squadron, who damaged an Fw 190 on 24 May 1944. (Credit: Thomas Thacker)

Lt. "Junior" Adams, 2nd Fighter Squadron, scored 4.5 aerial victories during his tour of duty with the Squadron. (Credit: Thomas Thacker)

P-51B/C Mustangs of the 4th Fighter Squadron on the flightline at Madna, May 1944. (Credit: Harding)

Lts. Junior Adams and James Hoffman who joined up with Lts. Curtis and Barry Lawler just in time to observe a formation of ten Me 109s flying north at 15,000 feet. In the ensuing encounter six of the Messerschmitts were destroyed, one was probably destroyed, and three were damaged. The victories in this engagement were credited as follows: Lt. Curtis, one Me 109 destroyed and two damaged; Lt. Barry Lawler, one Me 109 destroyed and one damaged; Lt. James Hoffman, 2.5 Me 109s destroyed and one damaged, and Lt. Junior Adams, 1.5 Me 109s destroyed. Lts. Alexander, Curtis and Lawler were awarded the Distinguished Flying Cross for this mission.

The 2nd FS scribe noted enthusiastically in the diary: *"A great day for the squadron. On today's mission to Vienna the pilots had a field day, destroying eight enemy aircraft, probably destroying one more, and damaging six others. Only fifteen enemy aircraft were encountered, but they were very well taken care of. A few more E/A might have been destroyed if the guns of Lts. Bryan and Curtis had not jammed."*

May 25th found the pilots flying a long-range mission to Lyon, France but again the *Luftwaffe* was conspicuous by its absence. Because of the length of the mission the aircraft had to make a refueling stop in Corsica, and two of them had to stay there for a while due to engine trouble. It was quite late in the day when the Mustangs landed at Madna and the hard-working ground crew had to begin work immediately in order to ready the aircraft for the next day's mission. The job was finally completed at 23.00 hrs.

The Group's Mustangs returned to Lyon on 26 May as an escort for heavy bombers attacking the marshalling yards located in the city. Again the *Luftwaffe* failed to make an appearance but the pilots still had to fend off a bounce by some overzealous P-38 pilots. Fortunately, no damage was done and all aircraft returned safely.

While the pilots flew the missions, work continued on the base at Madna. Italian laborers were brought in to help build Nissen huts on the base and to help in the mess hall. At this time the base was operating with just one common mess hall and the squadrons rotated duties. At the same time work began at the farmhouse that became Group Headquarters to convert the adjoining barn into a war room and staff offices for the S-2 (Intelligence) and S-3 (Operations) sections. The diary noted: *"At present the barn is deep in manure and filth. Italian workers are doing the cleaning and whitewashing."*

After flying another *"milk run"* to France on 27 May, the Group returned to targets in the Third Reich on 29 May, and this mission turned out to be quite eventful.

The target was an aircraft factory in Weiner Neustadt, Austria and Capt. James O. *"Tim"*Tyler, Commanding Officer of the 4th FS, led the 52nd FG as it escorted the bombers to the target. As the formation approached the target area the 4th FS was ahead of the bombers and scouting for potential threats from the *Luftwaffe*. Their wait was not long, and soon the Squadron was engaged in a big air battle with a mixture of single-engine and twin-engine enemy aircraft that were attempting to disrupt the bomber formation. In the ensuing dogfight three Me 109s and six Me 110s were shot down and two further Me 110s were claimed as probables. Capt. Tyler, Lts. Norman Gross and William Hanes each scored two confirmed kills in the engagement and individual kills went to Lts. Richard N. Evans, James D. McCauley and Bradley Smith. Unfortunately, Lt. Gross was later lost when he was shot down by an enemy fighter.

Next into the fray was the 5th FS when it encountered enemy aircraft at 26,000 feet near Altenmarkt. Capt. Edwin W. Fuller, Squadron Commanding Officer, led two flights of the 5th FS after the enemy aircraft only to lose them in the clouds. The other two flights from the squadron also headed down shortly afterward and Lt. Stanley Rollag spotted a He 111 bomber diving for the deck and headed south in an attempt to escape the attacking Mustangs. Rollag and his wingman headed for the fleeing bomber and Rollag managed to score a few hits on it before Lt. Henry J. Woods and Lt. Matthew Bruder joined in the attack. Lt. Woods made a close pass at the Heinkel – too close – and smashed into the bomber's right wing. The impact sent the bomber down in flames and ripped Woods' right wing in half. Seconds later, Woods died when his Mustang smashed into the earth.

Action continued when Capt. Fuller located another unidentified aircraft in front of him at 18,000 feet. As he turned to try and identify the aircraft; Lt. Walter Zelinski recognized it and tore into the Me 109 and blowing it up in mid-air with several long bursts from his .50 cal. machine guns. Upon completion of his turn Capt. Fuller spotted another Me 109 and sent it crashing to earth with a short burst. Two more Messerschmitts soon fell victim to the well-placed gunfire of Lts. James H. Johnson and Jim Empey, closing out the 5th FS scoring for the day.

Lt. Stanley Rollag, 5th Fighter Squadron. (Credit: Thomas Thacker)

Lt. James Johnson, 5th Fighter Squadron, who downed an Me 109 on 29 May 1944 for his third and last aerial victory. His totals were 3-0-2. (Credit: Paul Ludwig collection)

Two of the 2nd Fighter Squadron Aces. Left to right: Lts. Richard L. "Dixie" Alexander and James S. "Sully" Varnell. (Credit: C. G. Jones)

Lt. Fred Ohr's P-51B, QP-Q, 43-24860 showing the emblem of the "Ace of Spades" flight of the 2nd Fighter Squadron and two kill markings under the canopy. (Credit: Dwayne Tabatt)

The action for the most part passed the 2nd FS by and it had to settle with a total of one Me 109 damaged by Lt. James *"Sully"* Varnell. All told, it was a very successful mission with the Group scoring 14 confirmed kills and three probables against the loss of two of its own.

The Group returned to Austria on 30 May on a bomber escort mission to Wels. The unit took over the escort just as the bombers were departing the target area and encountered flight of about 10-20 Me 109s near Vordenberg. First on the scene was the 2nd FS and four of its Mustangs chased two of the Me 109s down from 23,000 feet to treetop level before Sully Varnell shot one of them down a few miles north of Linz. As Varnell pulled up he observed a Ju 88 heading east at 2,500 feet and gave chase. After his first burst apparently missed he closed to 200 yards and destroyed the Junker's right engine. His next burst hit the fuselage and the aircraft exploded, and crashed about 20 miles north-east of Linz. The final victory of the day was scored at about the same time when pilots of the 5th FS encountered three Me 109s at 23,000 feet and about 15 miles NW of Amstettin. The 109s were climbing to attack the Mustangs when Stan Rollag saw them and chased one of them down to about 6000 feet, firing bursts on the way down. As Rollag pulled out of his dive he saw the enemy aircraft crash just north of the Danube River.

The day was not with cost, though, as the 2nd FS lost its newest Ace, *"Dixie"* Alexander in the initial encounter. No one at the time knew what had happened to *"Dixie"* as his aircraft just disappeared from sight. *"Dixie"* was last seen by his wingman, Lt. Fred Ohr, as he chased an enemy aircraft up the Danube River between Amstettin and Linz. What happened to Dixie was later explained in his autobiography *They Call Me Dixie*. In the final moments of his mission Dixie chased and shot down the fleeing Me 109, but as he pulled up his engine suddenly sputtered and stopped. Since he was so low he had no choice other than to belly-land his Mustang into a small clearing. As he jumped out of his aircraft he could smell gasoline and then saw four to five bullet holes along the cowling and figured one of them had nicked his fuel line. Moments later as he was trying to set the charge to destroy his Mustang named *Chappie* , German troops arrived and he was taken prisoner.

The 2nd FS lost one of its unforgettable characters when Dixie Alexander went down. Dixie was one of the Americans who couldn't wait until his country entered the war. In October 1940 he traveled to Canada and joined the RCAF. After receiving his wings in September 1941 Dixie was sent to England and served with 133 Eagle Squadron until the Eagles transferred to the USAAF. During his stay with 133 Squadron Dixie destroyed one Do 217 and probably destroyed a Fw 190, both at Dieppe. Even though he had been successful in the air, Dixie's adventurous personality kept him in hot water with the brass. He was not transferred to the 4th Fighter Group and ended up in the 109th Tactical Reconnaissance Squadron for a short time. His further exploits in the 109th resulted in a transfer out of England and an assignment with the 52nd FG in April 1943. Even that did not go well initially. He was part of a ferry flight taking P-39s from England to North Africa and his aircraft developed engine trouble, forcing him to land in Portugal where he was interned for three months. In July 1943 he was finally released and continued his journey to join the 52nd. Once in North Africa he was assigned to the 2nd FS, and

P-51B-15-NA 43-24816, *Chappie/Dixie Mk X,*

Lt. Richard L. "Dixie" Alexander,
2nd Fighter Squadron,
52nd Fighter Group, Madna,
Italy, May 1944

"Dixie" Alexander's Chappie illustrates the 52nd Fighter Group's early unit markings – a red spinner, and a yellow band on the rear fuselage, stabilizers, and wings. This aircraft was lost on 30 May 1944 and Alexander became a Prisoner of War.

A German soldier, looking very pleased, poses with "Dixie" Alexander's fallen P-51 Mustang named "Chappie" and "Dixie MK X". It was coded QP-A, serial number 43-24816.
(Credit: J. Griffin Murphey III)

over the next 10 months *"Dixie"* destroyed four enemy aircraft in aerial combat, giving him a grand total of 5-1-0. During his tour of duty with the 2nd, *"Dixie"* Alexander earned the Silver Star, the Distinguished Flying Cross, nine Air Medals and the Purple Heart. [His full story can be read in his biography entitled *They Called Me Dixie*, published by Robinson Typographics, CA, 1988].

The 31st of May 1944 was described in the 52nd Fighter Group diary as a *"red letter day"* for the Group. The mission was to take them to the oil fields of Ploesti, Rumania and Axis fighters were up to meet them. These strategic oil fields were the lifeblood of the German war machine, and were vigorously defended by the Luftwaffe through this campaign. It was reported that the 52nd FG encountered about 34 enemy aircraft during the mission and before it left the area at least 15 of them lay as burning wrecks in the fields in and around Ploesti. The 2nd FS led the way with nine kills. Lt. Bruce Kellam first noticed the German formation consisting of four Fw 190s and two Me 109s and led the attack. At 16,000 feet he swept in behind one of the Focke-Wulfs and opened fire. His first burst missed and then Kellam closed to 150–50 yards and fired again, scoring fatal strikes on the fuselage. Lt. Riley, Kellam's wingman, witnessed the Focke Wulf roll over and crash near Bucharest. As this encounter was taking place Lts. Carl Bellis and Barry Lawler of the same flight went after one of the Me 109s. As the Me 109 half-rolled and headed for the deck Lt. Bellis lost sight of both the enemy aircraft and Lt. Lawler. At this point Lt. Lawler took over and followed the Me 109 down to 1,000 feet before opening fire. Lawler's bullets ripped into the Me 109 and its pilot bailed out. In the meanwhile Lt. Bellis had pulled up and quickly found a Fw 190 and shot it down.

Next Lt. Arthur Johnson quickly disposed of two Fw 190s while Lt. Fred Ohr was taking out another Me 109. Ohr chased the E/A down from 4000 feet to treetop level and sent it down in flames with a long burst from 200 yards.

The destruction continued when Sully Varnell shot down a Me 109 and a Fw 190 and Lt. Dan Zoerb then finished out the Squadron's scoring for the day with an unusual kill. The report stated: *"Lt. Zoerb saw a Me 109 trying to land at an airfield five miles north of Bucharest. He caught him with his wheels and flaps down. Lt. Zoerb got in a couple of hits on the left wing. The enemy aircraft pulled its wheels up and tried to go to another field but Zoerb cut him off again. The pilot either ran out of gas or panicked because he crashed in the field."*

In its action the 5th FS chipped in with six kills but at the cost of two of its pilots. Capt. Edwin Fuller led the scoring with two kills, and Lts. John Karle, Stanley Rollag, Charles Denham, and John Schumacher each claimed one kill. Lt. Denham scored his kill, unfortunately, by colliding with an Fw 190 and was last seen bailing out of his crippled Mustang. The other loss was Lt. Karle who began suffering engine problems after his victory over a MC200 and was forced to bail out over Yugoslavia.

The victories of 31 May 1944 pushed the 52nd Fighter Group past the 200 mark, with Lt. Fred Ohr being credited as the pilot scoring victory number 200. Lt. Frederick *"Ted"* Bullock of the 4th FS commented on the mission in his diary: *"31 May. Another mission to Ploesti today and really good one too. Beautiful clear day and the target really*

Lt. John Karle of the 5th Fighter Squadron, posing with his P-51C, "Sexy". This photograph was taken after Lt. Karle's escape and evasion from Yugoslavia after being shot down on 31 May 1944. This Mustang soldiered on after he completed his tour and ended its service career as a "war-weary" hack for the 5th Fighter Squadron. A fin strake was added late in its service life. (Credit: Robert Fulks)

Rumanian pilots of Grupal 6 vanatore and one of their IAR 81C fighters. (Credit: Denes Bernad)

An IAR 80 similar to the one shot by by Bob Curtis on 6 June 1944 (the IAR80 and 81 are virtually identical in appearance). (Credit: Denes Bernad)

P-51B-10-NA 42-106715, *Hey Rube! II*

**Lt. Daniel Zoerb,
2nd Fighter Squadron,
52nd Fighter Group,
Madna, June 1944.**

This aircraft was the second of four Mustangs Dan Zoerb christened Hey Rube. The name of these aircraft came from the carnival world. Zoerb played in a carnival band before the war, and the expression was used to indicate that trouble was about to break out. The name of this aircraft was applied before the red nose band was added to Group markings, and covered up the 'H' in 'Hey'. Dan Zoerb went on to score seven confirmed victories, rose to the rank of major and commanded the squadron during the last few months of his combat tour.

Lt. Daniel Zoerb's P-51B "Hey Rube! II". When asked about the origin of his aircraft's unusual name Dan Zoerb explained: "Before the war I played in a carnival band and if you heard some say 'Hey Rube', trouble was about to occur…" (Credit: Daniel Zoerb via Jeff Ethell)

Lt. Jack Schneider, 2nd Fighter Squadron (Credit: (Robert C. Curtis)

got clobbered. The oil fires came up to 20,000 feet – the smoke rather. Really a sight. We were top cover and didn't get any. The 2nd and 5th got 15 between them and the 5th lost two. Pretty fair day all told. Both of the 5th boys bailed out okay."

June 1944 began slowly for the 52nd Fighter Group. Only four missions were flown during the first eight days of the month and only one enemy fighter was claimed during this period. That kill, his third, was scored on 6 June by Lt. Bob Curtis during a mission to Brasov, Rumania. His encounter report read: *"While flying at 22,000 feet, at eight o'clock to the bomber formation which had just come off the target, I saw an enemy aircraft in a climbing turn, going from 12 o'clock to three o'clock relative to the bombers. I called a right turn and started to chase the enemy aircraft. I was cutting it off and closing on it when an Fw 190 flew across in front of me from three o'clock to nine o'clock and toward the bombers.*

"I made a sharp 90 degree left turn and fired a long burst from about 300-350 yards but saw no strikes. I closed rapidly to about 150 yards, fired a long burst and saw strikes on the left side of the enemy aircraft; on the aileron, the wing root, the cockpit, the side and bottom of the fuselage. The E/A flicked over on its back and went into an inverted spin and then into a normal spin, with the propeller windmilling. It was streaming white and black smoke as it went down. My wingman, Lt. Robinett, saw the E/A crash." (In the spring of 2002 Bob Curtis learned from Mr. Victor Nitu of Bucharest that he had actually shot down a Rumanian IAR-81C flown by Lt. Constantin Balta.

Curtis added: *"This type of plane had a radial engine and looked like a Fw 190. We didn't know such a plane existed, so anything with a radial engine we thought was a Focke-Wulf. Although the plane crashed it was later repaired and returned to service")*

Several important news items were reported during the first few days of the month, such as the fall of Rome, the Normandy invasion and the report that Lt. Bob Hoover (4th FS) who had been missing for several months had been reported as a POW. These were morale boosters to the Group. The Group diary entries for 6 and 7 June stated: *"Today's mission to Brasov, Rumania resulted in only one encounter and in that one the enemy plane was destroyed. But the mission couldn't have claimed the spotlight if we had won a score of victories, for this was Invasion Day. The joy throughout the Group over receiving this wonderful news is without precedent for everyone feels that we are now starting on the last leg of our war in this theater. Radios were on all day and everyone crowded around them to get each new scrap of information. To us overseas it seemed like a dream come true and that an invisible weight was lifted from our shoulders."*

Invasion fever continued in the entry for 7 June: *"The invasion and the date of the ending of the war monopolized the day's conversation. The fortunate ones who picked the date of the invasion within the correct month or on a certain date collected their winnings and went about looking smug."*

On 7 and 8 June the weather was in command and high winds prevented missions on both days. Everything on the field was covered in a fine dust and to add insult to injury a fire broke out during the evening of 7 June. A large pile of hay and manure behind the Headquarters burst into flames and it took the efforts of several fire crews to keep it from spreading to the dry grass and grain fields on the base. The high winds continued on 8 July to the point the runways had to be oiled down to keep the dust contained.

The 52nd FG returned to action on 9 June with an escort mission to Munich, Germany. The Operations Order called for the Group to rendezvous with the bombers at Traunstein and provide penetration, target and withdrawal cover for three groups of bombers from the 49th Bomb Wing. Things, however, did not go exactly as planned. As the 52nd FG approached Udine, Italy it encountered a number of enemy fighters that were attacking some B-24s and an element of all three squadrons became involved in this dogfight, leaving only 29 of the scheduled 55 Mustangs to continue the escort.

Elements of all three squadrons went into action over Udine at approximately the same time. The 2nd FS, led by Lt. Jack Schneider, attacked a flight of Me 109s and Fw 190s which were harassing five B-24s. Schneider overran his target, a 190, but his wingman, Lt. Fred Grey, hit the enemy aircraft with a series of telling bursts and its pilot bailed out of his doomed aircraft. Lt. Barry Lawler then attacked a lone Me 109 that was firing on a lone B-24 and after hitting it with several bursts the enemy aircraft rolled over at 5,000 feet and its pilot bailed out.

At approximately 09.20 hrs Capt. Tim Tyler, Commanding Officer of the 4th FS, saw four Me 109s attacking a lone B-24 and another formation of German and Italian fighters preparing to join in on the attack. He then ordered Lt. Robert L.Burnett III to lead a flight of eight Mustangs in a bounce against the enemy aircraft. The Germans spotted the oncoming P-51s and headed for the deck with four of the Mustangs hot on their tails. Dogfights then broke out and soon the enemy formation was dispersed, with five of its number going down under the guns of the 4th FS. Lt. Burnett was credited with two kills, and the remaining three were credited to Lts. Frederick "Ted" Bullock, Bill Hanes, and Robert Deckman. Lt. Bullock later noted his first victory in his diary: *"I'm no longer a virgin! Got into a dice over Udine, Italy today and destroyed a Me-109. We were on an escort mission to Munich. Got as far as Udine and saw about 20 E/A bouncing early return bombers. I took three short bursts at a 109, hit his glycol tank and he bailed out. Burnett got two and Shorty spun one in. Group score 14 and 1 probable. No losses. Not bad. Really a thrill and really good luck. I stayed with him fine—guess he wasn't too sharp a pilot. At least he didn't fly like it. Came home with Deck, alone and OK. Thanks Lord."*

The 5th FS entered into action over Udine at

Crew Chief, S/Sgt Elmer Dalebroux, congratulating Lt "Sully" Varnell for his fifth kill and for becoming an Ace. Behind them is their Mustang, "Little Eva II" coded QP-E, serial number unknown. (Credit: Tom Thacker)

P-51B, Serial Number unknown, *Abdul's Baby*

**Lt. Frederick "Ted" Bullock,
4th Fighter Squadron,
52nd Fighter Group,
Madna, Italy, summer 1944.**

The name of this aircraft was devised as the result of the nickname "Abdul the Bull" that one of "Ted" Bullock's squadron-mates gave him. Bullock scored his three confirmed victories in this aircraft. His second assigned Mustang, a P-51D, was unnamed.

"Abdul's Baby" was assigned to Lt. Fred Bullock, 4th Fighter Squadron. The aircraft name was a direct result of the nickname "Abdul the Bull" tagged on Fred Bullock. It was coded WD-A, serial number unknown. Note the Arabian baby shoes artwork under the name and the checkerboard landing gear covers. (Credit: Fred Bullock)

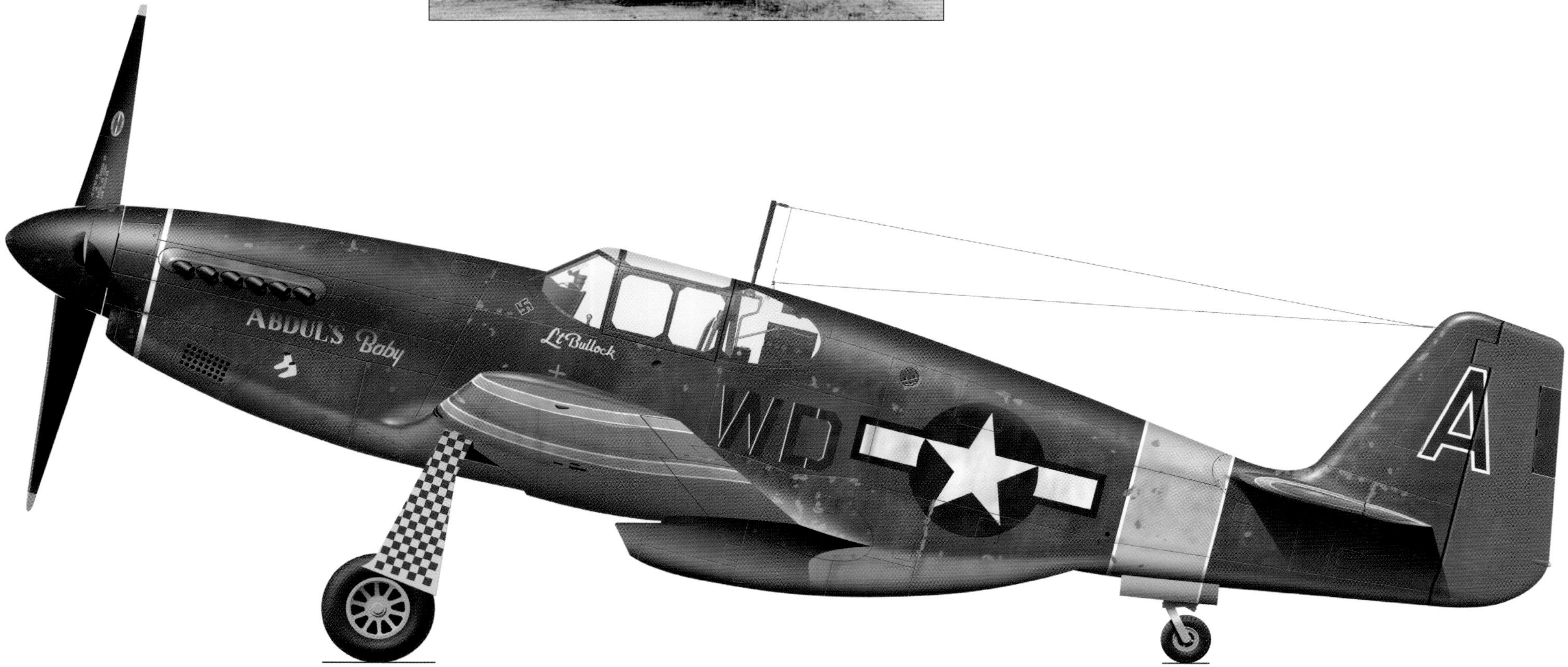

P-51B-15-NA 43-24818, *Little Joe*

Lt. Joe Blackburn,
5th Fighter Squadron,
52nd Fighter Group,
Madna, Italy, June 1944

The name of this aircraft is in reference to the height of its pilot, and while flying this aircraft Lt. Blackburn scored one victory, raising his total to three confirmed kills. The markings on this Mustang illustrate the second phase of the 52nd Fighter Group's unit markings, with the addition of the red nose band and the black borders to the yellow fuselage, wing and stabilizer bands.

Lt. Joe Blackburn's P-51B "Little Joe" of the 5th Fighter Squadron. Note the "Spittin Kitten" squadron emblem and the white 'A' inside a red square which was the Flight marking. Blackburn's Mustang provides a good view of the 52nd Fighter Group's unit markings. Note the band around the rear of the fuselage is now wider and bordered with black outlines. Yellow bands with black borders also feature on each wing tip. (Credit: James Empey)

Lt. Joe Blackburn of the 5th Fighter Squadron (Credit: Thomas Thacker)

Lt. Arthur Johnson also reached Acedom on 9 June 1944 when he downed an Me 109 for his fifth victory. His aircraft was P-51B QP-M, serial number 73-7061. (Credit: Dwayne Tabatt)

Lt. Richard Lampe, 2nd Fighter Squadron, achieved Acedom with 1.5 victories on 2 July 1944, raising his totals to 5.5-0-1 (Credit: Paul Ludwig)

about 09.15 hrs when Lt Joe Blackburn spotted another B-24 under attack by a gaggle of six Me 109s. Blackburn, Blue flight Leader, led his flight and two aircraft from Green flight after the enemy aircraft. The Messerschmitts headed for the deck and as one of them leveled out at 300 feet, Lt. Bob Karr hit it with two bursts and the Me 109 rolled over and smashed into the earth. Seconds later Lt. Carnie clobbered another of the Me 109s at 2,000 feet and it too rolled over and went straight into the ground. At this point the two flights headed toward Casarsa airfield where Lt. Holloman, leader of Green light, observed two Me 109s and attacked one of them. Firing from 300 down to 50 yards, Holloman scored strikes all over the fuselage and canopy, and the German pilot quickly took to his parachute. Moments later Lt. Blackburn caught two Me 109s as they were taking off and downed one of them after a five mile chase down the Tagliamento River.

Action against the *Luftwaffe* resumed as the 52nd FG approached the rendezvous point and sighted a formation of approximately 20 Me 110 and Me 410 twin engine fighters, with top cover of ten Me 109s and Fw 190s headed toward the bombers. As the enemy aircraft appeared to be forming for an attack Lt. Kellam, who had assumed leadership of the 2nd FS, led his flight into the German formation and scattered it. As the enemy aircraft broke, Kellam and his flight returned to the bomber formation. Simultaneously, Lt. Kellam ordered Lt. Art Johnson and his flight plus Lt. Sully Varnell and his wingman to chase and attack the enemy aircraft. Sully Varnell struck first and his encounter reported stated in part: *"I took after a Me-110 in the rear of a flight of three and closed to fire at about 700 yards. On my first burst I observed no strikes. On my second and third bursts I observed strikes on the left engine, wings and fuselage. Pieces came off the left engine, fuselage and the left engine stopped. As it was streaming black smoke the Me-110 attempted to level out to crash land, but went over on its back at 2000 feet and crashed to the ground, breaking apart on impact."*

Next Lt. Johnson locked onto the tail of a Me 109 and after his third burst the enemy aircraft went into a spin, its canopy came off, its engine exploded, and seconds later the entire aircraft exploded. With these victories Lts. Varnell and Johnson became the 2nd Fighter Squadron's newest Aces.

Twenty minutes later Lt. James Hoffman shot down an Me 109 as it pulled away from an attack on the bombers. When the bomber formation was one minute from the target, Bruce Kellam spotted a flight of six Me 109s attacking the B-24s. Kellam immediately broke into the enemy aircraft and dispersed them. He then latched on to the tail of one of the Me 109s and sent it down through the clouds trailing a dense cloud of black smoke and shedding pieces.

The mission of 9 June 1944 was a magnificent success for the 52nd FG. Its pilots claimed a total of 14-2-0 enemy aircraft with no losses to the Group or the bombers they escorted. In recognition of its masterful escort mission, the Group was awarded the Distinguished Unit Citation.

The Group flew an early mission to Ferrara airfield on 10 June, but the enemy was nowhere in sight and the mission was a milk run. The 2nd FS diary commented on the day by saying: *"As expected no E/A were seen. Although they didn't get any victories today, the 5th Squadron has been doing very well since we started operations in Italy. They are gaining steadily on the 4th Squadron which at one time was our arch rival. Four new pilots, who haven't had any O.T.U. training, were assigned to the squadron this evening. We wonder why pilots are assigned to a combat outfit with so little training. Group has plans to show movies every so often at HQ in the evening."*

The Group diary covered current living conditions at Madna by reporting: *"The Army's new insecticide bomb, used in conjunction with good screening, is keeping the building free of flies. The manure pile in back of the Headquarters building continues to smolder in a malodorous way."*

The 5th FS diary for 10 June also commented about the arrival of relatively untrained replacement pilots, *"Seven new pilots were assigned to the squadron. All of them had just come over two months*

The Headquarters of the 5th Fighter Squadron with the Mess Hall and tent area in left of photograph. (Credit: Lundgaard)

ago, with the exception of Lt.(John) Heller, who was formerly with the 82nd Fighter Group and has twelve combat missions to his credit. The others have very little fighter time and will require quite a bit of training before being sent on combat missions."

The mission of 11 June 1944 was a long-range escort mission to the oil storage facilities at Constanta, Rumania. So long range was the mission in fact that the 52nd's guidelines in the field order was "*... to provide escort on penetration to the prudent limit in endurance* [the target was about 680 miles from Madna] *for four groups of the 47th Bomb Wing.*"

It was not going to be a milk run on this date since enemy aircraft and Flak were encountered over Bulgaria and Yugoslavia. The bombers were late for the rendezvous and by the time they reached the RV point two of the three squadrons from the 52nd had already been forced to turn back because of fuel shortage after encountering Axis fighters at 08.45 hrs. Only the 4th FS was available for a 15 minute escort. The enemy force was apparently a combination of German and Bulgarian aircraft. The opposing forces collided at about 08.45 hrs and Axis lost 13 aircraft to the 2nd FS (10) and the 5th FS (3) against the loss of one aircraft and pilot. Lt. Bob Curtis led the way in scoring for the 2nd FS, destroying two Me 109s in this engagement and a third about 30 minutes later over Yugoslavia as he was heading back to base. Single kills were recorded by Lts. Jack Schneider, Dan Zoerb, Richard Lampe, Dennis Riddle, Art Johnson, Sully Varnell, Fred Ohr, and Barry Lawler. With these kills the 2nd Fighter Squadron's tally of enemy aircraft now stood at 102.33 confirmed victories. The three victories by Bob Curtis raised his total to six and he became the Squadron's newest Ace.

In this same widespread air battle Lt. James Empey, flying his P-51C *Little Ambassador* downed two Me 109s. The first encounter took place at 08.45 hrs north-east of Sofia when Empey, as 'Blue 3', spotted four Me 109s below them and attacked. His encounter reports states: *"I located a lone ME109 and got on his tail. He made a straight dive at the ground, I followed, giving him short bursts at about 250 yards. I saw the pilot bail out and the E/A crash into the ground."*

His next kill occurred about five minutes later and Lt. Empey reported his action as follows: *"About eight P-51s were at 15,000 feet forming to return home when a pilot ahead of me called out E/A below at 3 o'clock. We started down to attack 3 ME109s stacked to the right. Another P-51 took the middle one and I took the one on the right. I fired several bursts, observing hits on the wings and fuselage. The canopy came off and the pilot bailed out."*

In addition to Lt. Empey's victories, another Me 109 was shot from the sky by Lt. Calvin Allen of the 5th FS. The 5th FS also claimed two other enemy aircraft destroyed on the ground when Lts. Robert Carnie and Calvin Allen strafed a German airfield on the way home. On the debit side of the ledger Lt. Joseph Riley, 2nd FS, was shot down and killed during the air battle. Lt. James Hoffman's P-51, 2nd FS, was also badly shot up but he managed to get the battered

A smiling Bob Curtis poses with his P-51B "Julie" in this highly censored photograph taken after his sixth aerial victory. (Credit: Robert C. Curtis)

This P-51B, QP-F, serial number 43-7024, seemed to be cursed. It was damaged in this crash-landing in early June 1944, repaired and was then lost to enemy action on 11 June 1944 with its pilot, Lt. Joseph Riley, was killed. (Credit: Robert C. Curtis)

Lt. James Hoffman and his heavily damaged Mustang. The battle damage occurred on 11 June 1944, but Hoffman was able to nurse it back to Madna. (Credit: Robert C. Curtis)

P-51B-15-NA 43-24853, *Little Ambassador*

**Lt. James W. Empey,
5th Fighter Squadron,
52nd Fighter Group,
Madna, Italy, June 1944**

Lt. Empey, the 5th Fighter Squadron's first Ace, scored all five of his victories in this aircraft during the period of 29 May-28 June 1944 in this aircraft. The Mustang's name, Little Ambassador, was also Empey's nickname within the Squadron. He acquired the nickname because of his outgoing personality and his ability to interact with all the personnel on the 52nd's base. Little Ambassador soldiered on after Empey completed his tour of duty and was finally lost on 22 February 1945 when Lt. Robert Rhodes crash-landed the Flak-damaged Mustang in the River Rhine in Switzerland.

Lt. James Empey's P-51B "Little Ambassador". Empey scored all of his victories in this Mustang. (Credit: Dwayne Tabatt)

Messerschmitt Me 109 G-2s of the Bulgarian Air Force. (Credit: Joe Fregosi)

Mustang back to Madna. At least four of the victories were claimed at the expense of 5./JG 301 which was based at Wrasdebna airfield outside of Sofia. Fw. Gunter Iffert and Uffz. Heinz Gerling were KIA and Fw Paul Becker and Uffz. Hermann Erchen were wounded and bailed out of their Me 109 G-6s. Por. Ivan Bonev of the Bulgarian Air Force is also known to have fallen under the guns of the 52nd FG on 11 June. By all accounts both the German and Bulgarian units were aggressive and experienced pilots. The mission summary had this to say about the opposition. *"There was no disposition on the part of the enemy to avoid combat. In view of the evident ability of the enemy pilots there was some surprise expressed at the evidence of poor marksmanship on their part."*

No missions were scheduled on 12 June and the pilots enjoyed a well-earned day of rest. This was not the case, however, for the maintenance crews who spent the day going over the aircraft and preparing them for the next mission. The 52nd FG diary proudly reported that: *"A compilation of victories shows that since May 24 the Group has destroyed 70 enemy aircraft. Men returning from Wing Headquarters say that the record the Group is making is receiving a great deal of commendation there. Tonight the combat films of the big day over Constanta were shown."*

The Group also started a 10 day ground school and transitional flying course to help prepare the newly arrived and somewhat ill-prepared pilots for combat.

P-51C VF-Q, serial number 42-103852 was assigned to Lt. John Heller. Heller downed a Ju 88 in this aircraft on 26 June 1944, and Lt. Calvin Allen was flying it when he shot down four Me 109s and damaged a fifth Messerschmitt on 4 July 1944. (Credit: USAF)

The 52nd FG returned to action on 13 June with a mission to Munich and continued its devastation of enemy aircraft. The target was Neuabing Dornier Works and the *Luftwaffe* was up in force to defend the area. The 52nd FG alone encountered nearly ninety enemy aircraft and engaged them in a series of running battles. After two unsuccessful attempts by *Luftwaffe* fighters to lure the 52nd away from the bombers as the formation passed over northern Italy, the Germans finally made an attempt to strike at the bombers near Landshut. Five Fw 190s were observed by pilots of the 5th FS as they were closing on the bombers from the rear, and seven Mustangs dove on them. The enemy aircraft saw the bounce and headed for the deck followed by the Mustangs of the 5th FS. A dogfight, which continued down to the deck, then broke out and the original seven Mustangs were joined by four more 5th FS aircraft. As the air battle progressed ten more Fw 190s, two to three Me 210s and a Ju 88 joined in and paid for their efforts. Seven Fw 190s, and one Me 210 were destroyed and the Ju 88 limped away heavily damaged. Victory credits went to Lieutenants John Heller, Calvin Allen and Victor Tresvik who each destroyed two Focke-Wulfs, and the seventh Fw 190 was shared by Lieutenants Matthew Bruder and Robert Anderson. The Me 210 fell to Jim Empey who described his victory: *"I was flying number 4 in blue flight. East of Munich at 26,000 feet my flight leader called in a flight of Fw 190s. We started down on them. Close to the ground I saw a Me210 going 90 degrees to the Fw 190s. I made three passes at the Me210 from above, trying to lose my excess speed. On my fourth pass I got dead astern and shot up both engines and the cockpit of the E/A. E/A then crashed into the ground and burned."* This was Lt. Empey's fourth victory.

The remaining three victories of the day were scored by the 2nd FS and the 4th FS. Lt. Barry Lawler downed a Me210 for his fifth victory and Acedom, and Junior Adams a Fw 190 for victory 4.5. The 4th FS victory, a Me 109, was credited to Lt. Robert Burnett III.

Back at base another battle was shaping up in an effort to protect the ground echelon and this effort was noted in the HQ diary along with another memorable incident at the field: *"The Headquarters building was sprayed today by the fumigating squad to destroy the various vermin there. Following today's mission three B-24s made emergency landings at this base. One of them, after landing successfully, hit a ditch while taxiing and collapsed the left wheel, causing minor damage."*

The mission to Budapest, Hungary on 14 June was unopposed by enemy fighters and the bombers hit the oil refineries successfully. At Madna a number of morale boosters were the talk of the day. First was the report that Lt. Everett of the 5th FS, who had been shot down over Viterbo, Italy on 19 February, had been liberated by the advancing Allied armies and that he would rejoin the unit later in the day. From the enlisted men's standpoint, the highlight of the day was the announcement that 23 of them would be rotating to the USA after two years overseas. The HQ diary went on to read: *"The combination of this large*

Lt. Robert Anderson's P-51B "The Bar Fly". It was coded VF-A, serial number 42-106604. (Credit: James Empey)

Lt. Barry Lawler, 2nd Fighter Squadron, scored his fifth kill on 13 June 1944 and became the Squadron's latest Ace. (Credit: Barry Lawler)

number of men going home and announcement that large numbers are to leave each month from now on has caused much excitement in the Detachment."

Also on this date, the 52nd FG received its first new P-51D and the diary reported: *"Three more have been assigned to us and the Wing has assured Lt. Cummins that we will be the first Group to be assigned and fully equipped with P-51Ds."* (This statement turned out to be extremely optimistic since there were still quite a few P-51B/Cs in the unit at war's end.)

The mission of 15 June was canceled half way through the briefing and the squadrons used the lull in action to give the new pilots a little more training. The newly returned Lt. Everett entertained the 5th FS with his experiences after being shot down. The Squadron diary noted: *"He told a thrilling story of his escapades. In the furious action with enemy aircraft, in which we lost three other pilots, he was attacked by six Me-109s. A long running battle ensued in which his radio, then his instrument panel was shot out, and finally his engine quit, but not before he had accounted for two of the E/A. He bailed out, landed safely and took refuge with a friendly Italian family where he stayed until the Allied advance made it possible for him to make his way back. Through Lt. Everett's story we were able to confirm five more E/A destroyed on that day."*

Tom Thacker added a few passages to this story in his history of the Group: *"His report told how Lt. Gahagan, his plane damaged by Flak, returned to the fight, never to be heard from again. Lt. Everett also related that after downing two Me 109s, he was forced to leave his plane and landed in a large field where six wrecked German planes had already crashed from the activity overhead. His success in hiding out with the partisans enabled the Spitfire victory roll to be increased."*

Thacker also provides an intimate view of the life and daily events of those that stayed behind on the ground during the long and eventful missions being flown by the Group's pilots during the summer of 1944: *"There was a certain romance attached to this period of our lives. Early each morning we heard the roar of heavy bombers leaving their bases to the south and passing overhead. Group after group of B-17s and B-24s headed north before the fighters started engines. Then, depending upon the battle order for fighter protection, we might see one or two formations of P-38s or P-51s take to the sky, flying faster and climbing more rapidly to reach their proper positions when arriving over enemy territory.*

"Finally, then, squadron by squadron, our own P-51s began firing up, then taxied out for take-off. Two by two, allowing for the minimum safe clearance in case of a problem, they took off, usually circling once to check the plane's operation and to allow the last ship in the formation enough time to get into position. Soon, all were headed north and the sky became quiet once again.

"Suspense hung like a blanket while the planes were on a mission. A few spares or aborts soon returned, then several hours generally passed before more planes appeared. The first fighters out, Yellow tails, Red tails, stripes, checkers or whatever, were usually the first to return. Often their formation gave a clue as to the opposition encountered: Is it tight or scattered? Does anyone appear to be shot up?

"Finally, when the waiting became almost unbearable, our planes would appear over the water, heading for the landing field. One high speed pass over the strip, then a sharp pull up and a turn to lose speed and to provide the proper landing interval. If one was in trouble he landed first with rescue equipment standing by in case of trouble. Everybody was watching, counting the planes within each squadron, and attempting to identify each individual plane. Was anybody missing? The crew chiefs waiting at the end of the runway to climb aboard the wing and guide their plane to the proper revetment. It was a long, long wait for the mechanic whose plane didn't return from the mission that day. As a noncombatant I cannot attempt realistically to relate what the pilots felt during their relatively short tours of duty in which glory and death stood so intimately at hand. I am sure this varied greatly, for there were those who actually looked forward to tomorrow's mission when the next medal or the lifelong title of "Ace", he who destroys at least five enemy aircraft in the air, might be achieved.

"I am equally certain that many felt black depression during the evening and night preceding a combat mission, particularly those quite certain to include heavy defenses such as Ploesti or Regensburg. This concern—call it fear if you like—was especially apparent for Flak or weather, those dangers were actually beyond the control of the flyer. Especially after we received the P-51s, the feeling was general that 'our' equipment was superior to 'theirs'."

On 16 June the 52nd FG headed toward the oil refineries at Bratislava as an escort for B-24s of the 47th Bomb Wing. The Group arrived at the RV point at Balatonboglar eight minutes early and then, to its dismay, had to circle and wait for the bomber formation which was 42 minutes late. Five minutes later, at 09.35 hrs, the 2nd FS spotted a flight of 12 Me 109s at 28,000 feet, preparing to attack the B-24s. As the 2nd FS dropped its tanks and prepared to bounce the enemy aircraft a squadron of P-38s beat them to the punch. Disappointment was only to last ten minutes though, as a flight of about 25 Me 210s was seen approaching the bombers at 26,000 feet, and moments later eight of them broke off to attack the third bomber formation. Four 2nd FS Mustangs went after the twin-engined Messerschmitts and broke up the attack. The remaining Me 210s passed between the second and third groups of bombers and then prepared to attack the lead group. Seeing this action four 2nd FS Mustangs charged into the enemy formation and forced them to dive away to the right. Almost simultaneously 30 Me 109s latched on to the last group of bombers. As six of the Me 109s closed on the bombers from the rear the remaining Mustangs of the 2nd FS dove into the fray. Air battles quickly broke out all over the sky and when the dogfights had ended five Me 109s and five Me 210s had crashed to earth, and one other 210 limped away after taking some damaging hits. Sully Varnell led in scoring with the destruction of two Me 210s, and Dan Zoerb was a close second with 1.5 (a Me 109 and .5 Me 210 shared with Lt. John Clarke). The other six victories were credited to Capt. Fred Ohr (Me 210) and Lts. Richard Lampe (Me 109), Barry

The flight line of the 5th Fighter Squadron at Madna where groundcrews are preparing their Mustangs for the next mission. (Credit: James Empey)

P-51B QP-B of the 2nd Fighter Squadron after a bad landing. (Credit: Paul Ludwig)

Lawler (Me 210), Willard Pretzer (Me 109) and Jack Schneider (Me 109). The remaining kill was a Me 210 shared by Lts. Art Johnson and Dennis Riddle. The Group lost one pilot, Lt F. R. Crawford of the 4th FS, who was last seen breaking away from some P-38s that were attacking him.

On the following day, 17 June, the weather changed and the rains began, causing a six day stand down for the Group. As the rain continued to fall, dust around the field turned into mud and the discontent was noted in the diaries. The HQ 52nd FG diarist, Sgt. Arthur Hommel recorded in the entry for 18 June: *"Another mission is called off. It rained quite heavily throughout the day and settled the dust, but oh boy, what mud. It's a question now whether one gets madder at Madna from mud or whether it's the dust that dood it. The windswept hay and grain fields of this little corner of Italy give a picture of barren loneliness which the fellows of the 52nd will long remember with perhaps just a little bit of a shudder."*

In the 5th FS the outlook was a little brighter since another of its missing pilots returned to the base. Lt. John Karle, who bailed out over Yugoslavia on the mission of 31 May, was rescued by partisans immediately after landing. Lt. Karle's rescuers then helped him undertake a 14 day walking and horseback trip back to Italy. Upon his return to Madna Karle was notified he was eligible to go home, but refused and asked to be put back on flying status with the 5th FS.

The subject of *"General Mud"* surfaces in the Squadron diary which reported: *"Rain last night and this morning, the first for several weeks, made it impossible for flying. The dirt roads in this area become very slippery when wet and it was not an uncommon sight to see jeeps and trucks going crabwise down the road. The Group is trying hard to obtain 100 victories in one month. We got our first on the 24th of May and still have a number to go before the 30 days are up."*

The 2nd FS diary continued the weather lament. *"Another day without a mission. The pilots are anxious to get up there again for a crack at the wily Hun. The squadron received more new a/c today, including its first P-51D, which was assigned to the C.O."*

For the next several days the diaries registered the same weather-oriented complaints and the 2nd FS diary noted that the pilots felt that they were growing stale! The rains finally ended during the late evening of 21 June and the disgruntled men of the 52nd were able to return to operations on 22 June. The mission, however, turned out to be a milk run to Turin, Italy. The results were good news in that no losses were incurred, but bad news in the sense that they were running out of time to break the Fifteenth Air Force record of the most E/A destroyed in one month. The 2nd FS diarist worried: *"The trip was uneventful; the Group now has only one day to break the 15th Air Force record for the most victories in one month. 99 E/A destroyed has been the record so far, but at the rate our Group has been mowing them down, we stand a good chance to get the 11 E/A needed to break the record."*

The 52nd FG headed to Rumania on 23 June on an escort mission to the Romano American refinery at Ploesti as an escort for the B-24s of the 47th Bomb Wing. Upon arriving at the RV point the 52nd saw B-17s flying over the area and these formations, according to the field order, were scheduled 10 minutes after the 47th BW Liberators. The mission leader, Capt. *"Tim"* Tyler, concluded that the bombers were ahead of them and led the 52nd to the target area. Enemy aircraft were first sighted at 09.40 hrs 20 miles NNW of Bucharest. Twenty Me 109s were spotted by the 2nd FS and ten of the Squadron's

Lt. John Clarke, of the 2nd Fighter Squadron, with his P-51B "Dottie" (Credit: Tom Ivie)

14 Mustangs dove to attack. As they did so, their top cover saw another gaggle of Messerschmitts at 29,500 feet and climbed to intercept them. As the Mustangs swooped in on the Axis formations the enemy aircraft all headed toward the deck, and as they did, ten Mustangs from the 4th FS joined in. Soon another flock of enemy aircraft joined the dogfight. The new enemy aircraft were identified as 10-15 Fw 190s, 10 MC-205s, and three Fiat G-50s and they were of mixed nationalities. (In all probability the aircraft identified as MC-205a and G-50s were Rumanian IAR 80 or 81 fighters. Close examination of Lt. Bullock's gun camera film shows his victim to be an IAR 80 or 81). From the description of markings in the combat report these aircraft were from the Rumanian and Hungarian Air Forces. During the next 20 minutes 12 enemy aircraft were shot out of the sky with five of the kills being credited to the 2nd FS and seven to the 4th FS. The Me 109 pilots were described as experienced and aggressive. With two shared victories Dan Zoerb raised his score to five and became the 2nd Fighter Squadron's latest Ace. The remaining 2nd FS kills were credited to Capt. Bob Curtis, Lts. Dennis Riddle and Dick Lampe, (one each), and Lts. Jack Schneider and Willard Pretzer, who were each was given a half credit. Capt. Tyler and Lt. Frank Tribbett, with two each, led the 4th FS scoring. The remaining three enemy aircrafts were claimed by Lts. George Goettleman, Bob McCampbell, and Ted Bullock. Lt. Bullock described the day's events in his diary: *"Boy! What a day this was. Had a mission to Ploesti. As we neared the target we encountered more E/A than I've ever seen before. All types—109s, 190s, MA 205s, MA 200s. Really a sight. Dogfights all over hell, fires, parachutes and what-not. I was in McCampbell's flight. We got into a hell of a scrap with some MA 205s. Mac got one, spun him in. I took a couple of 90 degrees deflection shots, I didn't see anything, but Mac confirmed one for me when we got back. Said he blew all to hell. Tribbett got two, Tyler two, George one also. We lost Burwell somewhere in the deal. The 2nd got five, 5th none, lost one each."*

The missions of 22 and 23 June served as Capt. Bob Curtis' introduction to the P-51D, and he commented about it in his book *The American Beagle Squadron*: *"This was my first mission in a P-51D, with the bubble canopy that provided such wonderful visibility, but somehow fouled up the airflow in a high-speed dive and produced a porpoising effect that helped the diving 109s and 190s to get away. As C.O. I got the first D model on 18 June, but was never smart enough to give it up after learning of its limitations."*

With the 12 victories on the 23 June 1944, the 52nd FG set a new Fifteenth Air Force record for victories in a month – 102. The new record was not without a cost though. Lieutenants F. B. Fisher, 5th FS; D. C. Robinett, 2nd FS, and G. N. Burwell of the 4th FS did not return from the mission.

The pilots returned to Rumania on 24 June and this mission was a stark contrast to the previous mission. No enemy aircraft were seen during the long round trip to Ploesti, but several pilots had some tense moments as their fuel ran so low that they had to land at other airfields for refueling. The mission of 25 June sent the Group to France on another milk run. At base things were just as quiet on that Sunday and generated a little grumbling. The 2nd FS diary noted: *"Sunday morning: the pilots went on another milk run to France. Many of the men went to church at Group and at the small Catholic Church in Campomarino. We guess that the boys figure they need a little praying these days. Everyone is greatly disappointed by the lack of entertainment in these parts, except for the movies at Group three times a week. The beach is about the only other enjoyment. Once in a while we are treated to the sight of the two Red Cross girls going for a swim. They are not bad to look at in their bathing suits; any American girl would look good to us in any kind of suit these days."*

The B-24 escort mission of 26 June to Vienna, Austria was anything but a milk run as the *Luftwaffe* was up in force. The action began just after rendezvous with the bombers near Lake Balaton, Hungary when three Me 109s attacked the B-24s of the 304th Bomb Wing from five o'clock high. Lt. Ted Bullock, leading four Mustangs of the 4th FS, saw the Me 109s and broke up their attack. Bullock described the action in his diary: *"Had a mission today to Vienna. I led my first flight and got a 109. Chased three of them right thru the bombers and really blew him up. Glycol and smoke streaming from him and he went straight in. After I'd shot him and pulled up, a P-51 made a head-on pass at me and shot a bunch of holes in my right wing. Got back with not too much trouble. Tyler got 2, and Frye 1. The 2nd got 4, 5th got 7. No losses."*

As Lt. Bullock's fight ended, Maj. Wiley attacked a flight of enemy aircraft and he damaged one of them which he thought to be a Me 109. His film, however, showed his target to be Lt. Bullock's Mustang.

Bullock's kill, the first of 15 for the Group, was clocked at 08.55 hrs and began a running air

S/Sgt Richard Potter of the 4th Fighter Squadron, and his jeep bear witness to the ever-present Italian mud! (Credit: Richard Potter)

Lts. Frank Tribbett and George Goettleman describe their part in the air battle of 23 June 1944. (Credit: Thomas Thacker)

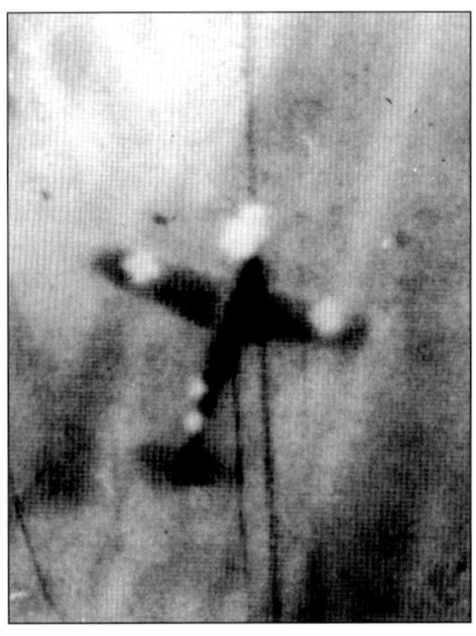

"Ted" Bullock's gun-camera films the Rumanian IAR 80 or 81 that he shot down north-west of Bucharest on 23 June 1944. (Credit: Fred Bullock)

Lt. Jim Empey, looking proud after receiving the Distinguished Flying Cross and an Air Medal. (Credit: Jim Empey)

Lt. Daniel Zoerb, 2nd Fighter Squadron, (in the cockpit) chats with his crew chief. (Credit: Dwayne Tabatt)

battle that lasted for another 35 minutes. Scoring honors of the day were shared by Captains Tim Tyler (4th FS) and Dan Zoerb (2nd FS) and Lt. Victor Tresvik (5th FS) with two each. Types of enemy aircraft claimed destroyed on the mission included Me 109s, Me 110s, Me 210s, Me 410s, and Ju 88s.

The reduction of the *Luftwaffe*'s inventory continued on 27 June when the Group traveled to Budapest. Ten enemy aircraft were destroyed on the mission and the 2nd FS claimed them all. Of particular note was Sully Varnell's triple. He downed three Me 110s and raised his score to 12, placing him third highest scorer in the Fifteenth Air Force as of this date. Lts. James Hoffman and Frank Grey were close runner-ups with two victories apiece, and the remaining five victories were claimed by Lts. Dennis Riddle, John Clarke and Bruno Dangelmaier. An obviously proud 2nd FS diarist summed it up this way: *"Ho Hum! The squadron's pilots got ten more victories on today's mission to Budapest. When will the slaughter cease? It is getting so that if the 2nd Squadron doesn't get any victories, the other squadrons don't expect to get any either. But today we got a wee bit hoggish and got the only victories for the mission. The squadron is mighty proud of its pilots; they deserve all the credit they can get."*

The HQ 52nd FG diary noted the arrival of some of the Eighth Air Force Mustangs that had flown the first shuttle mission from England to Russia: *"Some more metal strips were being laid on the runway at the south end of the field today. Over 20 P-51s from the 8th Air Force in England, which had flown escort for bombers on the shuttle to Russia, landed here for servicing before making a trip back to their home bases. They were in pretty poor shape, having been unable to get the necessary attention in Russia."*

The mission of 28 June took the pilots of the 52nd FG to Bucharest and although the Axis forces were not encountered in as much strength and were less aggressive as on the previous mission, the Group managed two victories and damaged a third enemy aircraft. The first of the encounters took place a few miles southwest of Bucharest when the 2nd FS bounced a number of Me 109s which were preparing to attack the bombers. Bob Curtis described the action: *"I was Red Leader on bomber escort when, near Bucharest at 28,000 feet and about 1010 hours, we saw six E/A at 3 o'clock attacking the bombers. I called a turn and dropped tanks and we started toward the bombers. As we approached them, 12 Me 109s passed us at 12 o'clock, slightly below us. Blue flight attacked the E/A while my flight provided top cover. (There was no dogfight as these 109s quickly fled the scene when they saw Blue Flight pursuing them.)*

"Shortly thereafter a Me 109 passed in front of me

P-51D-5-NA 44-13264, *Julie*

**Major Robert C. Curtis,
2nd Fighter Squadron,
52nd Fighter Group,
Madna, Italy, August 1944**

Major Robert Curtis named this aircraft after his younger sister Julie, and scored the majority of his 14 aerial victories in it. After Curtis left the Squadron, it was declared war-weary and converted to a two-seater. The codes were changed at this time to QP-?

Bob Curtis' P-51D "Julie", coded QP-C, displaying 12 of Curtis' 14 aerial victories which dates the photograph on or about 8 July 1944. (Credit: Robert C. Curtis)

P-51B-5-NA 43-6583, *Meg X* (Left side)/*Pat's Pet* (Right side)

Captain James O. "Tim" Tyler,
4th Fighter Squadron,
52nd Fighter Group,
Madna, Italy, June 1944

This Mustang was number ten in the list of James Tyler's assigned aircraft named Meg, and the number would rise to Meg XIII before he left the unit. The name Meg on the left side was for Tyler's girlfriend, and the Pat's Pet on the right, was in honor of Crew Chief, S/Sgt. Paul Lehman's girlfriend. Tyler served as Commanding Officer of the 4th Fighter Squadron during the summer and early fall of 1944, and was credited with eight confirmed kills.

Captain "Tim" Tyler of the 4th Fighter Squadron, watches as his crew chief, S/Sgt Paul Lehmann, paints on a fifth Swastika marking indicating Tyler's victory of 23 June 1944. (Credit: Paul Lehmann)

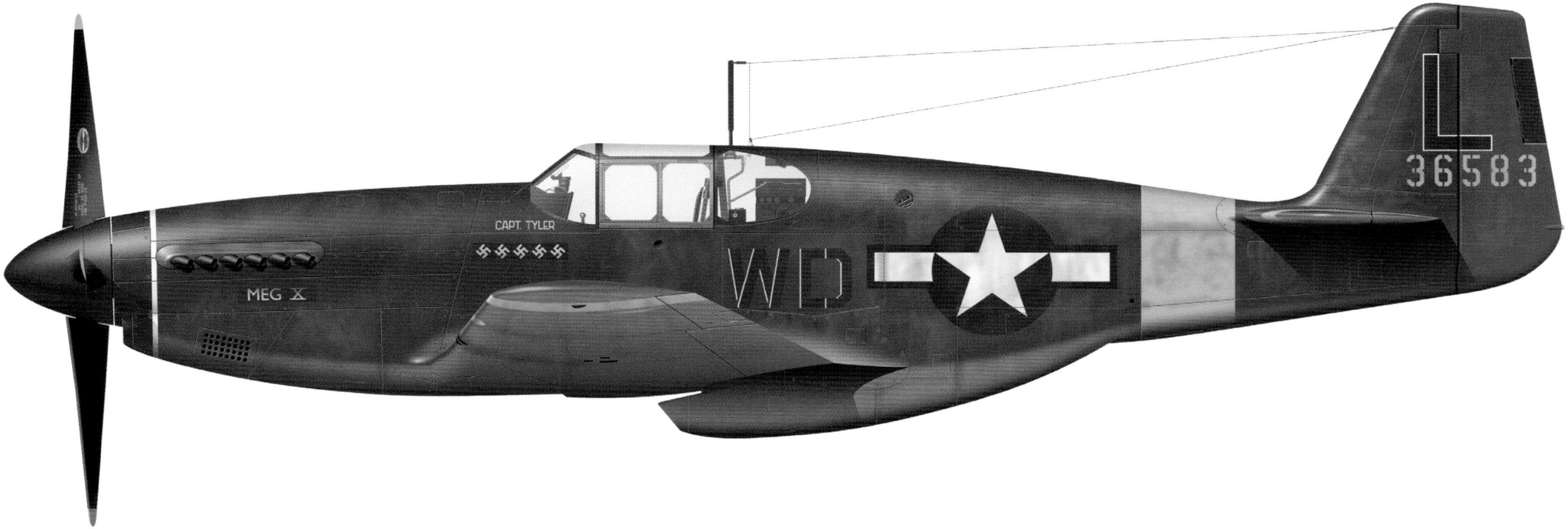

"Sully" Varnell and "Little Eva II". This publicity photograph was snapped after Varnell's triple victory on 27 June 1944 which raised his total to 12. (Credit: Thomas Thacker)

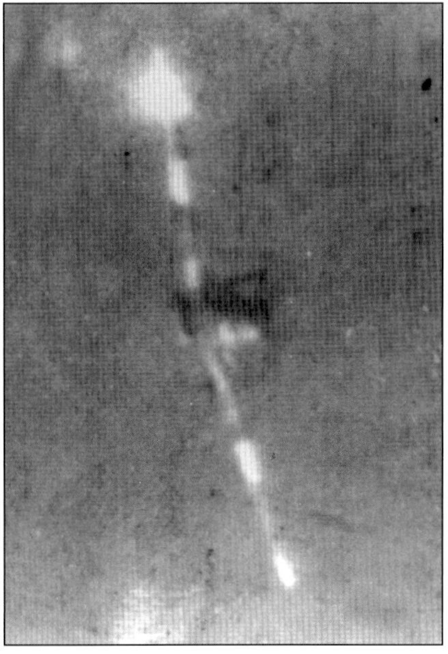

Bullet strikes from Major Wiley's gunfire can be seen in this out-take from his gun-camera film, hitting "Ted" Bullock's right wing. (Credit: Fred Bullock)

Lt. Robert Carnie, 5th Fighter Squadron, claimed his second of three total victories on 30 June 1944. Four days later, on 4 July 1944, Carnie was killed in action. (Credit: Thomas Thacker)

from 2 o'clock to 12 o' clock. I chased it and closed slowly in a dive. I fired at burst at 300 yards, slowing it down. I fired another burst at 200 yards and then overran the E/A. He turned into me and fired at me but stalled out and crashed in a field."

This Me 109 was Capt. Curtis' eighth victory.

The last victory of the day was by Lt. Jim Empey of the 5th FS and it was a very economical shoot down in terms of ammunition: *"I was number 4 in Yellow Flight. We were at 28,000 feet SW of Bucharest headed north when two Me 109s came from 9 o'clock to 3 o'clock and passed under us. We turned and dived on them. I fired a couple of bursts at one Me 109. It was way out of range, but I saw four strikes on the tail and wings. The Me 109 leveled out slightly at 18,000 feet, then to my surprise the pilot bailed out."*

This was his fifth victory and Lt. Empey became the 52nd Fighter Group's latest Ace.

The 29 June was a day of rest for the pilots. The 5th FS diary noted: *"Maintenance day and no mission scheduled. With the planes piling up the hours on those long missions, inspections come around quite often and the mechanics need time to perform them. Those that can, go down to the beach on the off day and most of us are acquiring a beautiful tan."*

Lt. Sully Varnell, the Fifteenth Air Force's third-ranking Ace, spent his day off a little differently by going to Rome to make a radio broadcast to the United States.

The Group returned to business as usual on 30 June and flew a very long mission to Blechhammer, Germany. The 52nd's assignment was to provide fighter cover over the target area and withdrawal for the bombers of the 5th, 49th, 55th, and 30th Bomb Wings which attacked the synthetic oil plants at Blechhammer, Germany. The 5th FS became separated from the others on the return trip and as it turned out were the only pilots to encounter the *Luftwaffe*. As they headed home, the 5th FS ran into a mixed formation of Fw 190s and Me 109s and in the ensuing dogfight claimed two of each shot down. Lt. Dwaine Franklin showed the way by downing a Me 109 and a Fw 190. The other victories were claimed by Lts. Bob Carnie (Fw 190) and Joseph Holloman (Me 109).

Thus ended a very busy and record-breaking period for the 52nd Fighter Group. In its first six weeks of flying Mustangs the Group had turned in a magnificent performance, claiming a total of 133-8-27 enemy aircraft during the period.

Chapter Eight

"Mixing it up"

Destruction of the Luftwaffe in Italy

July 1944

Richard Lampe's "Betty II" after the Swastika symbolizing his fifth victory had been applied. This aircraft was coded QP-X, serial number 43-24838. Note Lampe's non-regulation footwear in the photograph. (Paul Ludwig collection)

On 1 July the mission was canceled at the last moment and the pilots had a day to relax in the warm Italian sun. The 2nd FS diary gives an interesting insight of what was considered interesting and exceptional to young men at war on *"a day off"*: *"Another month has started and we all hope that it will be a fruitful one for the squadron record. The pilots got up early for a mission only to have it canceled at the last minute. No one seems to know the reason why. However, the entire Group got a day of rest, something that the personnel really deserved. Those who had no work in the evening went to the beach for a few hours of swimming. Although the beach is nothing to brag about, it certainly comes in handy on a hot, sultry afternoon. The mess hall had fresh meat on the menu in the evening; it was really the "cat's meow." Good steak is unusual these days and it is appreciated by all. Cucumbers and fresh salads are something else fairly new on the menu, and we are happy to say that the salads are well prepared, but not seasoned quite enough. Our mess halls are getting so classy these days that we now have paper napkins, sugar, salt, and canned milk on the tables. Now some of the men are expecting waiters to show up."*

The Group returned to action on 2 July, providing withdrawal support to B-24s attacking the Manfred Weiss marshalling yards and the Shell Oil refinery at Budapest. The 4th FS was to cover the front of the bomber stream, the 2nd FS the center and the 5th FS the rear. As the bombers were leaving the target area the 2nd FS encountered approximately 50 Me 109s and 12 Fw 190s which attacked the B-24s. The *"Beagles"* swept into the enemy aircraft and destroyed eight of them while breaking up their attack on the bombers. Barry Lawler shot down two Me 109s and damaged another. Lt. Cowan and Maj. Ralph *"Doc"* Watson each downed a Fw 190 and Dick Lampe destroyed a Me 109 and shared a second Messerschmitt with Dennis Riddle. Lt. Lampe's kills raised his total to 5.5 victories and brought him the title of *"Ace."* The final two kills of the day by the 2nd FS were credited to Bill Bryan who shot down two Me 109s. On the return trip to base, however, Bryan was forced to bail out over the coast of Yugoslavia after his aircraft took a Flak hit in the cooling system. He was rescued by partisans and returned to Bari.

The next action took place after the 5th FS heard calls for help from the bombers and rushed to their aid. The first gaggle of enemy aircraft was driven off without a fire-fight, but the second encounter resulted in a dogfight that saw the destruction of four enemy aircraft. In this action Lts. Dwaine Franklin and John McCarthy each downed a Fw 190, and Bob Carnie and Walter Zelinski each claimed a Me 109.

The mission was a rough one for the Fifteenth Air Force, however, as it suffered the loss of approximately 50 aircraft during the mission. The *Luftwaffe*, aided by the Hungarian Air Force, deployed approximately 170 fighters against the bombers and fought very aggressively during the day. American fighters composed of squadrons from the 15th and 8th Air Forces claimed a total of 29-4-7 enemy aircraft in the running air battles over Hungary. One of the American losses was the colorful Ralph *"Kidd"* Hofer of the 4th Fighter Group.

The Group flew to Rumania on 3 and 4 July as escorts to Fifteenth Air Force bombers attacking Axis oil producing facilites. The mission of 3 July to Bucharest turned out to be a milk run, but enemy aircraft were up in force on 4 July during the flight to and from Brasov. When the Group failed to make rendezvous with the B-17s of the 5th Bomb Wing it continued on and took up defense of a formation of B-24s. At 10.15 hrs two flights of about 15 Me 109s each were spotted and Mustangs from the 2nd and 4th Fighter Squadrons went after them. During the next five minutes three of the Me 109s were shot out of the sky, two of them by pilots of the 4th FS. They were credited to Lts. Ralph Peterson and Arnold Smith. The third Me 109 was downed by Lt. Edmund Gubler, a new pilot of the 2nd FS, who was flying his second mission.

The action continued at 10.25 hrs when the

Lt. Ralph "Kidd" Hofer of the 334th Fighter Squadron, 4th Fighter Group, an Ace with 16.5 aerial and 14 strafing victories, died on the 2 July 1944 mission. The 4th Fighter Group augmented by the 486th Fighter Squadron of the 352nd Fighter Group participated in this mission while on the return leg of the first Shuttle Mission to Russia. (Credit: Air Force Museum)

P-51D-5-NA 44-13428, *Cathy II*

**Captain John Barry Lawler,
2nd Fighter Squadron,
52nd Fighter Group,
Madna, Italy, July 1944**

Captain Barry Lawler scored his last five victories in this aircraft, named for his wife. After Lawler left the 2nd Fighter Squadron the aircraft was assigned to Lt. John S. Clarke. The codes were changed to QP–K, and the aircraft was renamed Dottie II.

Lt. Barry Lawler's P-51D "Cathy II". Note the Varga girl painting behind the 'V' on the rudder. (Credit: Barry Lawler

Bob Karr's P-51D VF-B displaying three Swastikas. More than likely this photograph was taken in the fall of 1944 after its previous pilot, Edwin "Chick" Fuller had departed the Squadron. The all-yellow rear fuselage and tail surfaces were adopted around October 1944. (Credit: James Empey)

5th FS joined in and scored five quick kills. The mission summary described the actions of Lt. Calvin Allen, who had borrowed John Heller's 'VF-Q' for the mission, and his wingman, Lt. Bob Carnie: *"Two P-51s dove on five Me 109s seen below the bombers. As these enemy aircraft where chased to the deck, Lt. Allen destroyed three in rapid succession. Lt. Carnie, at 15,000 feet, was seen by Lt. Allen to get strikes on another Me 109 which began leaking glycol. Lt. Carnie then overshot this E/A and got on the tail of the last Me 109 which he chased to the deck."*

From this point things went tragically wrong for Lt. Carnie and he crashed to his death while pursuing the Me 109. Lt. Allen reported the incident in the following statement. *"Lt. Carnie called to me to take the Me 109 to the right and that he would take the one on the left. I couldn't get into position to fire so I turned slightly left to cover him. I was at 4 o'clock to him and about 400 yards away. He was 200-300 yards behind an Me 109 and right on the deck. At about 1040 hrs he either hit a tree or the ground and his left wing came off. His aircraft went up to about 100 feet and traveled 200-300 yards. It then hit the ground and exploded in position 4505N/2503E approximately 18 miles NE of Pitesti, Rumania. He did not bail out."*

Angered and infuriated by seeing what had happened to his friend, Lt. Allen closed in on the Me 109 and shot it down for his fourth victory of the day.

The final kills of the mission were recorded by Maj. Franklin Robinson and Lt. Richard Evans of the 4th FS. Robinson and Evans had just left the formation and were heading back to base when they sighted two Fw 190 below them. The pair dived on the unsuspecting 190 pilots and shot them down on the first pass.

The 4th Fighter Squadron also lost one of its pilots on the mission when the wing of Lt. Jack Chidester's Mustang broke off during a high-speed dive after an enemy aircraft.

The mission of 5 July to the Toulon area in France turned out to be a milk run, but on the following day the 52nd met some opposition over Bergamo, Italy. In that encounter the 2nd FS downed four enemy aircraft. Two of the Me 109s were destroyed by Lt. Charles Botvidson, his first kills after flying in excess of 100 missions. Capt. Bob Curtis also claimed an Me 109 for his ninth victory. His encounter report noted: *"At about 28,000 feet near Lake Garda we saw eight Me 109s at about 26,000 feet flying from 1 o'clock to 12 o'clock. We dropped tanks and dived on them. I closed on a Me 109 and fired from about 500 yards. It rolled over and dived and I followed it to the deck, firing short bursts but seeing no strikes. I finally saw two hits on the fuselage and the pilot immediately jettisoned the canopy and bailed out at about 200 feet. The enemy aircraft crashed and burned."*

The final kill of the day was shared by Lts. Frank Grey and William Cowan. Frank Grey later related the action in *The American Beagle Squadron* as follows: *"This was by far my longest encounter with a single E/A, and the pilot was the best of all I encountered. The engagement seemed to last forever, maybe as long as fifteen minutes, with Cowan and I trading roles with him as hunter and hunted. Because of the difficulty of this victory Cowan and I didn't want to flip for it, so we shared it."*

On 7 July 1944, the 52nd FG flew a long mission to Blechhammer, Germany and encountered enemy aircraft. The 5th FS downed three Me 109s and damaged two others against the loss of one pilot. In this action Lt. Bob Karr destroyed two of the Me 109s and damaged a third. Lt. Stan Bricker destroyed one enemy aircraft and Stan Rollag closed out the scoring by

Lt. Calvin D. Allen, 5th Fighter Squadron – an Ace with seven victories. (Credit: Bill Hess)

Lt. Stanley Bricker, 5th Fighter Squadron, who scored the second of his three aerial victories during the mission of 7 July 1944. (Credit: Thomas Thacker)

damaging another of the German fighters. Lt. John Floyd was shot down during the air battle and reported killed in action.

Victories and casualties continued on 8 July during an escort mission to the Floridsdorf Oil Refinery in Vienna, Austria. Axis aircraft were up in an effort to defend the target area and several dogfights broke out. It was during these engagements that Capt. Bob Curtis of the 2nd FS had his best day of his long tour of duty. His encounter report provides the details of his day: *"At about 1100 hours, at 26,000 feet ESE of the target area, I was leading the squadron formation when we saw 15+ Me 109s attacking the lead bombers as they came off the target. I followed Blue Flight as they dived on the E/A, and attacked one of four Me 109s that were attacking the bombers from 6 o'clock. The E/A took violent evasive action and I followed it down to about 5000 feet, firing occasionally and seeing strikes. Then the windshield and canopy clouded over and I lost sight of the E/A. My wingman, (Frank) Grey, saw the pilot bail out, but his parachute caught fire.*

"After my canopy and windshield cleared I closed on what I thought was the E/A that I had followed down, but Grey later said it was a different plane. I fired several bursts, saw strikes on the wings and fuselage, and as I turned up and away I saw the Me 109 crash and explode. Grey later said that he saw me destroy two E/A in about one minute.

"Grey and I then climbed back toward the bombers. When we reached about 14,000 feet we saw 8 Me 109s attacking a bomber at about 17,000 feet and at 2 o'clock to us. We attacked them but they were very aggressive and skillful. A dogfight ensued and we eventually were forced to hit the deck. A Me 109 followed me down, firing at me, with Grey following and firing at it.

"After I leveled out on the deck, and after about three minutes of aggressive, skillful flying by the Me 109 pilot, I was able to get in a position to fire a few bursts and get enough strikes to force the pilot to bail out."

Bob Curtis was later awarded the Distinguished Service Cross in recognition of his exploits on this mission.

During this engagement Maj. Ralph *"Doc"* Watson shot down another of the 109s and Barry Lawler claimed a Me 109 as a probable. The remaining victories of the day were claimed by the 5th FS. Lt. John Schumacher downed one Me 109, and Maj. Edwin Fuller damaged three, while Lt. Lindsey Lundgaard damaged one. On the down side of the action Lt. Glenn Grewe was reported missing in action and Lt. Charles Botvidson, 2nd FS, was forced to bail out near Vis. Fortunately Lt. Botvidson was rescued and returned to base on 15 July.

When the Group flew to Ploesti, Rumania on 9 July 1944, Sully Varnell picked up where Bob Curtis left off the day before and scored a triple. His were three of the six kills scored by the 2nd FS on this mission and Lt. Varnell's total score now stood at 15. The mission summary described the 2nd FS encounter but did not detail the actions of Lts. Varnell, Fred Ohr, John Clarke, or Jim Hoffman: *"As the last group of bombers were coming off the target some P-51s were at 27,000 feet*

A happy Captain Bob Curtis, Commanding Officer of the 2nd Fighter Squadron posed for this photograph after returning from his triple victory mission of 8 July 1944. Note that Crew Chief, S/Sgt Gilbert, has already added three new German crosses to "Julie" to reflect Captain Curtis' new total of 12. (Credit: Robert C. Curtis)

Major Ralph "Doc" Watson, pictured here after he had transferred to the 5th Fighter Squadron from the 2nd Fighter Squadron. (Credit: Paul Ludwig collection)

Captain "Chick" Fuller's P-51D "Shoot Jerry, You're Faded". (Credit: James Empey)

Lt. Fred Ohr, 2nd Fighter Squadron, downed an Me 109 on 9 July 1944 for his fifth aerial victory. (Credit: Thomas Thacker)

flying parallel to and east of the bombers. When the last bomber had made the right turn toward the rally point at 1025 hours, P-51s of the 325th came upon the 52nd P-51s from the NE. In turning into these P-51s, the 52nd sighted between 10-12 slate gray Me 109s which were at 28,000 feet diving toward the target area. These E/A may have been planning to intercept a third wing of bombers coming off the target or possibly they were going to attack the B-24s from the right beyond the target. Eleven P-51s immediately turned into and dove on the Me 109s as they headed east. Within a period of five minutes, six of the eight Me 109s were destroyed. One of the E/A was a Me 109E, having struts on the tail. In general the pilots were not too experienced but rather cagey; occasionally cutting their engine while being chased so that the P-51s would over run them."

In addition to Varnell's three, Lts. John Clarke, Jim Hoffman, and Fred Ohr each shot down a 109, and for Lt. Ohr, it was his fifth and he was now the 2nd Fighter Squadron's 10th Ace. Lt. Ohr described his fifth victory in his encounter report: *"I saw nine E/A at 8 o'clock. We made a climbing turn into them and I closed on four of them, firing two short bursts at each. Three of them turned left and one broke down toward the deck. I followed it (an Me 109) and on the way down fired a long burst from astern and saw several strikes on the fuselage and wing root. I saw pieces fly off the wing and coolant began to pour out. I broke away because of a cloud and then saw the E/A on the other side of the cloud. I fired two more long bursts and saw strikes on the fuselage and wings. The E/A then burst into flames, went into a spin and crashed."*

Thirty minutes later Mustangs of the 5th FS went into action against a pair of Fw 190s and Lt. Stan Rollag sent both of them down in flames. Lt. Ralph Peterson of the 4th FS then closed out the day's scoring by downing a Me 109 30 miles north-east of Nis. All of the 52nd FG's pilots returned safely to base after this excellent mission, but their report carried this one caustic note at the end: *"A flight of P-51s with red tails (332nd FG) crossed over some 52nd P-51s at the target area and made passes at us. Pilots took a dim view of this."* (Bob Curtis also commented *"…that we also took a dim view of the P-38s that did this."*)

The Group stood down during three of the next five days. There was a little excitement around Madna on 11 July, however, when a film crew showed up to film the Group. That evening 16 aircraft representing the three squadrons flew formation shots for the camera. The films taken at Madna were to become part of a movie illustrating the activities and progress of the 15th Air Force. Lt. Varnell, the 15th Air Force's second leading Ace at the time, also received a lot of attention from the cameramen who took numerous photographs of him and his Mustang. The 12th of July was a quiet day at the base and the 2nd Squadron diarist became a food and movie critic noting: *"Steak for supper once again; it was a little on the tough side but the men didn't mind and it was eaten eagerly. The movie "Buffalo Bill" was shown at Group in the evening and was fairly well enjoyed. The scenes, in Technicolor, were beautiful but the story dragged too much."*

When the 52nd returned to action on 14 July its mission was a free-lance fighter sweep over the target while the bombers attacked oil installations and marshalling yards in the Budapest area. Numerous enemy aircraft were encountered in and around the target area, but only the 2nd FS engaged them. Two Me 109s were claimed as destroyed in the action, one by Lt. James Hoffman and the second by Capt. Bob Curtis, but both were later changed to probably destroyed. The combat report noted that some of the Me 109s carried Italian Fascist markings on the wings.

The mission of 15 July found the 52nd FG returning to Ploesti as an escort to bombers attacking the Romano Americano oil refineries. As the Group reached the Yugoslavian coast, dense clouds were encountered and the squadrons became widely scattered. The 2nd FS found itself north of the briefed route, and all but three of its ships found themselves in a dogfight with a formation of about 20 Rumanian Me 109s near Turnu Severin. During the battle that followed, three of the Me 109s were shot down and a fourth limped away damaged after Lt. Frank Grey shot it up. The confirmed kills were credited, one each to Capt. Curtis, Lt. Art Johnson, Lt. Willard Pretzer and Lt. Elmer Mendonca. Even though Capt. Curtis was successful in engagement, his encounter report again alludes to *"porpoising"* problems with the P-

On 9 July 1944 "Sully" Varnell scored a triple in his new P-51D "Little Eva III" and raised his score to 15. In this photograph his groundcrew proudly poses with its aircraft. From left to right: Sgt. C. G. Jones, Asst, CC; S/Sgt. Elmer Dalebroux, Crew Chief (in the cockpit) and Armorer Sgt. Murrell Fleming (Credit: C. G. Jones)

P-51D-5-NA 44-13263, Jo-Baby

**Lt. Robert McCampbell,
4th Fighter Squadron,
52nd Fighter Group,
Madna, Italy, August 1944**

Lt. Robert McCampbell scored his third and last victory in this aircraft on 4 August 1944 when he downed an Me 109. After his departure, the aircraft was used by various pilots until it was lost on 11 November 1944 with Lt. J.W. Frankoff at the controls.

A still from a movie taken by USAAF film crews on 11 July 1944 of 4th Fighter Squadron Mustangs. The photograph to left shows Lt. Robert McCampbell's "Jo-Baby". (Credit: USAF)

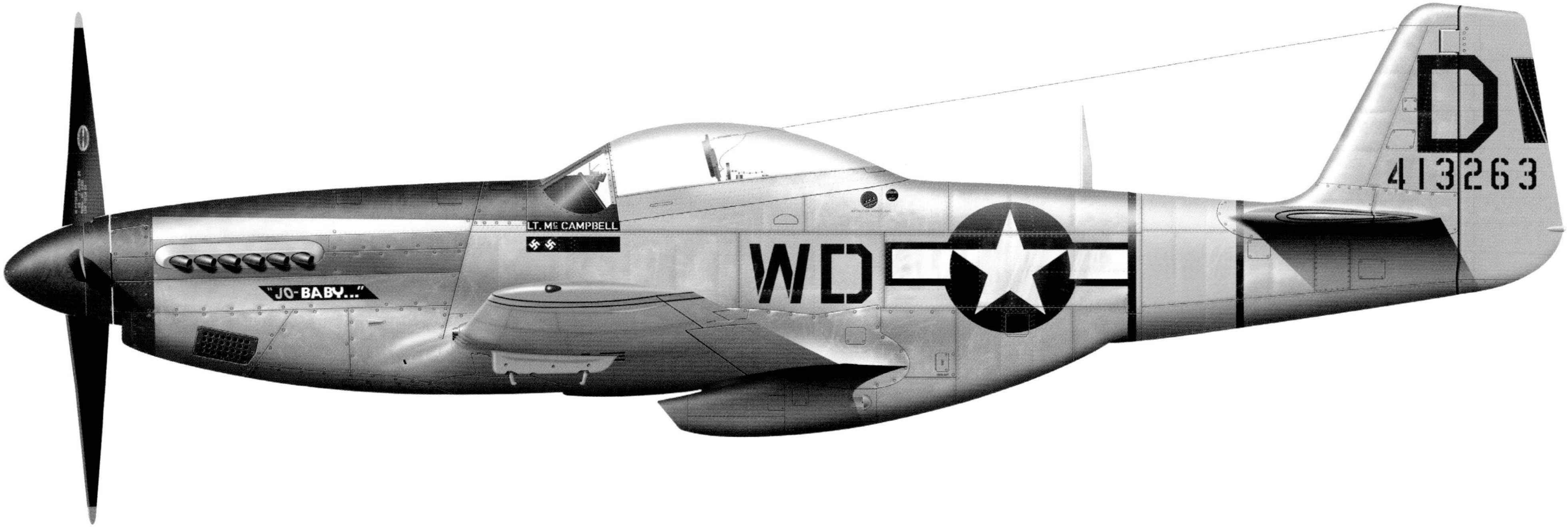

Captain Thomas Thacker watching incoming B-17s from the control tower. (Credit: Thomas Thacker)

Seen here from left to right: Lieutenants Dwaine "Bird Dog" Franklin and Lin Lundgaard of the 5th Fighter Squadron. (Credit: Lin Lundgaard)

This P-51D, WD-I, was assigned to the 4th Fighter Squadron Ace, Lt. William "Shory" Hanes. (Credit: Paul Ludwig collection)

51D: *"We were east of Turnu Severin, Rumania at 26,000 feet when I saw 20 Me 109s at about 27,000 feet coming toward us from 9 o'clock. We dropped tanks and climbed above them, turning to the left with them and then diving on the last three E/A of the group. I closed on one of them to about 200 yards astern of it and fired a two second burst. I saw numerous strikes all over the fuselage, engine and wing roots. The E/A then rolled over and started down, with small pieces flying off of it, and glycol and black smoke streaming from it. I was unable to follow it down to the deck because of the violent tail buffeting of my aircraft. Lt. Johnson, number three in my flight saw the plane crash and burn."*

Tom Thacker also touched upon some of the problems the Group encountered with the new P-51Ds in his unpublished history of the 52nd Fighter Group: *"The new "D" models were especially welcome, with the beautiful bubble canopies for improved visibility. Still, mechanical problems continued to appear, sometimes resulting in loss of planes and even the loss of pilots. Wing weakness during a high speed pullout apparently cost the life of Lt. Raymond H. Irvine, Jr., while chasing a Jerry on the 18th. Capt. Bruce L. Morrison, 5th Squadron, was slightly more fortunate a couple of days later when his engine failed. He became a POW after only four days with the Group."* (Lt. Irvine somehow managed to free himself from his crippled ship and bail out. He was soon captured and became a POW.)

Thacker went on to record some general problems with the Mustang that required correction: *"The liquid-cooled Packard-Rolls engines required radiators which were located under the belly of the P-51. A small electric motor automatically opened and closed shutters to regulate coolant temperatures. Oil dripped into the motors occasionally, causing malfunction. Engines then overheated. Several early returns resulted and losses due to unknown causes may have been due to this engineering defect.*

"As each problem was identified and the cause isolated, a technical order "T.O." would be developed to correct the situation. Much of our logistic support was concentrated toward eliminating these troublesome items. Nothing must prevent sending up the very best fighting machine possible on every mission.

"Little could be done to provide relief for the pilot's bottom during missions which grew progressively longer, and taxed the stamina of the most durable flyer. Unlike the bombers, moving around inside a fighter plane was impossible. A couple of our boys tried to find a solution. Perhaps, they reasoned, a shot of morphine carried for emergencies might eliminate that tired feeling. Inserted where the body made contact with the seat cushion, the results proved dramatic. Sensitivity was lost, as had been desired. An un-programmed side effect killed the experiment, however. A critical muscle was relaxed and the pilot ended his mission sitting on more than he had bargained for."

The 4th and 5th Fighter Squadrons both had a good day by scoring a combined eight kills, two probables, and four damaged on the mission to Münchendorf airfield on 16 July. The action began after a feint attack by several enemy aircraft on elements of the 5th FS. When the 5th FS challenged the bounce, the unidentified bogies fled. They were both described in the mission summary as Me 109s: *"These 109s dived very fast and the P-51s were gaining on them very little. They also had an elliptical wing. It was not as broad as the Spitfire at the root, but was definitely pointed at the tips. The fuselage and outboard six to eight feet of the wings were cream colored or silver. The rest of the wings were dark gray or black. No markings were seen although it was thought to have possible German markings."*

Minutes later the 5th FS turned its attention to some Me 109s that had apparently shot down two B-24s of a group escorted by P-38s. One flight had to split-S away when the P-38s turned on them and opened fire. Ten minutes later another gaggle of enemy aircraft comprising about 30 Me 109s and Me 110s were spotted. Two of the 5th's Mustangs jumped in to assist four Mustangs from the 325th FG that were attacking the enemy formation and culled a few bandits from the sky. As the 110s attempted to dive away Lt. Dwaine Franklin fired at a 110 and it collided with its wingman and both aircraft exploded. Franklin then fired on a third 110 that immediately broke into flames.

At that point Lt. I. P. Franklin, 5th FS, chased a Me 109 downed toward the deck and when the German pilot tried to split-S away from Franklin, he lost control and smashed into the ground and exploded. As Lt. Franklin pulled up after this kill, he spotted a formation of five Me 110s. At 13,000 feet he made a pass on the Me 110 just as it entered a cloud. Franklin went around the cloud for another pass and as the Messerschmitt came out of it the *"Keystone Cops"* routine continued. Just as he was about to fire another burst at this Me 110, it collided head on into a Ju 88 and both enemy aircraft went down in a ball of flame.

Now it was the 4th Squadron's turn to watch the next *"Keystone Cop"* act. Bill Hanes and Frederick Straut spotted a formation of Me 110s and as they closed in on the two trailing enemy aircraft, the Germans swerved into each other. One enemy aircraft exploded and the other snapped in half. Lt. Hanes then chased down a flight of five Ju 88s and shot one of them down in flames while Lts. Robert Deckman and Fred Straut were attacking another group of Me 110s. By the time they broke off their attack, Lt.

Lt. William Parent's P-51D "Pendaja". (Credit: USAF)

Captain Barry Lawler of the 2nd Fighter Squadron, scored his 10th and 11th aerial victories on 25 July 1944, and in this photograph he is seated in "Cathy II" with its its up to date scoreboard. (Credit: Barry Lawler)

Deckman had shot one of them down and damaged three others. Lt. Straut was hot on the tail of another Me 110 and scored quite a few strikes before he lost it in a cloud.

The day was not a complete success for the 4th FS, however, because it lost two of its pilots on the mission. Lts. Ralph Peterson and Robert Hyde fell victim to Flak and were forced to bail out over enemy territory. Hyde was killed and Peterson became a POW.

No mission was flown on 17 July, and when the Group flew to Memmingen airfield in Germany on 18 July it did not have the best of days. The *Luftwaffe* was up in great numbers to defend the target areas, and before the day was out it had accounted for 14 of the B-17s of the 5th Bomb Wing, but had lost 40 of its own aircraft in doing so. The day's scoring honors went to the 27th FS, 1st FG with 14 kills, and the 31st FG 12 and the 332nd FG downed 11. The 52nd FG claimed the final three of the day, one each by Lts. Art Johnson and Barry Lawler of the 2nd FS and one by Lt. William Parent of the 4th FS.

The Group returned to southern Germany on 19 July and in stark contrast to the day before, the *Luftwaffe* sent only a few aircraft up to defend the target areas. Only eight kills were claimed by 15th AF fighters during the mission, one of which was scored by Lt. Ralph Gassman of the 4th FS. On the trip back to base Lt. Gassman spotted a lone Fw 190 about 10,000 feet below his Mustang and dove to the attack, catching the unwary German by surprise and quickly shooting him down.

During the remainder of July 1944 fighter groups of the Fifteenth Air Force flew ten escort missions to various targets and on at least five of the missions met vigorous opposition from the *Luftwaffe*. These air battles resulted in the destruction of 190 enemy aircraft, (17 probables, and 70 damaged), but somehow the 52nd FG's assignments placed them at the wrong place at the wrong time. The Group was only able to claim 6-0-1 during this period and all of them were scored by pilots of the 2nd FS. The first of these kills occurred on 25 July when Barry Lawler destroyed two Me 109s and Willard Pretzer shot down another. On the following day Sully Varnell shot down a Me 109 during a mission to Austria and Bob Curtis could only claim a *"damaged"* when his Mustang went into compressibility during the dive after a Me 109.

It is interesting to note that these aircraft were identified at the time as 'Messerschmitt 309s', an aircraft which never saw operational service. The description of the aircraft was as follows: *"One pilot obtained a very good view of the wings of the enemy aircraft. They were, as he described them, elliptical wings, just like those of a Spitfire. For this reason and their superior maneuverability at that altitude, it is believed that the enemy aircraft were Me 309s. The enemy aircraft had black crosses with a white background on the upper sides of the wings, and a black cross with a square green border on the fuselage. They were painted a greenish gray with a light gray underside. They had no belly tanks."* (This is the third encounter mentioned in 52nd FG reports of encountering this type of aircraft.)

The Group flew to Budapest on 27 July and met minimal opposition from Axis air forces in the area. After some encounters with Me 109s that turned away when the Mustangs of the 2nd FS approached them, Fred Ohr finally had the opportunity to attack. His encounter report stated: *"At about 1005 hours, a few miles southwest of the target, I saw six E/A at about 24,000 feet approaching the bombers from about 5 o'clock as the bombers were going into the target area. Although we were about to return to base because my wingman's plane had developed engine trouble, we turned into the E/A. As they broke away from the bombers, I closed on one of them to firing range and fired several short bursts at about thirty degrees deflection. I saw a few strikes on the wing and fuselage. I identified the E/A as Fw 190s. The one I hit dived to about 10,000 feet and I followed it, firing several long bursts and seeing strikes on the wings, engine, fuselage and tail section. Only three of my guns fired. The E/A snapped over on its back and the pilot bailed out. I lost sight of the pilot before his parachute opened."*

The Group's final victory of the month occurred on 31 July when James Hoffman of the 2nd FS downed a Me 109 for his fifth victory making him the Squadron's 11th and final Ace. The mission summary provides a brief description of the encounter: *"At 1140 hours when the bombers were going over the target, (the Prehova Oil Refinery in Burcharest, Rumania), three light gray Me 109s with red*

Lt. Hans Zachmann's P-51B "Dody", coded QP-S, serial number 43-25133. (Credit: C. G. Jones)

Lt. John Ondocsin, 2nd Fighter Squadron, and his P-51B "Michelle Marie" which was coded QP-Z. (Credit: R.C. Curtis)

The Reggianne Re 2005 was the only Axis aircraft which fitted the description provided by 2nd Fighter Squadron pilots. Only 48 of these aircraft were manufactured, 13 of which, went to the Luftwaffe, and a few were operated by the Italian RSI units. Possibly the aircraft encountered by the 2nd Fighter Squadron on 26 July 1944 were some of these aircraft on temporary assignment to the Vienna area. (Tom Ivie)

crosses on the wings were seen at 26,000 feet about three miles east of Bucharest. Four P-51s of the 2nd Squadron which were flying at 3 o'clock to the bombers at 24,000 feet climbed to attack. As the 51s climbed, the 109s dived for the deck. The flight split into elements, each chasing one Me 109 while the third Me 109 turned off to the east. One of the 109s was destroyed."

In this same action Lts. Dennis Riddle and Edmund Gubler went after the another Me 109 and as Riddle closed on it the enemy aircraft went into a cloud. Riddle followed the Messerschmitt into the cloud bank and continued his pursuit, losing Gubler in the process. Lt. Gubler skirted the cloud and waited for the enemy aircraft to reappear. When the first aircraft broke out into the clear he opened fire and that was an unfortunate mistake. His bullets ripped into Lt. Riddle's aircraft, setting it ablaze and forcing Riddle to abandon his aircraft. As Lt. Riddle jumped from his burning Mustang, Gubler circled and watched and as soon as Riddle touched down, Gubler landed nearby. Both men squeezed themselves into the small cockpit and attempted to take off, but the soft earth would not support the P-51's weight and it dug into the dirt and flipped over on its back. Moments later the two were taken prisoner and remained so until October 1944 when they were liberated.

Tom Thacker summarized the last few days of July at Madna with these comments: *"A busy July was coming to a close. Lt. Roy W. Smith, 2nd Squadron disappeared while mixing it up with enemy aircraft on July 28th. On the final day of the month, Lts. Dennis R. Riddle and Edmund V. Gubler, 2nd Squadron, failed to return from an engagement over Bucharest. Others reported hearing Lt. Riddle call on the radio: 'Get that one off my tail'. Five weeks later both returned to relate their experiences which included a short stay in a PW camp until it was overrun by the Russians.*

"The heavy brass continued to visit, often with a new package of medals to be distributed. Lt. General Barney M. Giles, deputy chief of the AAF was the top in rank, followed by Major General Frank O'd. Hunter. With such a full schedule of flying, some pilots were heard to remark that they would have preferred to have their extra time free to relax on the beach.

"The Adriatic was nearby and visited during the summer months whenever work loads permitted. Weekends and holidays were no different from other days in this respect. Just to lie on the hot sand followed by a cooling dip was a real treat. Even the use of swimming trunks was optional in that remote spot. This carried a slight risk from jelly fish, as our chaplain learned the hard way, getting stung in a most sensitive location."

Chapter Nine

"Burning aircraft and twisted wreckage"

The Luftwaffe Vanishes

August 1944

Lt. Robert McCampbell's "Jo-Beth" in the foreground of the 4th Fighter Squadron flight line. (Credit: Paul Ludwig)

August 1944 saw a definite downturn in the 52nd Fighter Group's encounters with Axis aircraft, and as a result its scoring continued to suffer. The same was true for most of the other fighter groups within the 15th Air Force. The 2nd Fighter Squadron reported a drop from 49 kills in 9 encounters in June to 34 kills in 12 encounters in July culminating with only six victories in four encounters during August. The same was true for the 5th FS as it claimed only 4-1-0 during the month. The 4th FS, however, did a little better and closed out the month with 14-0-6.

The month, however, did offer some new types of missions for the pilots, including a shuttle to Russia, and a number of strafing missions. The shuttle to Russia began on 4 August 1944 and it was somewhat different than the earlier shuttle missions in that instead of escorting heavy bombers, the 52nd FG would be escorting P-38s as they strafed and bombed enemy installations. The P-38s were from the 82nd Fighter Group and they were assigned to bomb targets at Ploesti on the first leg of the shuttle and strafe airfields at Focsani, Rumania on the return trip. However, during the trip to Ploesti and on into Russia, the attack force ran into enemy opposition in the forms of Flak and fighters as it approached the target area. The 4th FS was bounced from out of the clouds by a flight of 15 Me 109s and before the Squadron could react Lt. Stewart, flying *'Yellow 4'*, took hits in his glycol tank and started streaming coolant. His wingman told him that his Mustang was in bad shape and that he should jump, but Stewart radioed back that he was *'OK'*. He was last seen as his Mustang disappeared into a cloud. He did survive the shoot down, however, but was captured. The enemy aircraft all headed for the deck after the initial attack, with Lt. Bob McCampbell hot on the tail of one of them. He fired a long burst at the Me 109 and it immediately started trailing a stream of coolant, then burst into flames as it went into a cloud. Two other 4th FS pilots confirmed McCampbell's victory, noting the enemy aircraft was heading straight down into a mountain. As this encounter was taking place Lts. Roy Frye, Ralph Gassman, Ted Bullock, Henry Montgomery, and Joe Fitzpatrick followed Me 109s down and each of them damaged one before the fleeing enemy aircraft vanished into a large cloud bank.

A few moments later as the 2nd FS passed by just north of the target at 2,000 feet, Capt. Sully Varnell spotted a Rumanian Ju 52 transport and shot it down for his 17th and final victory of the war. This 'kill' ended contact with enemy aircraft but the squadrons were all experiencing continuous fire from Flak guns until they crossed into Russian held territory. The 5th FS by now had broken into two sections while dodging Flak and the section led by Lt. Schumacher became somewhat disoriented and tried following the Dnieper River to its assigned landing field in Russia. Somewhere along the way, Lt. John McCarthy's Mustang was hit by a Flak burst that severed its tail and he crashed to his death. Lts. John Schumacher and John Heller landed in a wheat field and were interned by the Russians for a few days.

Bad weather along with the Flak over the target area contributed to the confusion that resulted in the aircraft becoming scattered as they tried to fly into Russia and increased the navigational problems. However, it transpired the 33

Lt. "Ted" Bullock's P-51D did not retain the "Abdul the Bull" artwork that adorned his P-51B. (Credit: Fred Bullock)

P-51D-5-NA 44-13431, *Little Eva III*

**Captain James S. "Sully" Varnell,
2nd Fighter Squadron,
52nd Fighter Group,
Madna, Italy, August 1944**

"Sully" Varnell scored the last five of his 17 victories in this aircraft during the period 9 July-4 August 1944. The aircraft is illustrated with red code letters, but later thin black outlines were added. The aircraft was lost as QP–V with Lt. James Hoffman at the controls.

This photograph, taken 19 August 1944 at Madna, is an excellent view of "Sully Varnell's P-51D "Little Eva III" displaying Varnell's final score of 17 aerial victories. (Credit: USAF)

The 4th Fighter Squadron bar at Madna airfield. (Credit: E. Torvinen)

Mustangs which completed the flight to Russia landed at eight different locations. The 5th of August was spent getting the aircraft repaired, refueled and rearmed for the return trip and fraternizing with the Group's Russian hosts. Drinking, eating and dancing was the order of the day for many of the men during the evening of 4 August and part of the next day. By the 6th of August the Mustangs had all found their way to either Poltava or Piryatin and began preparations for the return trip. Thirty-one Mustangs made the return trip to Madna without incident on 6 August, and about a week later the two detained pilots, Schumacher and Heller, were allowed to head for the base. Tom Thacker noted that, *"No report of their status was provided to other Americans despite assurance to the contrary by the Russians."*

In addition to the slight change in some of the missions, August 1944 also produced some changes in the facilities at Madna. With the help of the local Italian work force a number of improvements were taking place around the base. Some of the improvements came about due to the language problems between the Americans and the Italian locals; Tom Thacker recounted of some of the results: *"We were encouraged to employ as many local civilians as possible due to high unemployment and the low cost of such labor. Local help dug and maintained latrines along with other sanitary facilities. Shelters were constructed and winterized largely by this crew who also erected our community shower.*

"One of the best services provided in this manner was the carpenter shop. Its abilities were limited only by the availability of materials and the language barrier. Tony was picked as the foreman largely for his linguistic ability but it was less than perfect. For the first time in two years, I worked at a desk, a product of Tony's crew.

"Capt. Camhi saw what was being accomplished and desired something of the sort. He prided himself in being able to communicate in Italian and described the item of his dream by raising his voice and with lots of arm waving. The term "cabinetto" was repeated several times. The carpenters finally nodded in agreement and enthusiastically began construction as they understood it. About three days later the finished product was delivered. Capt. Camhi's "cabinetto" proved to be the first four-hole privy of the Italian campaign, complete with hinged lids. It was truly a work of art."

He closed out his commentary on the changes in August with a few points about the war in the air: *"Overall, combat operations during August were on the level of the two prior months. Aerial victories were becoming more difficult to achieve as the enemy was beginning to react from heavy losses from both the Mediterranean attack and from western Europe. Constant bombing of oil fields and refineries was helping to cause a fuel shortage and many more planes were located on the ground. Thus the air battle was changing, with longer and more varied missions becoming commonplace. With the requirement for top cover for the bombers diminishing, the fighter planes were striking more frequently at ground targets. This was essential but dangerous work."*

Missions were limited during the early days of August 1944 due to weather conditions in the Group's usual zone of operations and as a result contact with the *Luftwaffe* was negligible. The middle of the month, however, would find the Group temporarily returning to its former role of air support for the troops on the ground.

The long overdue invasion of southern France was now about to take place. The plan, originally called Operation Anvil, had been scheduled to coincide with the Normandy Invasion, but was postponed due to Britain's objections. Churchill believed that the Italian campaign should take precedent over the invasion of southern France and the other Allies reluctantly delayed this plan. Now, with the Italian campaign progressing well, the invasion of southern France, renamed 'Operation Dragoon', was on again. Air support for the upcoming invasion began on 12 August when bombers of the Mediterranean Allied Air Force hit targets in both southern France and Italy in an attempt to disguise the proposed

Aircraft of the 5th Fighter Squadron taxiing out for the day's mission. (Credit: James Empey)

P-51Ds of the 4th Fighter Squadron on the flight line at Madna. (Credit: Paul Ludwig)

The 5th Fighter Squadron's scoreboard in the bar. (Credit: James Empey)

The 2nd Fighter Squadron flight line at Madna. QP-2 "Sit" was Lt. David Emerson's Mustang. (Credit: C. G. Jones)

invasion area. During the night of 12 August, B-24s of the 885th Bomb Squadron (Heavy) (Special) dropped 67,000 pounds of arms, ammunition and supplies to the French Forces of the Interior, generally referred to as the FFI. Along with the arms and supplies, the Liberators dropped in agents to guide the FFI during the invasion and leaflets to alert the French citizens. The bombing attacks along the French and Italian coasts continued on 13 and 14 August, knocking out 35 gun positions and bridges in the invasion area between Toulon and Cannes. The 52nd Fighter Group joined in the pre-invasion assault on 14 August and its pilots were ordered to strafe radar positions along the French coast and they continued this operation on 15 August. The yellow-tailed Mustangs thoroughly worked over installations in the area of Nice and all aircraft returned to base in spite of heavy anti-aircraft fire.

Not all of the Fifteenth Air Force fighter groups were so lucky. The 1st and 14th Fighter Groups, flying P-38s, had been assigned to fly close ground support to cover the landings and during the period 13-20 August they lost 23 aircraft. On the positive side they managed to destroy over 100 German vehicles, 12 bridges, and a number of gun and headquarters positions. With the invasion now proceeding reasonably well the Fifteenth Air Force units returned to their normal strategic missions, flying to Ploesti on 17 August and 19 August 1944. These missions turned out to be the last bombing attacks on this crucial target. A total of 20 attacks on these facilities had reduced their output to a mere trickle, and now with the Russians quickly closing in on them, the Fifteenth Air Force began looking at other targets.

Late in the month the 2nd FS went through a tough period losing several of its pilots in accidents and combat. On 20 August one of its newly arrived pilots, Lt. Charles Kelly, was killed when his wing came off during some violent maneuvers on a transitional training mission and two days later, the Squadron lost one of its old timers in a combat mission to Blechhammer, Germany.

During the escort mission to the Blechammer oilfields of 22 August, the 52nd FG found the enemy back in the air in force and attempting to defend its territory. High head winds had delayed both the bombers and fighters in route to the rendezvous point over Lake Balaton and possibly gave the *Luftwaffe* the opportunity to scramble a large force of fighters. The 52nd FG first crossed paths with enemy aircraft at 11.20 hrs. As they approached the rendezvous point elements of the 2nd FS saw a huge formation of about 100 Me 109s approaching a flight of B-24s. The mission summary stated: *"The dark slate gray Me 109s were sighted NNE of Brataslava, Czechoslovakia approaching the bombers from the southeast at 28,000 feet and about ten miles behind the B-24s. The enemy aircraft were in no particular formation but two definite groups were noted. The P-51s, which were at 29,000 feet, turned up sun of the E/A and dived on them from the rear. At least half, if not all, of the E/A split-essed for the deck. Two Me 109s were destroyed and one damaged in the ensuing combat."*

Lt. Frank Grey led the attack and his encounter report noted in part: *"Most of them split-essed for the deck but I was able to fire on several of them before they took this evasive action. After damaging one E/A, I saw a Me 109 at 3 o'clock. I turned and closed on him from dead astern. He rolled over and dived and I followed him down to 10,000 feet where I had to break off because of an E/A behind me. But I was able to return to my attack on this E/A and fire several bursts at it. I saw strikes on the left wing root, the left side of the cockpit and fuselage. The Me 109 then went down from about 5000 feet and crashed."*

Grey's wingman, Lt Elmer Mendonca, who seconds earlier warned Grey of the Me 109 on his tail, also jumped into the fray and added another Messerschmitt to the Squadron's score for the day. In the meanwhile, however, things were not going well for the other element of Grey's flight. Lt. James Hoffman and Lt. Harry West also followed the Me 109s into the dive and somehow got separated from each other. Hoffman was last heard to say, *"I have lost my wingman; I see a perfect bounce. I am going down alone."* He was flying P-51D 44-13431 coded QP – V, which had previously been Sully Varnell's QP-E, *"Little Eva."*

Another engagement took place almost simultaneously when the 4th FS encountered about 50 enemy aircraft north-west of Ostrava, Czechoslovakia. Seven of the squadron's Mustangs then turned to the right and climbed to about 24,000 feet. As they reached the attack altitude the mixed force of Me 109s and Fw 190s were positioning themselves to attack the bombers, and the Mustangs of the 4th FS rushed in to break them up. They dived upon a group of about 15 Me 109s which quickly dispersed upon seeing the American fighters honing in on them and headed for the deck. For two of the Me 109s, however, it was an exercise in futility as Lt. Don Stinchcombe closed in and shot them down.

The 4th Fighter Squadron flight line at Madna. (Credit: Paul Ludwig)

After this encounter Stinchcombe's flight continued its return to Madna on a course 15 miles west of the briefed course. As they were nearing the airdrome at Sombatheley, Hungary someone looked down and noticed the field was packed with about 40 aircraft. When no Flak appeared as they closed on the airfield Lt. Bill Hanes then gave the order to go down and attack. During three passes across the field the four Mustangs saw numerous strikes on at least 18 aircraft, eight of which were already burning hulks as the P-51s departed the scene.

Fifteenth Air Force despatched a large force of bombers consisting of the 49th Bomb Wing and four Groups from the 55th Bomb Wing to attack Markersdorf airdrome near St. Pölten, Austria on 23 August and the *Luftwaffe* again made an appearance. The 52nd FG's assignment was to provide high offensive cover over the target area and during the withdrawal of the bomber forces.

A mixed force of Me 109s and Fw 190s struck just as the bombers were crossing the target area and a flight of Me 109s shot down at least one B-24 on a diving pass. A second pass by the enemy aircraft followed soon after but apparently did no damage. The Messerschmitts then escaped into a cloud. About this time the 325th FG intercepted several of the enemy aircraft and shot down six of them, and shortly afterwards the 4th Fighter Squadron got its chance to further reduce the enemy force. At about 12.20 hrs pilots of the 4th spotted a mixed flight of about 25 Me 109s and Fw 190s approaching the bombers from nine o'clock at 24,000 feet. The enemy aircraft circled to the rear of the bombers and began an attack from 3 o'clock level, but broke away when they observed the Mustangs heading toward them. As the Fw 190s tried to reach the cover of clouds they were overtaken and three of them fell to the guns of Lts. Richard Evans, Roy Frye and George Nash. Evans also damaged another Focke-Wulf before it escaped into the clouds. Lt. Nash then completed the 4th Fighter Squadron's scoring for the day by diving to the deck and destroying a Ju 52 parked on the airfield.

At about the same time the 2nd FS encountered German fighters which were preparing to attack the bombers and went after them only to lose them in the clouds. As these bandits disappeared into the clouds, Maj. Bob Curtis observed another flight of Fw 190s and this time one of them did not escape. Curtis' encounter report said in part: *"Then I saw five Fw 190s approaching the bombers on the far right from dead astern. As one of them went in to attack a B-24 I closed on it from 6 o'clock. The E/A then broke off to the left, skidding so the pilot could look behind. When he saw me he rolled the plane over, diving toward the cloud tops. I followed, closing rapidly, and fired a burst from 100 yards, scoring strikes on the fuselage and wing roots. I closed to fifty yards and fired another burst as the E/A went into a cloud. I overshot it in the cloud, pulled off to the left and came out at the side of the cloud. The E/A came out of the bottom of the cloud and went straight into the ground."*

This enemy aircraft was Curtis' 14th and last victory of the war.

The day's action had seen the destruction of 20 German fighters, but at the cost of nine B-24s. The mission summary reported that a spirited defense had been exhibited by an experienced and aggressive enemy force which made maximum use of the clouds to cover its attacks upon the bomber forces. After action reports from the fighter escort commanders stated: *"Pilots reported*

P-51D WD-Q, serial number 44-13261, became Colonel Marion Malcolm's aircraft when he assumed command of the 52nd Fighter Group in late August 1944. The aircraft was named "Queen Marjorie" (Credit: Richard Potter)

that the bombers could have and should have stayed away from the clouds. As it was the bombers flew so close to the clouds that it was virtually impossible to prevent the E/A from attacking the bombers and getting away."

The 4th FS continued its scoring when the 52nd FG traveled to the Paradubice Oil Refinery in Czechoslovakia and claimed three Me 109s in aerial combat. The action took place at 12.40 hrs as the bombers were leaving the target area. A flight of 60 enemy aircraft crossed in front of the bombers at 27,000 feet and then made a 180 degrees diving turn and came up under the bombers from three o'clock. Fifteen Mustangs, which had been flying on the bombers right, immediately dived on the enemy aircraft forcing them to split-S and head toward the deck. This evasive action failed for three of the Me 109s as Lts. Bill Hanes, Bob Deckman and Charles Hudson closed quickly and each of them shot down one German fighter. Seven other enemy aircraft fell in skirmishes with the 325th and 332nd Fighter Groups.

Although the mission was completed without casualties, the 2nd FS lost one of its veteran pilots in a freak accident. Sully Varnell and Robert Confer had flown to Naples and as they were taking off for the return flight to Madna, Confer's Mustang became caught up in the prop wash of a bomber that was warming up its engines and he crashed into a parked B-17. Confer had originally joined the 2nd FS in North Africa as a flying Sergeant and was later commissioned as an officer. The accident happened just a few days after he had returned from a leave in the United States as a newly married man.

A close-up of the name and artwork on Lt. Jim Empey's 5th Fighter Squadron P-51B "Little Ambassador". (Credit: James Empey)

Enemy resistance, on a smaller scale, continued on 25 August during a mission to Czechoslovakia. Thirteen enemy aircraft were claimed that day by Fifteenth Air Force P-38 and P-51 pilots, two of which were credited to Lt. Dwaine Franklin of the 5th FS. In this instance two Fw 190s went under Franklin's flight and apparently the Germans thought they had not been noticed, so they turned and started climbing to attack. Unfortunately for them, they had not gone unnoticed by Franklin who dived upon the Focke-Wulfs and quickly shot them both of them down in flames.

"Scotty III" was assigned to Lt. Bruno Danglemeier of the 2nd Fighter Squadron and coded QP-J, serial number 44-14463. (Credit: USAF)

Lt. Colonel Charles M. Boedeker, who led the raid on Rechlin on 31 August 1944. (Credit: Thomas Thacker)

During the next four days the 52nd Fighter Group flew a fighter sweep, two escort missions and a special mission by the 5th FS and did not encounter any opposition from Axis air forces. The special mission occurred on 29 August. By this date the Russians had overrun and occupied part of Rumania, and the opportunity to rescue some American POWs had now presented itself. With this in mind, pilots of the 5th FS escorted two B-17s delivering supplies to Popesti airdrome and these same Flying Fortresses brought back the first increment of American POWs to be liberated from Rumania. Several of the 52nd FG's pilots were returned on this mission and an additional group was picked up and returned on similar flights during the next few days.

Since the *Luftwaffe* and its Axis partners had not come up to fight in recent days, Fifteenth Air Force fighter groups were dispatched on a series of strafing missions, beginning 30 August, to destroy enemy aircraft and transportation targets on the ground. The mission of 30 August took the 52nd FG to airfields around Kecskemet, Hungary and numerous targets were found. The attack met with tremendous success. Tom Thacker noted in his unpublished history of the 52nd FG: *"A ranging fighter sweep across Hungary left a trail of smoking locomotives, planes burning on the ground and destroyed Flak batteries. On only one of several airfields visited, 24 enemy planes were destroyed or damaged, including ten six-engine Me 323s destroyed. Lt. James Empey, 5th FS, returned that day with his plane covered in soot from an exploding locomotive."*

Bob Curtis recalled that: *"Many Me 323s were parked along one edge of the field, which was bordered by an apple orchard, I fired at one of the 323s through the trees and saw strikes on one of its wings. Then my plane went through the top of a tree and picked up some leaves, twigs and apples in the radiator scoop, but not enough to cause serious trouble. I pulled up and started a sharp turn to the right, but my hand slipped off the stick because the plane was going quite fast and the controls were stiff. The last few frames of the gun camera film showed the plane rolling nearly onto its back. My approach was much too fast because I was worried about ground fire. But no one was hit and we damaged or destroyed several of the Me 323s."*

All aircraft returned safely from this very successful mission which was only a preview of what would unfold on the strategically important mission of 31 August 1944. At this point the Red Army was smashing its way into the Balkans and the Fifteenth Air Force was striking hard at the enemy's lines of communications and oil installations. To further isolate Axis forces in these areas and to prevent their escape Fifteenth Air Force prepared plans to strike enemy held airfields in Rumania. The plan stated: *"Fifteenth Air Force is to strike at the enemy held airdromes in Rumania, destroy their fighters and transport aircraft, thus denying enemy aircraft opposition to our bombers, and prevent not only the bringing in of supplies to bolster their crumbling forces, but deny evacuation of key personnel, with the added effect of rendering valuable assistance to the Russian breakthrough."*

Reconnaissance aircraft had photographed Reghin airdrome and their photographs revealed the airfield was crammed with at least 175 aircraft of various types. It was immediately obvious that a devastating strike against this *"fat"* target would severely cripple Axis forces operating in the area. The 52nd Fighter Group was selected to carry out this important assignment and Lt. Colonel Boedeker, Deputy Group Commander, was selected to lead the mission.

The mission began at 07.40 hrs when Boedeker led 48 Mustangs out of Madna enroute to Rumania. The 5th FS led the flight with the 2nd Fighter Squadron in center position and the 4th FS bringing up the rear. The Group flew at 15,000 feet until it had crossed the mountains of Yugoslavia and reached the Danube River. At this point the 5th and 2nd Fighter Squadrons started a

Lt. Hans Zachmann, 2nd Fighter Squadron, who scored the first of his three kills on 31 August 1944. (Credit: C. G. Jones)

P-51C-10-NT 43-25133, *"Dody"*

**Captain Hans Zachmann,
2nd Fighter Squadron,
52nd Fighter Group,
Madna, Italy, fall 1944**

This is the first of two Mustangs assigned to Hans Zachmann and named for his wife. The second was a P-51D, Dody II, coded QP–H, 44-15116. Zachmann is credited with three aerial victories during his tour of duty with the 2nd Fighter Squadron.

A beautiful view of Hans Zachmann's P-51B "Dody". (Credit: Hans Zachmann)".

Lt. Al McCraw (L) and his P-51B "Mac's Little Squaw". The full code (QP - ?) and serial number are unknown. (Credit: R. Curtis)

gradual descent to the deck while the 4th remained at 14,000 feet to provide top cover. As the Group approached the target, it was apparent that surprise had been achieved and Chuck Boedeker led the 5th FS in the first pass over the field. Just as they came into firing position three Fw 190s appeared in the landing pattern with flaps and wheels down. Boedeker shot one of them down and Lt.Lloyd Hargrave claimed a second, but it was later changed to a probable. The third Fw 190 crash-landed and it was subsequently strafed and destroyed.

The 2nd FS was close on the 4th's heels and destroyed targets on the ground and in the air. Two Me 109s were knocked out of the sky, one each by Lts. Hans Zachmann and Willard Pretzer, while their squadron-mates were attacking targets on the ground. As this encounter was taking place, several other dogfights broke out and three other Me 109s were downed at the cost of one pilot from the 2nd FS and one from the 5th FS. These kills were split among all three squadrons; Lt. Robert Schween, 2nd FS, and Lt. Ralph Gassman, 4th FS, were credited with one Me 109 each, and the third Messerschmitt was shared by Lts. Herman Gardner and Howard Poulin of the 5th FS.

Aerial encounters continued for another 10-15 minutes and resulted in two more kills and three damaged. The victories were credited to Lts. Joseph Klerk (a Do 217) and George Nash (a Me 109), 4th Fighter Squadron. The damaged claims, two Me 109s and a Do 217, were credited to Lts. William Dorsman, Albert McCraw, and John Clarke, 2nd Fighter Squadron. In this series of encounters Lt. Robert Davis, 2nd FS, was killed and Lts. Paul Fraser, 4th FS, and Frank Tomlinson, 2nd FS, became POWs after parachuting from their stricken Mustangs.

All in all, pilots of the three squadrons made at least 12 passes over the airfields at Reglin and destroyed 60-plus aircraft on the ground. (The 52nd FG was officially credited with 60 enemy aircraft in the strafing attacks.) Strafing claims by squadron were as follows: 4th Fighter Squadron – 31, and 15 each for the 2nd and 5th Fighter Squadrons. In addition to these claims, Frank Tomlinson also claimed two more enemy aircraft after being released from his POW camp, bringing the total claims to 63.

So successful was this mission that the 52nd was recommended and later received its second Distinguished Unit Citation for its great victory. Brigadier General Dean Strother included these comments in his recommendation for the award. *"Upon completion of the strafing attacks the group leader reformed his group and led them safely back to base. Sensational success was achieved by the pilots by their superior and skillful attacks as shown by combat films and photo reconnaissance. Airplanes consisting of 29 single engine fighters, 6 twin engine fighters, 10 bombers and dive-bombers, 10 transports and five unidentified type were claimed destroyed on the ground. Many additional aircraft were damaged by the attacking pilots. Nine enemy aircraft were also destroyed and three additional enemy aircraft were damaged in aerial combat.*

"In spite of enemy aircraft and anti-aircraft opposition during the whole period of attack, only one pilot was lost and two were reported as missing. Only the skillful execution and brilliant leadership prevented severe losses on this dangerous mission. The pilots then returned to base, leaving the enemy field a mass of burning aircraft and twisted wreckage.

"The conscientious and devoted efforts of all ground personnel of the 52nd Fighter Group contributed in a substantial measure to the outstanding success of this mission. The painstaking care of the airplanes, their engines and armament by the line personnel proved invaluable. Too much credit cannot be given the pilots themselves who as a result of their aggressive and accurate attacks inflicted such severe damage to the enemy's aircraft and installations."

August 1944 had also been a full and interesting month for the Group's ground personnel. Several notable events took place and probably the two most memorable were the party commemorating the Group's two years overseas service on 18 August and the ceremony on 19 August when the 52nd Fighter Group was presented its first Distinguished Unit Citation. Emil Torvinen, 4th FS, commented about these events in his war diary. *"This evening, August 18, was a time for celebration. The squadron bar was open and free drinks were served for everyone. It was to commemorate our two years on foreign soil. A speech was held by our former commanding officer, Major Robert Levine (now Lt. Colonel). He tried to tell us what a good bunch of boys we had been when we were under his command. Also in the evening's program were singing by our famed doughnut girl (ARC), and strumming on the instruments by remnants of the former Cactus Club which had a number 1 'crack' orchestra."*

Tom Thacker also covered the festivities in his

General Dean Strother presenting Lt. James Empey of the 5th Fighter Squadron, the Distinguished Flying Cross at Madna, 1 July 1944. (Credit: Thomas Thacker)

P-51D-20-NT 44-13160, *Spare Parts*

**Major Ralph "Doc" Watson,
5th Fighter Squadron,
52nd Fighter Group,
Madna, Italy, summer 1944**

The origin of this aircraft's name is not known, but it was assigned to "Doc" Watson shortly after his transfer from the 2nd Fighter Squadron to the 5th Fighter Squadron during the summer of 1944. This aircraft illustrates the third and last phase of the 52nd Fighter Group's markings that featured the yellow rear fuselage and all tail surfaces.

P-51D "Spare Parts" was Major Ralph W. "Doc" Watson's aircraft, coded VF-V, serial number 44-13169. This is one of three Mustangs assigned to Watson while he was a member of the 5th Fighter Squadron. (Credit: Lindal)

High-ranking visitors to Madna: Major-General Nathan Twining (left), Commanding General, Fifteenth Air Force, and Lieutenant-General Barney Oiles, Deputy Chief of the AAF, USA, at Madna, 17 July 1944. (Credit: Thomas Thacker)

history of the group: *"Not only was August a busy month, it marked our second full year overseas. Celebrations were in order. The 5th Squadron threw a beer and watermelon bash of the highest order. HQ detachment opened a new bar, built with native labor and volunteer help from the Amis. Corporal Winn, always versatile, created murals to add a bit of class to the place. The first rain of the autumn season underscored the need for improved roofing but did little to dampen the festivities. Bartenders Patterson and Berry continued to pour as long as a glass was held upright."*

Emil Torvenin's diary provided these comments about the DUC ceremonies: *"On August 19, the 52nd Fighter Group was awarded the Presidential Citation by Major General Nathan Twining, of the 15th Air Force, of which we are part. As it read in the general order, it was for the great achievement of the group in escorting heavy bombers on a mission to Munich, Germany, June 9, 1944."*

Changes of command also took place in August and included the posts of Group Commander and 5th Fighter Squadron Commander. Command of the group was turned over by Lt. Colonel Levine to Colonel Marion Malcolm on 27 August and Major Ralph *"Doc"* Watson replaced Major Edwin Fuller as Commanding Officer of the 5th Fighter Squadron at the end of the month. Lt. Colonel Levine, during his long service within the 52nd FG served as Commanding Officer of the 4th Fighter Squadron and later became Group Commanding Officer on 25 February 1944. He scored three confirmed kills and one probable during the North African campaign. Major Fuller first saw duty in the 2nd Fighter Squadron before transferring to the 5th Fighter Squadron. Fuller's record included four confirmed victories and he damaged three other enemy aircraft.

Now that nearly four months had passed without a move, the 52nd FG personnel began looking at the base at Madna as *"home"* and were constantly working on the shelters and other facilities to try to make life as pleasant as possible. Tom Thacker painted a good picture about life at Madna at this stage of the war: *"Nearly eighteen months earlier, back in Africa, we witnessed convoys of British troops emerging from the desert where they had spent years in combat. We commented on the fact that they looked like gypsy caravans with kitchen equipment and homemade furniture hanging everywhere. They appeared to have as many implements accumulated for comfort as for fighting a war.*

"Late in 1944, we were becoming more like those veterans and, I suspect, like old campaigners from the beginning of history. We were finding ways to make life in the field tolerable, if not enjoyable. Now that we were fairly sure that no moves were imminent, we could create a little comfort for ourselves. Besides, we had seen two winters in the Med and knew how cold, wet and muddy conditions could become. We set to work preparing for it.

"Somebody has remarked that there are only two fit places to fight a war: at an extreme distance or close-up. When at the front, though preferably just out of the line of fire, you gain the freedom and excitement that only some real danger can provide. Sitting in a blacked-out tent listening to an enemy bomber overhead, knowing that its pilot is searching for a glimmer of light to direct his bombs – fear and thrill mingle in your thoughts.

"Supplies are limited near the front but what are available are freely issued and freely shared. Sometimes there were surpluses of certain items. At one time in North Africa we accumulated so large a stock of free cigarettes that exchange rates for eggs and oranges fell substantially. The arrival of a few cans of beer or issue of a couple of candy bars, on the other hand, was a major event.

"We usually had enough coffee but it was often prepared in a five gallon "flimsy" container after the gasoline was rinsed out. Balanced on three stones with a can of raw fuel underneath the water was soon boiling, ready for a pound of coffee. Wait three minutes, add a cup of cold water to separate the grounds and serve. Coffee so prepared was strong and slightly chewy.

"Now, civilization once more was reaching out her clutches to us. With the acquisition of gasoline mini-stoves, we seldom had to heat C-rations on our jeep manifold or drain radiator water for shaving. Boxes over slit trenches reduced the danger from falling in and cut down fly infestation. Toilet tissue was now in ample supply. PX rations were arriving regularly now, though we had to pay for them. Officers even were permitted to buy two bottles of stateside liquor per month, most months.

"The price of these luxuries was that a certain decorum was expected of us. No longer was a pair of underwear shorts considered adequate for the necessary early morning trip out back. Bathing from an iron helmet while standing in front of a tent before God and everybody was discouraged. Some degree of neatness in uniforming was now expected, now that laundry and dry cleaning service was available. Dry cleaning was returned from local facility smelling of the high octane gasoline which we furnished but, in appearance at least, the garments were presentable.

"The military custom of saluting was encouraged, particularly when there were high ranking strangers in camp. After an embarrassing experience involving the Group Commanding Officer and a visiting general, formations were called in each squadron and everybody was warned to salute anything above a captain, particularly around Group HQ. So, for the next 24 hours military tradition was strictly observed. Then matters once more settled back to normal.

"Anyhow, September became much too busy for non-essentials. Added to a heavy flying schedule came the realization that the winter season with its heavy rains and mud was just around the corner. Hammers and saws were worked overtime to erect shacks for protection from the elements. Tents were elevated and plywood outer walls were constructed from drop tank boxes. As this source of material became even more important, rumors were rife that 'on occasion' fuel tanks were jettisoned when not absolutely necessary.

"Bricks too also gained an even higher priority as everybody attempted to install a floor in tents and huts. No abandoned factory or railway station was safe from our roaming demolition crews. The HQ officers had initially appropriated a villa about three miles from the field. The first rain made it apparent that this arrangement would be impossible in a short time, so various structures were constructed to provide living space for the HQ officers adjacent to the flying field.

"Colonel Malcolm and his senior staff members erected a house from tufa block, a rock of volcanic origin quite common in Italy. It was roofed with ceramic tiles from an old barn. Some of us obtained British Nissen huts thanks to the cooperation of some engineers nearby. Soon we were installed more permanently than at any time since Selfridge Field."

Colonel Marion Malcolm, who assumed command of the 52nd Fighter Group in August 1944, replacing Lt. Colonel Robert Levine. (Credit: Thomas Thacker)

Chapter Ten

"Wings in the hedgerow"

Down to Earth

September–1944

During September 1944 the Luftwaffe and its diminishing Axis partners seemed to vanish from the skies over Europe, at least as far as the 52nd FG was concerned. As a result the Group did not score a single aerial victory during the month, and was forced to search for targets on the ground. The first mission of the month was made famous by the unorthodox rescue of Lt. Charles Wilson, 4th Fighter Squadron. The Group, which had just been released from its escort duties, was now free to look for targets of opportunity on the ground and the saga began. Charlie Wilson relates the story in his own words: *"It was September 1, 1944 and we had just unhooked from escorting a formation of B-24s back from a raid on Szelnsk, Hungary. Our eight P-51s were part of 4 Squadron, 52nd FG. I was flying #4 in the second element as our leader, Major James O. Tyler, took us back to an airfield that we had hit two days previously. After destroying a Me 323 on the ground Tyler and his wingman, Major Wyatt P. Exum (on his first ETO combat mission) led us to a large nearby rail marshalling yard. Meeting only sporadic Flak and no enemy air opposition Tyler and Exum went in first, then my element leader, Lt. Fred Straut and I followed. After twenty minutes of strafing, using short bursts, we were low on ammo and fuel. So with a lot of rolling stock in flames, Major Tyler ordered us to form up and head for home. Just then Lt. Straut spotted a moving train and requested permission to attack, and one pass was approved. As we rolled in Straut took the locomotive and I lined up on the #10 freight car. As Straut opened up the engineer blew a gout of steam through the smokestack to simulate a blown boiler. I recognized this old trick and redirected my own attack to the locomotive as Straut broke off. I hosed the cab area with my last 200 rounds of .50 caliber armor piercing/incendiary and the whole thing blew up just as I arrived overhead. Suddenly I had a major problem as the flying debris took out my coolant system and started an intense fire. I zoom-climbed to 5000 feet with the control surfaces mostly burned through and flames from the engine coming back over the cockpit canopy. Time to get the hell out! I cut the switches and fuel off, rolled back the canopy, unstrapped and swung one leg over the side. Just then the fire blew out. New situation! So I climbed back in and radioed Straut that I intended to force land as far away from the nearby town as I could possibly stretch my glide. Just before I pancaked into a plowed field in a cloud of dust, I heard Major Exum transmit, 'I'll be down to get you Charlie!' No shoulder straps, no seat belt and a gun sight inches from my face. I made my best landing to date and my teeth missed the gun sight and the dust flew. I tried to get out and bumped my head on the canopy that had closed during my slide in the dust. Major Exum passed over as he dropped his gear and landed 90 degrees to me. When I got to him I saw a real problem, there was a drainage ditch just ahead of him. The tail wheel was in a rut and he couldn't turn the ship 180 degrees. I put my back under the tail and lifted while he poured the power to it. The tail went the 180 degrees and I was blown about 30 feet away. We tried to get me into the cockpit but it was not going to work. Now another problem arose as men on horseback were getting close and put three holes in the plane with rifle fire and I could see the whites of their eyes. Out came my old .45 and Exum decided it was now or never. I was straddling his neck when the engine hit 60 inches and 3,000 rpm. Away we bounced, finally staggering into the air just in the nick of time and with me about 1/3 out of the cockpit with my loaded and cocked .45 in my hand. Major Exum asked me to throw it overboard and started climbing west with Lt. Straut on our wing. Major Tyler spent his last ammo burning my P-51.*

"We had no radio, and the CO was our wingman as we climbed to 12,000 feet. Lt. Straut climbed to 25,000 feet and got 'Big Fence', our radar to give him a direct heading to Madna. Now 400 miles later we had to make a choice. The right wing tank and fuselage are dry and I read about 25 gallons in the left wing tank. We have (to fly) 100 over water to Madna and we had to decide whether to try it or make an emergency landing in Yugoslavia. I told Exum that we could make it! As we touched down on a straight in approach from the Adriatic Sea, we were forced off the runway by Major Tyler and Lt. Straut who were landing "dead stick" from the opposite direction. Major Exum received the Silver Star for his heroism and my undying gratitude and admiration."

Lt. Charles E. Wilson, 4th Fighter Squadron. (Credit: Charles Wilson)

The tower operators were upset at first because they were not fully aware of the situation, but since everybody got down safely and no damage was done, all was forgiven.

On 2 September, the 52nd FG escorted B-24s attacking airdromes near Nis, Yugoslavia, met no aerial opposition and when released from the bombers, began looking for targets on the ground. In doing so Lt. John Ondocsin, 2nd FS, had a hair-raising experience as the Mustangs swooped in low over Yugoslavia. As he and his element leader, Lt. Willard Pretzer, flew along some valleys, Ondocsin was kept busy watching both his leader and the terrain. At one point he looked over to check his leader's position and then looked back, only to find himself heading straight for a tree on top of a hill. He jerked the stick back, quickly enough to completely avoid the tree. However, the bottom of his Mustang hit the treetop and shortly afterwards Ondocsin noticed his engine temperature was increasing rapidly. In an attempt to bring it down, he opened

Two views of how Major Exum and Lt. Wilson squeezed into the single-seat cockpit of a Mustang during Exum's daring rescue of Wilson who had been shot down. (Credit: Thomas Thacker)

Captain Fred Ohr, Commanding Offiver of the 2nd Fighter Squadron and George, the Squadron mascot looking over the Squadron emblem. George was named after General George S. Patton. (Credit: Thomas Thacker)

the air scoop shutter as far as it would go and this action at least kept the engine temperature under the red line. After nursing his crippled ship across the Adriatic Sea he prepared for a requested straight-in landing at Madna or bailing out, whatever the case might be. The tower told him to *"come on in"* but as Ondocsin landed his engine froze. After the Mustang was towed off the runway and parked he saw the problem. The radiator was jammed with leaves and tree branches, the carburetor scoop was also full of foreign objects, and the bottom of his aircraft was *"painted leaf green from nose to tail."*

This mission also turned out to be the last combat mission of the war for Maj. Bob Curtis, Commanding Officer of the 2nd FS. At the completion of his tour of duty Curtis, with a record of 14-1-5, ranked as the 52nd FG 's second highest scoring Ace and still remained so at war's end. He joined the squadron in April 1943 and during the course of flying 148 combat missions earned the Distinguished Service Cross, the Silver Star, two Distinguished Flying Crosses and nineteen Air Medals. Replacing Curtis as commanding officer of the 2nd FS was Capt. Fred Ohr. The squadron diary noted: *"Capt. Ohr, our veteran pilot, took over command of the squadron when Major Curtis went off operations. A better choice could not have been made."* Capt. Ohr, an Ace himself, joined the Squadron in North Africa and scored his first victory in April 1943.

The mission of 3 September turned out to be a costly one for the 52nd FG. The Group had returned to the area of Nis, Yugoslavia on an escort/strafing mission and although it succeeded in destroying numerous targets on the ground, six aircraft and pilots were lost in the process. Three of these pilots were killed and the other three eventually returned to Madna. Two of the aircraft lost were assigned to the 2nd FS and apparently Lt. Cowan (KIA) was a victim of target fixation. His wingman later reported that Cowan had spotted a tank column and went after it in a head on attack. Lt. Leary recalled: *"I was on his left, but not very far out, and saw him fly right into the lead tank. The plane and tank exploded and the impact started a chain reaction down the line, destroying several tanks and other vehicles."*

Joe Randerson of the 2nd FS was strafing trains and highway traffic near the town of Tresnjevia, Yugoslavia when his Mustang was hit by small arms fire from the ground. Just as he was pulling up from strafing a locomotive his engine suddenly stopped. Being far too low to bail out, Randerson selected an open field and made a wheels-up landing. The field turned out to be a sandy marsh and his aircraft quickly came to a halt,

Lt. Joe Randerson, 2nd Fighter Squadron, who was shot down and seriously injured on 3 September. He was rescued by partisans and eventually returned to Madna. (Credit: Joe Randerson)

smashing his face into the gun-sight and knocking him out for a short period. Upon awakening, he realized that his aircraft was on fire; he had to get out of it quickly. After freeing himself of the harnesses and climbing out he discovered two Serbian farmers standing at the end of the wing. Convincing them that he was an American, they agreed

Captain Fred Ohr's P-51D "Marie". The Mustang was coded 'QP-Q', and also displays the "Ace of Spades" flight emblem. (Credit: Dave Menard via Fred Bamburger)

Lt. Robert D. Fulks, 5th Fighter Squadron, who was shot down over Yugoslavia and eventually evaded back to Madna with help from Chetnik partisans. (Credit: Robert Fulks)

to help him. Lt. Randerson knew that he had been badly burned, but did not realize the extent of his burns until the Serbs grabbed and raised his arms so that he could wave back to Capt. Schween, who was circling, and the skin came off his arms. Then his badly burned hands and arms began to swell and it was necessary to cut his gloves and bracelet away. The farmers then loaded him into a two-wheeled cart and he was taken to a barn where he stayed for the first two weeks of his two month stay in Yugoslavia.

Horribly burned, Lt. Joe Randerson fell under the tender care of Nada Vidasave Mihalovich, the daughter-in-law of Draza Mihailovich, who had been the leader of the Yugoslavian resistance until Tito pushed him aside. With a minimum of medical supplies and only two bandages which she washed and rotated after each use, she did her best to nurse the ailing flyer back to health, and at the same time keep him hidden from the Germans. After a move to Glavinci, Serbia he was placed in a real bed which was a definite morale booster. As he began to recuperate and feel better the locals began to pay visits and try to give him gifts of food, in gestures of thanks for helping liberate their country.

Sometime in October the Russians came and instructed Nada that Randerson should go with them for better medical care, but after three days of no care from them, he returned to Nada. Eventually he was well enough to travel to Belgrade and on 7 November he attempted to get help at the American Embassy, but without much luck. (Here he met Robert D. Fulks, 5th FS, who had been shot down on the same date). Later that same day, however, his luck took a dramatic and positive change, as Draza Mihailovich had arranged for a C-47 to land and take him to Italy. Before leaving Lt. Randerson, gave Nada the chocolate candy and cigarettes that he received at the Embassy along with a one dollar bill with his home address on it. During the evening of 7 November 1944 Joe Randerson was flown back to the American lines, hospitalized, and after a long stay during which he underwent numerous skin grafts and other treatments, he turned down an offer to go home and returned to his Squadron. Returning to combat he completed 49 missions by war's end.

(A wonderful postscript to this story is that Joe was later able to repay the debt to Nada by helping get visas for her and her two children to move to the United States in 1949. Sadly before this happened both her husband and her father-in-law had been murdered by Tito's police).

The mission flown by Robert D. Fulks, 5th FS, on 3 September ended very similarly to Joe Randerson's, except that his injuries were not nearly as severe. His diary noted: *"Each of the squadrons had sixteen aircraft and would fly as a group to an area near Sarajevo, then each squadron would proceed to their assigned targets. Our target was to be a marshalling yard at Lapovo, a small town south and a little east of Belgrade. Each leader explained their mission. Capt. Schaub, the intellegence officer, explained what we could expect if we were shot down and issued each of us an escape kit with a map, $48.00 in American money, five pieces of quick energy candy and three no doze pills to keep us awake.*

"We were taken to our planes where we planned an 0830 takeoff. I was with the group leader and the first to take off. Major Watson and his wingman, Lt. McCloskey were the first to take off. Seconds later, as element leader, my wingman, Lt. Varnum and I took off to join Major Watson's flight. We made one big circle around the field while the other 44 planes of the 5th, 2nd, and 4th Squadrons joined us in about ten minutes.

"We then headed for our targets in Yugoslavia which took a little over an hour's flight. When we were about 75 miles from our target, each of the squadrons headed toward their assignment. We turned toward Lapovo where Major Watson's flight was to make the first strike with the 12 other planes acting as top cover. As we approached we could see one steam locomotive, two oil cars and several boxcars. We made three passes without any evidence of ground fire. Steam was pouring out of the locomotive where 50 caliber API's had pierced the firebox causing it to explode. The terrain allowed us to attack 90 degrees or across the target from east to west, let down low and return from west to east. The Germans, most of the time, used tracer bullets, which can be seen. Because we did not see any signs of ground fire we took the liberty to make several passes even though the targets had been hit and apparently destroyed.

"I made one more pass over the locomotive and was letting down to about nine feet above the ground when my airspeed indicator exploded. I felt a thud and my engine had no power. My airspeed was over 400 mph so I was able to glide over a mile from the target. I was headed east and found a cornfield that was only hope for a wheels up landing. Without flaps and an airspeed indicator I could tell I was too hot to land. I could hear the wings clipping the tops out of the corn but it did not want to settle in. I don't suppose it did much good but I fired my four 50 caliber guns to help slow it down and then flew it into the ground. All this time a hedgerow began to loom in front of me and was coming up fast. The fuselage found an opening and went through, leaving the wings in the hedgerow.

"Somehow my radio was still working. I called to say I was okay and was getting out of my plane. I started to leave but went back for my parachute. After my squadron saw I was safe and clear, came down and strafed my plane and destroyed the radio crystal to keep the Germans from getting the frequency."

At this point, Lt. Fulks, did not realize that he had taken a severe blow to the head and

Lt. Gordon Varnum, 5th Fighter Squadron, and his P-51B "The Dirty Dirk". The aircraft codes VF - ? and serial number are unknown. (Credit: James Empey)

Lt. Robert Fulks, 5th Fighter Squadron, and his Chetnik rescuers. (Credit: Robert Fulks)

Colonel Marion Malcolm's "Queen Marjorie", coded WD-Q, serial number 44-13261. Note a fin strake has been added to this P-51D. (Credit: Air Force Museum)

his scalp was laid open when he crash-landed. Suddenly he began to feel extremely tired and laid down to rest. After awakening from a short nap, he thought he had gone blind because his eyes were *"glued shut"* by dried blood from his scalp wound. Before long he had his wits about him again and cleaned his eyes and face and moved out of the cornfield and on to a road. As he came to a curve in the road he heard voices, retreated back into the cornfield and peeked out. What he saw was two families having a picnic and he decided to approach them. It was an excellent decision as the people gave him food and drink and then took him to a farm house and cleaned his wound. Later on in the day a number of curious neighbors dropped in to see the American. From here he was taken to another home several miles away and began a two month stay living among the Chetnik resistance fighters of Yugoslavia.

The situation in Yugoslavia at this time was, to say the least, unstable. The Chetnik partisans led by General Mihailovich and the communist resistance fighters loyal to Marshall Tito were both fighting the Germans and each other at the same time. Robert Fulks recalled: *"We had been briefed before the mission that there were two political factions in Yugoslavia but I had no idea they were having a civil war. I was with the Chetnik resistance fighters led by General Draza Mihailovich, who was the military leader of Serbia after King Peter fled the country to England, in exile. The other factions were communists backed by Russia. Both fought against the Germans, helped Allied airmen, but it seemed that most of their fighting was against each other.*

"I spent the next two months living with several different Serbian families, avoiding Germans, waiting for evacuation to Italy and getting involved in some of their civil war battles. (All this time) The Chetniks were making arrangements for me and several other American airmen to be picked up by American C-47s at a pre-determined point."

Finally, on 7 November 1944 he was taken to the American Embassy in Belgrade and met Joe Randerson. That night they were flown back to Bari, Italy for a medical check-up and debriefing. Since his wound was not serious, he was approved to return to Madna, and arrived there on 10 November. After spending the next two weeks at Madna undergoing interrogations about his escape and conditions in Yugoslavia, Lt. Robert D Fulks said his good-byes to his friends in the 5th FS and headed back to the USA.

Escort missions resumed on 4 September when the Group escorted B-24s to Trento, Italy but Axis air forces did not make an appearance. Some bombers were lost to Flak, however, as noted in his log by Lt. Emerson of the 2nd FS: *"B-24 exploded when hit by Flak in the target area."*

Records are not clear as to whether or not the Group flew missions on 5 and 6 September, but during the evening of 7 September, the 4th FS was selected to fly an unusual mission in support of RAF Beaufighters. The orders stated that eight Mustangs would take off early in the morning of 8 September and proceed to an RAF base near the front lines in Italy. The orders were cryptic in that they stated only that after arrival at the British base, a joint mission with Beaufighters was planned. Major James O. *"Tim"* Tyler of the 4th FS was selected to lead the mission and the second element of the eight Mustangs would be led by Group CO, Colonel Marion Malcolm. *"Tim"* Tyler described the early stages of the mission. *"The temporary strip at our base (Madna) had no lights for night operations, so for their early departure, vehicles were lined up along the runway with lights turned on to guide the planes during take-off. All eight aircraft left the strip without incident and landed at the assigned British field just at sun-up. The American pilots were taken directly to an operations room where they learned for the first time what was expected of them."*

The mission, they learned during the briefing, was to sink the Italian liner Rex. Intelligence sources had determined in August that the Germans were planning the destruction of the important harbor at Trieste, and they did not want it to fall into Allied hands. The German plan was to scuttle the Rex at its entrance, thereby blocking the port from further use. As increased activity around the Rex was noted during the last few days of August and Allied photo-reconnaissance aircraft kept a close watch on this work. On 4 September, an RAF B-26 crew noticed that the Rex was being towed away from her pier and out to sea. This action triggered the attack plan.

The attack was launched from Falconara Airfield on the Adriatic coast and the initial attack wave comprised eight Mustangs of the 4th FS and eight Beaufighters from 272

P-51D-5-NA 44-13442, *Little Eva*

**Lt. Charles E. Wilson,
4th Fighter Squadron,
52nd Fighter Group,
Madna, Italy, fall 1944**

Lt. Charles Wilson scored one aerial victory, over an Me 109 on 12 October 1944, during his tour of duty with the 4th Fighter Squadron. On the right side of the nose is the name Miss Betty B, and on the right side of the canopy rail is the name Lt. ? Lyon.

Lt. Charles Wilson's P-51D "Little Eva" coded WD-Z, serial number 44-13442 awaiting its next mission form Madna.
(Credit: Charles Wilson)

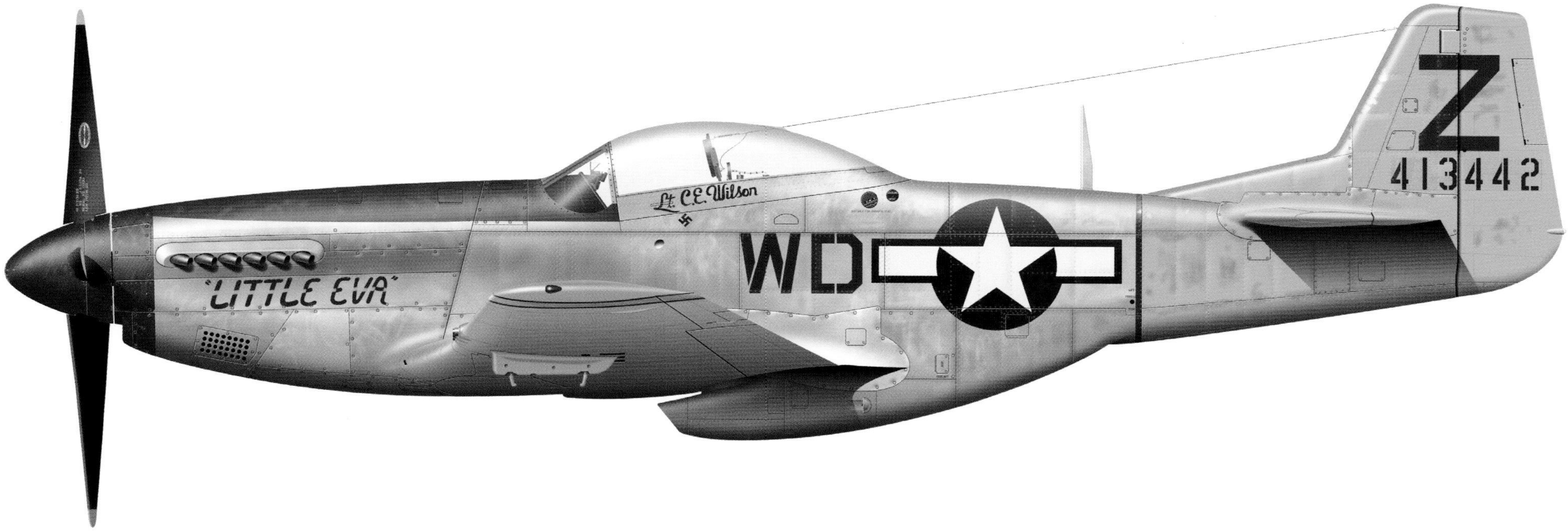

The 2nd Fighter Squadron's Captain Daniel Zoerb, in his P-51D "Hey Rube! IV". This aircraft was coded QP-U, serial number 44-14227. (Credit: Daniel Zoerb via Jeff Ethell)

Dan Zoerb's "Hey Rube! IV" after its hard landing in Rumania on 8 September 1944. (Credit: Denes Bernad)

Squadron, Royal Air Force. The pre-mission briefing was a little disconcerting to the pilots, as Lt. Charles Wilson noted: *"The briefing was typically British, crude and to the point. I did not expect to come back."*

The briefing officer had stated that the Rex would have an escort of one or two destroyers, and the Rex itself was armed with anti-aircraft guns. The attack was to be initiated with a strafing attack by Major Tyler's element of four Mustangs in the hopes that it would clear the way for the Beaufighter's rocket and strafing attack. With the anticipated Flak defenses, the pilots were justifiably concerned about their chances of survival.

With these thoughts in mind the attack force took off and headed at wavetop-level toward the Rex. Major Tyler gave this account of what followed: *"The possibility that single-engine fighters might be called upon to attack destroyers and perhaps other defenses as well was not a comforting thought. However, we took off as directed and followed the prescribed course at minimum altitude until we arrived in the target area. We climbed to 6000 feet. Directly in front of us was one of the largest ships I had ever seen. It was moving, though slowly. Then came the best possible news: there were no destroyers or other craft in the area."*

After radioing the Beaufighter crews of this news Tyler told Colonel Marion Malcolm to cover him and then took his flight of four Mustangs down to strafe: *"We peeled off and approached the vessel at a fairly steep angle and at right angle to her course. I had attacked vessels before and so opened fired at what I thought was the proper distance. Curiously, I didn't see any hits. Then I discovered that I was shooting into the ocean. The huge size of the target had created an illusion of proximity that was confusing."*

After making some corrections he and his flight continued the attack and raked the ship with machine gun fire. As they passed over the Rex, Maj. Tyler noticed that there were no anti-aircraft guns on her and that all personnel that had been on deck had disappeared. He then relayed this information to the Beaufighters and they began their assault while Colonel Malcolm's flight covered them. During the next 40 minutes 272 Squadron ripped the helpless liner apart. The Rex took 59 rocket and 3,200 20 mm cannon hits and burst into flames. Numerous hits below the waterline also resulted in flooding within the ship and she slowed as her crew fought desperately to put out the fires and stop the flooding. With all of their ammunition expended, the Beaufighters and their Mustangs then headed back to base. The Rex had a few minutes of peace, but it was shattered about an hour after the first attack was completed. Beaufighters of 39 Squadron RAF and 16 Squadron, South African Air Force arrived on the scene and put another 64 rockets and 4,000 rounds of 20 mm fire into her. When they departed the scene, the ravaged ship was already in its death throes and that afternoon the Rex rolled over and sunk in the shallow waters off Capodistria. All of the attacking aircraft returned safely to their bases.

The other squadrons also flew special missions on 8 September. The 2nd and 5th Fighter Squadrons escorted B-17s from Bucharest, Rumania after they had picked up Americans and other friendly personnel. One aircraft was lost due to accident when Dan Zoerb's Mustang, *"Hey Rube IV"*, experienced fuel pressure problems just as he was making a low pass over the Rumanian airfield to observe the loading of the former POWs into the B-17s. The engine lost power, and he tried to drop his wing tanks prior to making an emergency landing. The tanks refused to fall away and *"Hey Rube IV"* landed hard, buckling both wings. After reviewing the sad sight of his Mustang, he stayed overnight with the Rumanians and was asked by Rumanian pilots to join them that night for a banquet of sheep's head soup! The next day he returned to Italy as a passenger on a B-17.

Three of the 2nd FS's Aces, Captains Sully Varnell, Barry Lawler, and Art Johnson, departed for the United States during the first week of September and a few days later they were followed by another Ace, Major Bob Curtis. This outstanding quartet would be missed. Between them they had destroyed a total of 50.5 enemy aircraft and probably destroyed or damaged many others. At about the same time new pilots reported in at HQ, 2nd FS to take part in future actions. This was also happening in the 4th FS in September as eight new pilots reported in and several of the veteran pilots rotated back to the US. The same rotation policy applied to the enlisted men as numerous men from all three squadrons earned their points and had the chance to go home after a long overseas tour. Others took the opportunity to go to a rest camp Emil Torvinson, 4th FS, noted in his diary of the war: *"Rest camp had become quite popular with the men of our squadron by*

The He 111 used by a Hungarian delegation to fly to Italy. American engineers have already removed the engine and the outer left wing, possibly in preparation for shipment to the USA. (Credit: Thomas Thacker)

now. If one was lucky, he was able to go to the Isle of Capri, where there was comfort even for the most war-weary. The most common and enjoyable place, however, was in Rome, where two or three men usually left for a five-day period of recuperation. Most of the fellows seemed to need another five days to recuperate from the hectic life of the rest camp."

The missions of 10 and 13 September were both uneventful bomber escorts to Linz, Austria, and Odertal, Germany. The next mission was on 17 September and it was another special mission to pick up downed pilots in Czechoslovakia. This mission was carried out to perfection, with the B-17s delivering supplies to the underground forces in the area and bringing back the American aviators that they had rescued. One of the Group's Mustangs experienced troubles on the trip and had to be left in Czechoslovakia, and its pilot returned in one of the B-17s. During the remainder of the month, the 52nd FG flew six escort missions to various targets and encountered no opposition except Flak. Lt. Paul Swanson, 2nd FS, was downed by Flak on 20 September on the mission to Malacky, Czechoslovakia while the squadron was at low altitude in search of strafing targets. After bailing out of his crippled Mustang, Swanson was rescued almost immediately by members of the Czech underground and after a few days arrangements to evacuate him were made and Lt. Swanson was flown back to Italy.

A very unusual event unfolded on 23 September and it was noted in several diaries. The most detailed version of this event was provided by Tom Thacker in his unpublished history of the 52nd Fighter Group, and later augmented in an article he wrote for the Friend's Bulletin of the Air Force Museum:

"Several, including myself, were riding in a jeep, destined for the briefing room where a movie was scheduled. Overhead, a multi-engined plane was flying with no apparent pattern. Also, the engine sounds were unusual—one gets to recognize different aircraft in this manner. I leaned out to see past the top of the jeep and recognized it as a German Heinkel 111. Since it appeared not to be threatening, we continued on our way.

"As we approached the flying field, the plane had dropped to perhaps 1000 feet and appeared to want to land. Just then an anti-aircraft battery commenced to fire. (Until then most of us didn't realize that there were any guns around our field). The He 111 went into a descent away from us to the south.

"We followed. It was getting dark, but about a half an hour later we located the plane where it had landed, wheels up, in a field. Its occupants, the pilot, his wife and two other men, were standing beside it. In broken English they asked to speak to a senior officer. They admitted to being Hungarian, but otherwise were noncommittal.

"They were closeted with our Group CO for a short while later. He placed a call to HQ, 15th AF and was instructed to talk to nobody about his 'guests'. They were strictly isolated until the next morning when General Twining's plane came to pick them up. We never saw them again or learned who they were.

"If rumors are to be trusted, we had observed an attempt by one or more senior Hungarian officials to negotiate a separate armistice with the Allies. Very likely, the Germans learned what was happening and took over the Government to prevent such an action. History only confirms that Hungary capitulated at the same time as Germany, about eight months later. The He 111 was moved to the base "bone yard" where it remained for about two weeks when specific orders were received from 15th AF to destroy it."

Years later, in 1991, Tom Thacker learned the rest of the story. The rumors had been true. The occupants of the He 111 were Hungarians seeking a separate peace. The crew consisted of the pilot, Capt. John Majoros and his wife, General Naday, emissary of Admiral Horthy of Hungary, and Lt. Colonel Charles T. Howie of the South African Army. Lt. Colonel Howie was brought along to add credence to the Hungarian delegation. He had been captured in North Africa, sent to Germany as a POW and escaped from a Stalag in Silesia to Hungary. In Hungary, Howie had joined an underground organization and later made contact with members of the Hungarian Government. His daughter-in-law, Clareran Howie, related the story to Tom Thacker in a letter in which it was stated that he was asked by Admiral Horthy during the summer of 1944 to go with General Naday to try and negotiate a separate peace. Their search for someone to talk to continued until they made it to the office of Field Marshal *"Jumbo"* Wilson, the Supreme Allied Commander in the MTO where they were debriefed and finally delivered the message from Admiral Horthy. Negotiations were carried out, but the surrender of Hungary could not be arranged. Lt. Colonel Howie, on the other hand, now had his ticket home.

The Hungarian delegation at Madna. From left to right: Lt. Colonel Charles Howie, a South African former German POW who escaped to Hungary and worked with the underground forces; Colonel Marion Malcolm; and General Naday, a Rumanian emissary. (Credit: Thomas Thacker)

Chapter Eleven

"Mud almost everywhere"

General "Mud" Becomes the Enemy

September 1944–March 1945

Captain Paul Steinle's P-51D "Vicious Aloysius" at rest at Madna during the fall of 1944. The code is WD-T, serial number 44-13323. (Credit: Paul Ludwig)

Missions, for all practical purposes, ended on 23 September when heavy rains began to fall and clouds grounded the 52nd FG. As the torrential rains continued, Madna and its surrounding area were turned into a sea of mud. The incessant mud affected everything including morale. Productive activity was severely hampered, as was any vehicular movement. Tom Thacker noted: *"Ground transportation became a major problem. Since Palermo our pipeline for spare vehicle parts had been very slim. The move in May plus heavy activity since had just about worn out our trucks and jeeps. Most of our 'liberated' fleet from North African days had long since been abandoned. Now the weather was just about the last straw. Brakes, particularly, became inoperative as the mud ruined the linings and drums. Luckily in the mud we could operate without brakes; we simply had nothing that could be safely driven on the paved roads."*

The grumbling about morale was also prevalent in the 2nd Fighter Squadron's monthly report: *"The morale of the squadron was at its lowest this month, mainly because of the marked drop in mail. After receiving the best mail service since being overseas the squadron is at a loss to discover what in hell has caused the scarcity of letters. The bad weather and the resultant operational inactivity also has had its effect on morale. If there were a fair-sized town nearby we would at least have a place to go and get out of camp. We also take a very dim view of the announcement by 15th AF that stoves will not be available for tent quarters. Recreation is practically nil due to the bad weather."*

Seen from left to right in this photograph are Major "Doc" Watson, Commanding Officer, 5th Fighter Squadron, and Lt. Colonel Charles Boedecker, Deputy Group Commander. They are seen with Boedecker's P-51D "Doris Fay II", coded VF-H, serial number unknown. (Credit: Robert Fulks)

Another veteran pilot and Ace, Major James O. Tyler, 4th FS, left the Group and headed for home at the end of September. At the time of his departure, Tyler had destroyed 8.5 enemy aircraft in aerial combat and many others on the ground during his 125 combat missions. Major James Wiley became the 4th's next commanding officer on 2 October 1944.

The foul weather continued into October 1944 and disrupted missions for the first days of the month. The first engagement with enemy aircraft since 31 August occurred on the mission of 7 October. On that date the 52nd FG escorted B-17s to Czechoslovakia during the penetration and over-target phases, and then were responsible for shepherding six B-17s on a *"special mission"* to Hungary on the return trip. The 5th FS led the penetration escort and upon reaching the target area, one flight led by Lt. Colonel Charles Boedeker went down and circled over the target at about 800 feet. The mission summary related the encounter: *"At 1405 hours as a single flight of P-51s (2 had left due to fuel shortage) was circling the target, four brown mottled Fw 190s were observed heading west at 700 feet. These enemy aircraft were about four miles south of the target. The P-51s gave chase, causing one to crash and explode. (This kill was credited to Lt. Colonel Boedeker). Two additional Fw 190s got on the tail of one of the P-51s which successfully eluded the enemy aircraft by going up*

The photographer certainly did not have the later day historian in mind when he took this photograph! The Mustang in the right foreground is more than likely Robert Anderson's "The Bar Fly" and the next aircraft is Walter Zilinski's "Lou Lou Belle" with its name neatly covered by the prop of the "Bar Fly"! (Credit: James Empey)

through a solid overcast, which was at 1000 feet. The P-51s had no difficulty in overtaking and also drawing away from the E/A."

All of the 52nd's aircraft returned safely to base.

The miserable fall weather continued to plague 15th AF during the next few days. The bombers attacked targets in Italy on 10 October, but available records do not indicate the 52nd participated in the mission. On the following day the Group headed to Hungary to strafe enemy airdromes, but severe weather turned them back south of Lake Balaton. Lt. Roy Carlson, 2nd FS, even noted that he saw St. Elmo's fire dancing around the propeller of his Mustang.

The return trip to the enemy airdromes around Seregelyes, Hungary on 12 October was a roaring success. Fifty-four Mustangs departed Madna at 11.57 hrs enroute to the target. Three turned back as the flight progressed, one was an abort due to mechanical problems and the other two were spares. The remaining 51 held course for the attack scheduled for 14.00 hrs. The 5th FS led the formation while the 4th trailed and the 2nd FS provided high cover. The formation flew at 12,000/13,000 feet until reaching Lake Balaton and then started a gradual descent through the overcast and leveled off on the deck. The haze in the target area was so dense that the 2nd FS, as high cover, flew at about 15,00 feet. As the two attacking squadrons neared the target they split up as planned but the thick haze caused further separation of flights within the two squadrons. The 5th FS, flying line abreast made the first pass on the airfield, but the 4th FS, which was following, became split in the haze and only six of its aircraft strafed the airdrome on the first pass.

Major Wiley's flight, which had become separated, happened upon a flight of 25 enemy aircraft that were apparently preparing to land and attacked just a few moments prior to the beginning of the strafing attack. Four Me 109s fell under the guns of Major Wiley's flight, with Wiley claiming two of them. The other kills were credited to Lts. Charles Hudson (who also claimed a He 111 as damaged), and Lt. Charles Wilson. Lt. Wilson reported his kill as follows: *"We were approaching the target close to the ground when approximately 25 enemy fighters were sighted, flying at 100 feet. My wingman and I veered to the right and became separated. I circled and was suddenly joined in formation by two Me 109s which flew beside me for a short time. I immediately made every effort to get behind them and as I did so, one of the aircraft broke away and disappeared. I chased the remaining one, firing short bursts and getting strikes on his fuselage from 300 yards to point blank range. Catching up with him on the other side of a hill, he pulled up and attempted a loop, but the plane couldn't make it and crashed into the ground and burned."*

One other enemy aircraft was shot down, at about the same time, by Lt. Stanley Bricker of the 5th Fighter Squadron.

While these aerial engagements and strafing attacks were proceeding, Capt. Ohr, leading the 2nd FS, decided that the wrong airfield had been attacked and led six Mustangs of his squadron onward for a short distance. He then made a 180 degrees right turn and approached the target from the northeast. The remainder of the action is described in the mission summary: *"Before reaching*

An excellent photograph of Lt. James Johnson's "Hazel II" undergoing some maintenance at Madna. (Credit: Paul Ludwig collection)

"Little Butch" was assigned to Lt. John Beard of the 2nd Fighter Squadron, and was coded QP-R, serial number unknown. (Credit: R. C. Curtis)

the airdrome these latter (Ohr's) planes thoroughly strafed six trucks, a bus, and an odd looking locomotive, then proceeded to make repeated attacks on the airdrome. A fact that appears to bear out Capt. Ohr's original conclusion that an airdrome north of the briefed target had been attacked by the lead squadrons is the observation that only one aircraft was seen burning in the center of the field when Capt. Ohr's flight made their first pass. The 5th and 4th Squadrons reported that on their very first pass many planes were set afire. The single burning plane seen by Capt. Ohr is believed to be one of the two planes shot down by Major Wiley in aerial combat just before the strafing attack. Capt. Ohr reports that after his first pass, he saw other formations attacking the same airdrome.

"All pilots that strafed airdromes are agreed that irrespective of whether they were on the same airdromes from 70 to 100 A/C were seen dispersed in revetments and in the open, both around the perimeters of the A/D and in the fields, which were well camouflaged. Ju 88s predominated, with many Fw 190s also observed. Hangers at the target were observed to contain A/C; these were thoroughly shot up during the strafing, as were barracks and a radar station.

"All pilots are agreed that a very large number of aircraft were burning when the 51s finally left the area, after making four to eight separate attacks. Other targets which received effective attention were river barges, pilot boats and locomotives.

"One flight of the 5th Squadron while returning from the target made one strafing attack at an airdrome 12-15 miles south of the target and observed that P-51s of the 332nd were also attacking this same target; where at least 20 undamaged aircraft were parked in deep revetments. Eight fires were seen on this A/D before the 5th Squadron made its attack. A locomotive with 25 cars at 4705N 1842E was strafed and the locomotive was seen to burst."

The attack had produced tremendous results. The 52nd Fighter Group was credited with the destruction of five enemy aircraft in aerial combat, 53 enemy aircraft destroyed in strafing attacks, plus numerous highway, rail and water vehicles. Not a single aircraft was lost in this attack, but several of the Group's Mustangs returned to Madna with bullets holes to be repaired. For his leadership and initiative during the attack, Capt. Fred Ohr was awarded the Distinguished Flying Cross.

The mission of 13 October to Blechhammer, Germany cost the 2nd FS Lt. Willard Pretzer,

The flight line of the 5th Fighter Squadron at Madna. Note the first two aircraft do not yet have the 'VF' applied to their fuselage, but personal markings are already there. The first aircraft is named "Winsome Gal" (pilot unknown), and the second is Major "Doc" Watson's "Spare Parts". (Credit: James Empey)

Lt. Matthew Bruder's P-51D "My Ronnie" at Madna. It was coded VF-J. Bruder was killed in action while at the controls of this Mustang on 23 October 1944. (Credit: Robert Fulks)

who had to bail out over Czechoslovakia because of a glycol leak and he became a POW. An escort mission to Blechhammer on 14 October was already in process when the 52nd FG received a mission cancellation message by R/T as it headed toward the target. The rest of this mission contains a little controversy due to conflicting recollections. In his unpublished history of the 52nd FG, Tom Thacker stated that after the mission was canceled the Group was instructed to proceed toward the original target area and strafe any worthwhile targets. His commentary noted:

Lt. Hugh Ottley, 4th Fighter Squadron, flew his first combat mission on 21 October 1944. (Credit: Hugh Ottley)

"South of Lake Balaton, in the vicinity of Szekesfehevar, Hungary, they found good hunting. Destroyed were 31 aircraft on the ground, 28 locomotives plus 14 more locomotives damaged, along with three trucks, four oil cars, and 47 freight cars. Our cost was two P-51s: Lt. Raymond H. Mann, 5th Squadron, missing and later declared dead; Lt. Thomas C. Leary, 2nd Squadron who was hit by Flak, bailed out, became a POW and was freed by Patton's Third Army at the end of the war."

In the book *The American Beagle Squadron* Capt. Fred Ohr and Lt. Jack Beard were of the opinion that only the 2nd Fighter Squadron continued onwards. Both Ohr and Beard stated that a blinding thunderstorm blew in from the Adriatic while the 2nd FS, the lead squadron, was lined up on the runway for takeoff. A request was made to Colonel Marion Malcolm to delay the take-off, but it was denied and somehow the 2nd got off the ground and finally popped out of the storm clouds at 20,000 feet. Lt. Beard noted at this point that he thought he heard a recall to base message from the Commanding Officer through the static on his radio, but Capt. Ohr, whose radio wasn't working properly, heard things differently.

Fred Ohr, in the *American Beagle Squadron*, noted: *"We were the first squadron to become airborne. Before the other two squadrons could take off, or while they were in the process of taking off, the Group CO radioed us that the mission had been canceled. But the transmission was full of static and although I heard him say that the mission had been scrubbed, I thought that he then said we could proceed to targets of opportunity. But the later transmission might have been the suggestion of one of our eager pilots and not that of the CO."*

Capt. Ohr then switched the Squadron to a different radio frequency and led it towards Hungary. When it arrived over Yugoslavia the weather was much better and it looked as if would be a *"good day for hunting."* As they approached the target Capt. Ohr led his flight down to the deck, while the other two flights flew top cover. The targeted airdrome at Seregelyes in Hungary, was found to be loaded with aircraft parked wing-tip to wing-tip and in they went. Capt. Ohr's Mustang took hits from a machine gun mounted on the control tower, but he continued his run and fired at a line of 15 aircraft. Jack Beard *"torched"* a Fiesler Storch as it was taxiing and then exploded a Ju 88 on his first pass. After Ohr's flight had used up most of its ammunition, the other two flights came down and continued with the destruction of the air base.

Leaving the airfield covered in burning aircraft Capt. Ohr then led his squadron back to Madna to report its outstanding day only to find an incensed Group Commander who was threatening to court-martial Capt. Ohr. Fortunately, cooler heads prevailed and the threatened court-martial was forgotten.

Escort missions were flown on 16 and 17 October to Brux, Czechoslovakia, and Blechhammer, Germany without encountering enemy aircraft. A secondary mission was also flown on 17 October by a flight of eight aircraft, four each from the 2nd and 5th Fighter Squadrons, and met with some unexpected opposition. This flight was sent on an armed reconnaissance mission to an area east of Budapest, Hungary to check on German troop movements in the area. When it reached the target area, a thick overcast was encountered and the the 2nd and 5th aircraft separated. The 5th FS pilots followed a course from Miskeles to approximately 4750N, 2210E, while the 2nd FS pilots flew east along a route believed to be 20-30 miles south of the briefed course.

As they closed on the assigned target area things went awry. The mission summary stated: *"No E/A were seen or encountered. However, both flights were prevented from carrying out their missions by interference from Russian planes. The 5th Squadron was attacked from behind at 5000 feet at 1115 hours by three YAK-9s at 4750N, 2210E. The P-51s immediately recognized the planes by their star emblem. Although the*

P-51D-20-NA 44-63799, *Seneca Chief*

Lt. Hugh Ottley,
4th Fighter
Squadron, 52nd Fighter Group,
Madna, Italy, winter 1944.

Records indicate that Lt. Hugh Ottley was assigned this aircraft around December 1944 and flew it throughout the remainder of the war. He related that when he flew it to Naples depot at the end of the war it was like "saying goodbye to an old friend". He named the aircraft after his hometown of Seneca Castle, New York. This area was the home of the Seneca Indian tribe, part of the Iroquois nation in the time before the Revolutionary War.

Lt. Ottley's assigned Mustang, "Seneca Chief" was coded WD-L, serial number 44-63799 (Credit: Hugh Ottley)

'Main Street' in the 5th Fighter Squadron bivouac area at Madna, 18 October 1944.

A winterized tent in the 5th Squadron area, 18 October 1944. (Credit: Thomas Thacker)

Lt. Barnett Chaskin (center), 4th Fighter Squadron, his crew Chief, S/Sgt Richard Potter (left) and his assistant crew chief, Pfc. John Hubbard at Madna, 5 October 1944. Their Mustang is "Miss Dottie" coded WD-V, serial number 44-13489. (Credit: Paul Ludwig)

P-51s dropped their wings in the prescribed signal the YAKs opened fire with machine guns and cannon. The P-51s went into a Lufbury, consistently avoiding combat and finally decided to break away. P-51s [pilots] *voiced the opinion they could have easily shot down the Russian planes which were noticeably slow. The 2nd Squadron's flight decided to turn back when two A/C, believed from a large Russian A/D, took off from the field as though to come up and make an attack."*

In spite of the interference from the Russians, pilots from both squadrons were able to observe heavy German rail and highway movement in the area and noted the locations.

The 52nd FG escorted bombers to Czechoslovakia and Hungary on 20 and 21 October without incident, and flew two special missions on 21 October. The special mission, led by Capt. Fred Ohr, was a flight of eight to ten (the records are contradictory) Mustangs ordered to Naples for further instructions. Upon arrival in Naples, Capt. Ohr learned that they would be escorting an RAF bomber carrying Prime Minister Winston Churchill back to London. The flight was without incident and after the PM was safely in the ground the pilots of his escort spent the night in London and enjoyed themselves taking in the city's night life. The return trip, however, was not as smooth and was to cause the deaths of two of the pilots. After leaving England for Madna Capt. Ohr's flight encountered bad weather and landed in Paris. After spending the night in Paris the journey was resumed. After taking off the flight again ran into thick clouds and mist and Lts. Clarence Carson and Albert McCraw collided in mid-air, killing both pilots. It transpired that this was to be Capt. Ohr's last mission. He received orders returning him to the USA for a well earned rest from combat and left the Squadron on 1 November 1944.

The other special mission of the day was an air search and rescue mission flown in the Venice-Trieste area by four pilots from the 4th FS. For one of the pilots, Lt. Hugh Ottley, it was his first combat mission. He described the emotions of that day in a personal diary: *"Possibly, one of the most memorable experiences of a fighter pilot is the first combat mission. When I first saw my name on the mission board, I had an uneasy feeling, probably like stage fright. I was to fly as wing-man to Shorty Hanes, a six victory Ace who had a reputation for being able to seek out enemy airplanes. Our mission of four planes was to escort a Navy PBY on an air-rescue mission over the Adriatic Sea, picking up airmen in the water who were shot down the previous day. We spent about three hours escorting the PBY during which he picked up about a dozen people from life rafts. He then returned home. We proceeded across the sea and began looking for targets of opportunity. Over Trieste we encountered some Flak and proceeded inland. Suddenly one of the pilots radioed that he had sight of eight airplanes below us that looked like German Me 109s. We circled around a large cumulus cloud and dove on them. All I could think: 'on my first mission'. We closed on them, they spotted us and broke up at us. When they did, the first thing we noticed was the elliptical shape of their wings – English Spitfires. What a relief: I was disappointed at the time, but as I grow older, I feel very fortunate."*

The right side of Lt. Chaskin's Mustang photographed undergoing maintenance. (Credit: Toppen)

An excellent aerial view of Lt. Al Anderson's, 4th Fighter Squadron, unnamed P-51D. (Credit: Hugh Ottley)

P-51D QP-H was Lt. Hans Zachmann's second Mustang named "Dody" Its serial number was 44-15116. The name on the Chief's side of the nose is "Donna" for S/Sgt Dalebroux's girlfriend. (Credit: Hans Zachmann)

The thirteenth and last mission of October was flown on the 29th. Weather again had limited operations and the relative inactivity had an effect upon morale within the unit. High on the top of the enlisted men's complaints was the Group rotation policy. The 2nd FS diary, for example, noted in the section on Morale: *"The continued bad weather and consequent stand downs have not helped morale. A discussion of rotation was held in the EM's mess hall under the supervision of Major Cook, Executive Officer and Capt. Harris, Orientation Officer. The men were permitted to voice their opinions of the squadron system of rotation. After they were told that they could see the rotation list of their section, they were more or less satisfied. Apparently the main bitch had been the secretiveness of it—no one knew where they were on the list and therefore could not even speculated about the time they would be going home. It is believed that the outlook of the EM has now changed for the better."*

Tom Thacker also touched upon the thoughts of the ground personnel at Madna, both officers and enlisted: *"For those of us who remained in camp, winter quarters, rest camps and possibility of rotation were the principal topics of interest. A few trial 30-day furloughs to the States were being tested, but most preferred to remain overseas if necessary and rotate permanently. The limited quotas for stateside transfer created a problem of fairness, since nearly everyone began his overseas tour at the same time.*

"Higher HQ largely left the question of 'Who wins?' to the local command. In some cases a lottery was established. In others, an effort was made to qualify based upon promotions and job performance. As a morale factor, rotation was an important and sensitive subject."

Lt. Robert Searl's P-51D "Winsome" coded WD-7, serial number 44-15681. It appears that the panel bearing the name "Winsome" may have been salvaged from the 5th Fighter Squadron Mustang "Winsome Gal". (Credit: Hugh Ottley)

P-51D QP-B was assigned to Lt. Joe Randerson after recovering from his ordeal in Yugoslavia. The aircraft, named "Julie" was a continuing tradition by its crew chief, S/Sgt Gilbert. Gilbert had been Bob Curtis' Crew Chief and since Curtis had named all of his assigned aircraft "Julie" (after his sister), Gilbert saw no reason to change the name of the aircraft he serviced just because a new pilot was flying it. (Credit: Joe Randerson)

Of poor quality, this photograph does show the artwork on Captain Walter Zilinski's "Lou Lou Belle". (Credit: James Empey)

The lack of missions in October did, however, provide the men extra time to try to prepare their tents and other facilities for the winter months ahead. Wood from drop tank crates was used to make lower walls and floors for many of the tents. Home heaters from oil drums were also quickly manufactured for heating purposes since issue heaters were provided only for offices and shops at the base. Along with improving the *"housing"* new facilities such as clubs, mess halls and game rooms were constructed at Madna. Tom Thacker provided these thoughts about the new facilities: *"Everyone now had at least one location where a bit of socializing was possible and some of the local beverages could, for a very modest price, be obtained. Strange mixtures such as egg cognac surfaced, not too bad to the taste, but best consumed in a dim light."*

November 1944 saw the marginal flying weather continuing, a change in command in the 2nd Fighter Squadron, and a few encounters with enemy aircraft. On 1 November, Capt. Daniel Zoerb replaced Capt. Fred Ohr as Commanding Officer of the 2nd FS and led his first mission as its CO. On that date the 52nd FG provided penetration, target, and withdrawal escort for three bomb groups of the 49th Bomb Wing attacking munitions facilities at Vienna, Austria.

Forty-nine Mustangs took off for the mission and 12 returned early, leaving 37 aircraft to carry out the escort mission. Weather became a factor and accounted for seven of the early returns. The mission summary noted: *"From rendezvous the course as briefed was followed except that the squadrons became separated as did flights within the squadrons because of extremely bad weather. Some flights covered the general area without actually seeing the bombers or the target. Other P-51s took the bombers through on penetration, target, and withdrawal, while still others lost the bombers while still short of the target, but picked them up again to the east of Vienna. On the whole, insofar as being able to provide penetration, target, and withdrawal, it was a decidedly unsatisfactory mission, entirely because of weather."*

The only encounter with enemy aircraft occurred at 14.00 hrs when a flight of five Mustangs from the 4th FS observed a single Me 109 preparing to attack a lone B-24 that they

Lt. DeForest's earlier "Myrtle" was the 2nd Fighter Squadron's reliable old P-51B, QP-7, serial number 43-7061. (Credit: C. G. Jones)

were escorting. They went after the Me 109 and chased it from 16,000 feet to the deck before Lt. Barnett Chaskin closed in and shot it down.

Things had not gone entirely well at Madna on 1 November. The 4th FS lost one of its ground personnel in a freak accident. As two of the 2nd FS Mustangs were taking off one of them suddenly went out of control and collided with a 4th FS Mustang which was alongside the runway waiting for its turn to takeoff. Pvt. Cashmere, sitting on the wing, was killed instantly, and Pvt. Chudy was seriously injured in the accident.

About 45 minutes later a crippled RAF B-26 Marauder made an emergency landing at Madna and gave fright to several members of the 4th FS flight line when it appeared that the bomber might hit some of their parked aircraft and the men working on them. The men made a hasty retreat from the oncoming aircraft, which fortunately stopped in time and no further damage was inflicted upon the squadron.

The next mission was an escort to Regensburg on 4 November and it was unopposed by enemy aircraft, a night and day change from only a year before when the *Luftwaffe* had wreaked havoc upon 8th Air Force bombers over Regensburg. When the Group traveled to Vienna on 5 November, the *Luftwaffe* did make a limited effort to defend the city and paid a price for doing so. The weak German effort was made in opposition to the largest 15th Air Force raid against a single target to date. The few German aircraft were up against a force of 500 B-17s and B-24s that were escorted by 337 fighters. The 52nd FG's assignment was to escort B-24s of the 49th Bomb Wing to the target and back home again.

Engagements with a small number of enemy aircraft began shortly after the bombers unloaded 1,100 tons of bombs on the target and had started the return trip back to their bases. The first encounter occurred at 13.15 hrs when four Mustangs of the 4th FS bounced a single Me 109 that had made a pass on a straggling bomber. The enemy aircraft tried the *Luftwaffe*'s standard escape technique of diving for the deck from 15,000 feet, but without success. Lt. James D. Callahan pulled in behind it and sent it crashing to earth with well-placed bursts from his machine guns. Five minutes later it was the 2nd FS's turn. This time it was a flight of six Me 109s which attacked a straggling B-24. The mission summary related: *"The B-24 was at 16,000 feet and the Me 109s were making passes from 6 o'clock high and low, singly, closing to 100/200 yards. After making their passes the E/A would pull up to the left or right, doing a chandelle and coming around for another pass. The B-24 did not appear to be damaged. The P-51s dived on the Me 109s from 23,000 feet and after breaking up their attacks, destroyed two Me 109s. The pilots lost sight of the other Me 109s after initiating their attacks*

The cockpit of the Group's two-seat Mustang. This Mustang, now coded QP-? was the former QP-C "Julie" flown by Major Bob Curtis. In this photograph, Lt. Dwaine Franklin, a 5th Fighter Squadron Ace, is preparing to take Army exchange officer, Lt. Stanley Gullion, for a ride. Lt. Gullion, had been wounded in action, and after recovering, he was selected to spend a week with the 52nd Fighter Group as part of the Army's "exchange-scholarship" plan. Under this plan Air Force officers would spend a week on the lines with the "ground-pounders" and vice-versa. (Credit: USAF)

Bill DeForest (left) and his Crew Chief pose in this fuzzy photograph with their P-51D "Myrtle" QP-3, serial number unknown. (Credit: American Beagle Squadron Assn)

Going home! From left to right: Captain James D. McCauley, 4th Fighter Squadron, Captain Bruno Dangelmeier, 2nd Fighter Squadron, and Captain Robert Deckman, 4th Fighter Squadron, with the 52nd FG's B-25 hack just prior to heading for the US, 28 November 1944. (Credit: Thomas Thacker)

P-51D-5-NA 44-13469

Captain Robert A. Karr, 5th Fighter Squadron, 52nd Fighter Group, Madna, Italy, December 1944

Captain Robert Karr scored a triple victory in this aircraft on 17 December 1944, raising his total to six and giving him the title of Ace. He scored five of his six victories in this aircraft.

Captain Robert A. Karr (left), 5th Fighter Squadron, receives congratulations from Colonel Marion Malcolm after shooting down three Me 109s over Blechhammer, on 17 December 1944. (Credit: USAF)

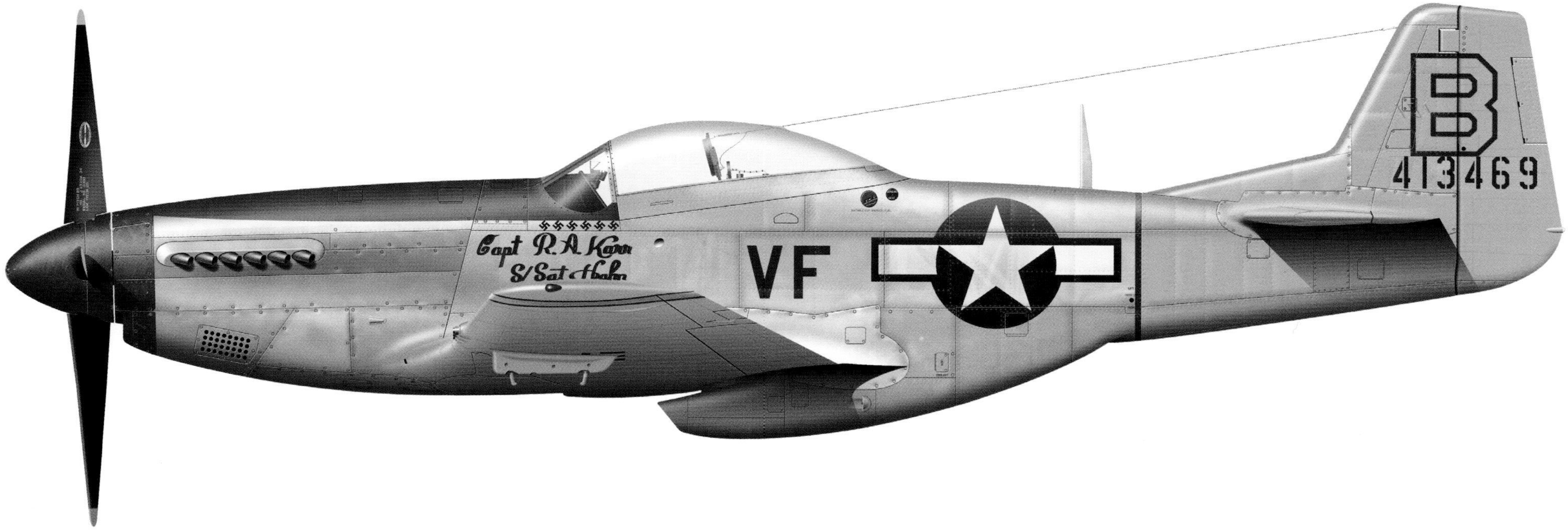

In this photograph Dave Emerson's "Sit" appears to be a little worn and weary with its yellow paint peeling. (Credit: Air Force Museum)

on the two of them."

The Messerschmitts were destroyed, one each, by Capt. Robert Schween and Lt. Hans Zachmann. Unfortunately Lt. Horace Hudson, flying P-51C QP - L, was killed during this encounter, possibly shot down by one of the four Me 109s that disappeared.

About an hour after these encounters Lt. Warren Lockwood, 5th FS, came upon a Ju 88 and promptly shot it down for the Group's fourth kill of the day.

Escort missions, without aerial oppositions were flown on 6, 7 and 11 November. The mission of 11 November turned out to be a day of tragedy for the 4th Fighter Squadron, however, when it lost three aircraft and pilots to bad weather or engine trouble. Lts. Edward Dzurnak and John Farnkopf disappeared over Yugoslavia and Lt. James Callahan vanished after bailing out over the sea.

The continual rain during the month forced the 52nd FG personnel to continually struggle with the legendary Italian mud. The Group HQ diary noted that: *"Traffic often became bogged down in deep mud holes or in ruts and ditches off the sides of the slippery roads which link up several squadron areas with Headquarters. Officers and men were obliged to slog through mud almost everywhere within the Group area and, besides causing depressed spirits, this condition brought on additional fatigue since it made more work for everyone and proved a definite handicap in maintaining daily schedules."*

On the positive side, the 52nd had completed the steel-matted runway and this enabled the aircraft to take off on days that missions or training flights were scheduled.

The mission of 16 November was to escort bombers to Munich and it got off to a bad start. The rendezvous was hampered by the late arrival of the bombers and when they did arrive, the formations were badly mixed. Four of the bomb wings were to strike marshalling yards in Munich and two were to bomb oil facilities at Innsbruck, Austria. Because of the badly mixed bomber formations, elements of the 52nd FG, in effect, provided escort coming off the targets for both strike forces. Enemy aerial opposition was almost non-existent, but Flak did take a toll of bombers and one of the 2nd FS's Mustangs. Group pilots saw four bombers go down and no chutes appeared from three of them. Flak also downed

A visiting Italian Air Force P-39 at Madna on the 5th Fighter Squadron flight line. "Doc" Watson's "Spare Parts" can be seen in the right background. (Credit: Al Gelo)

Lt. Don Ferch's 4th Fighter Squadron P-51D "Ravaging Rudolph", WD-C, serial number 44-15656. (Credit: Hugh Ottley)

Lt. Roland Dumais near Innsbruck. He radioed his Squadron that he was bailing out, but no one observed a chute. His aircraft, QP-4, was last seen in a glide by Dave Emerson. On their trip back to Madna, two pilots of the 4th FS were at 12,000 feet when they noticed an Me 109 circling over a downed B-17 from a very low altitude. They dived on the unsuspecting enemy aircraft whose pilot was apparently checking out his victory, and Lt. Junior Hanson shot it down. The Messerschmitt's pilot did not get out of his burning aircraft.

After uneventful escort missions on 17 and 18 November, the Group flew a strafing mission to Hungary in support of the advancing Russians on 19 November. Targets were plentiful and the Group's pilots shot up numerous targets including trucks, trains and parked aircraft. However, it was a costly victory for the 2nd FS. Three of its pilots, Capt. Cleo Bishop, Lt. John Beard, and F/O Haden Bourg, went down during these attacks. Fortunately, all three survived and became POWs. It was a steel cable, not Flak, that brought Jack Beard down. He and his wingman were on the deck strafing a train, so low according to Lt. Burdick, that Beard was *"plowing the ground."* As they pulled up from the strafing run Jack Beard called out that he had hit something and asked Burdick to come in close and look him over. Trailing from his tail was a long cable which Lt. Burdick at first thought Beard would be able to eject by slipping his aircraft. That thought was suddenly dampened when Burdick noticed the cable had sliced into the radiator scoop and that flames were starting to appear. Moments later Lt. Beard took to his chute.

Bishop and Bourg both rode their stricken aircraft in for crash landings, and in Bourg's case it was a little hair-raising! When his engine stopped, he jettisoned the canopy, released his harness and started to jump and then realized he was too low. Because his Mustang was still trimmed for the strafing run, it started downward and before he knew it his aircraft was glancing through some treetops. When the Mustang hit the ground, Bourg was catapulted out of it and he landed on a rough, unmade track. As he collected his wits, he noticed that he was directly in front of his burning aircraft and that there was a real danger that its .50 caliber gun rounds would explode in the fire. In great pain from several injuries, Lt. Bourg managed to haul himself out of the possible line of fire and into some woods, narrowly missing capture by some approaching SS troops. After they passed by, he searched for help and found a farmhouse where his wounds were cleaned. His freedom was short-lived however, as his hosts turned him over to the Hungarian authorities. Bourg was first taken to a makeshift hospital in Sumeg, Hungary where he stayed for a few days before a succession of transfers and threats by Hungarian police. Finally he was turned over to the Germans for a long stay in a POW camp.

Escort missions were flown on the 20, 22, and 23 November and each of them was a milk run for the 52nd FG since the *Luftwaffe* refused to show its face. Heavy rains and bad weather virtually shut down Group operations for the remainder of the month.

Tom Thacker gloomily recalled that: *"Meanwhile, the Madna mud grew deeper and vehicular traffic practically ceased. Either you waded through on foot or you didn't go. The engineers who supported us were supposed to maintain the roads, but were engaged full time just keeping the flying field operational. Someone did point out, however, that the dust and flies of a few weeks earlier seemed to have disappeared."*

The foul weather that had continued for over two months was deepening the morale problems among some of the enlisted men and was spreading to the pilots as well. Many of the veteran pilots were anxious to complete their combat tour and go home for a little rest and recuperation. The constant rain was limiting the missions and replacement pilots continued to stream in, further limiting their mission accumulation. The situation was clearly stated in the 2nd FS diary for November: *"The morale of the pilots, however, has reached its lowest level. With such bad weather and infrequent missions, the outlook for early completion of their tours of duty is not promising. With the arrival of 27 new pilots this prospect is worse than black. On days of stand down the pilots are at a loss for something to do. Although living conditions in the camp are relatively comfortable, there is no decent town within a short travel time where they could go for entertainment."*

Things did work out, however, for a few of the veteran pilots and November saw the departure of Captains Robert Anderson, Walter Zilinski and Merle Ney of the 5th FS; Captains Bofinger, William Hanes and Robert Deckman of the 4th FS and; Maj. Fred Ohr, Captains John Clarke, Bruno Dangelmaier, Robert Schween and George Burden of the 2nd FS. Eleven NCOs from the three squadrons also headed for home.

With the continuing bad weather, the diaries

Lt. Albert Mannella, 4th Fighter Squadron, and his P-51D "Jersey Bounce", code and serial number unknown. (Credit: Paul Ludwig)

changed from operational notes to those of celebrating Thanksgiving Day with a grand turkey dinner and most of the traditional trimmings. Another item of note was the war-weary P-51 that was converted to a two-seater by the 2nd Fighter Squadron. According to Tom Thacker the work was done in cooperation with the 55th Service Squadron. In the process of converting it the crew removed the guns (to lighten the aircraft) and its fuselage gas tank. A second seat from a salvaged Mustang was installed behind the pilot's seat and now some of the Group's ground personnel could get an opportunity to fly in a P-51. The *"new"* two-seater was given the code of QP*?. On 29 November, the 2nd FS's new Commanding Officer, Daniel Zoerb, was promoted to Major and Dwaine Franklin and Lawrence Fuller, both of the 5th FS, were promoted to Captain. For the officers of these two squadrons this was a wonderful opportunity to drink to their limit at the Officers Club at the expense of the newly promoted!

The rotten winter continued into December 1944, but the number of the Group's missions increased in spite of it. During the first two weeks of the month the 52nd FG escorted bombers to targets in Germany, Austria, Yugoslavia, and Czechoslovakia without engaging aerial opposition from the *Luftwaffe* or other Axis air forces. The lack of enemy aircraft, however, did not mean that the Group did not suffer any losses during the period. The 2nd FS lost Lt. James Swindel who was killed during a test flight on 5 December and Lt Paul Keyser, who disappeared during a reconnaissance mission on 8 December. Keyser's loss was attributed to oxygen failure. Lt. Roy Carlson reported that he had seen Lt. Keyser's Mustang start to drift out of formation and go under Lt. DeForest's P-51. He called Keyser numerous times and received no response. Moments later Keyser's Mustang went into a cloud bank and he disappeared forever. The Squadron's bad luck did not end here and it lost another aircraft upon its return to Madna. Something went wrong as Lt. DeForest was letting down at the base. He missed the runway and hit the ground hard, breaking the left wing off of his P-51. Fortunately he wasn't injured, but his severely damaged aircraft was relegated to the spare parts yard.

The 2nd FS experienced another change of command on 6 December when seven victory Ace, Major Daniel Zoerb, received his orders to head Stateside for a well earned rest and reassignment. He was replaced by Major James G. Curl who returned to the MTO for his second tour of duty. In his first tour of duty Curl was assigned to the 66th Fighter Squadron, 57th Fighter Group, and was credited with 3-0-3. Two other veteran pilots of the 2nd FS, Captains Schween and Burden, also departed to the US after completing their tours of duty. Lt. Fitzpatrick and Lt. Lutry of the 4th FS also headed for the US during December. December was a lucky month for 39 NCO and other enlisted ranks and they departed for the US, some for reassignment and others on a 30-day furlough.

Weather resulted in the loss of another 2nd FS Mustang on 9 December. On the trip back from Brux, Czechoslovakia, Lt. Greg Burdick became disoriented in a dense cloud bank as the Squadron began its let down over the Adriatic and Burdick had to bail out. In the process of jumping he broke his arm. After landing in the sea, Burdick watched as his friends circled to pin-point his location for the Walrus rescue aircraft. An hour and a half later, the Walrus arrived and pulled him out of the water, but his problems were still not over. The Walrus' engine had blown a cylinder on the way to pick him up and was unable to take off in the rough sea. After a harrowing night in the Walrus, which was being tossed around like a toy, a British destroyer came to the rescue. Burdick later noted: *"Once aboard the destroyer things were not at all bad. I arrived in time for early tea, followed by cocktail time, tea, dinner and a nightcap. I slept well."*

Uneventful escort missions were flown on 11, 15 and 16 December, but on the mission of 17 December the *Luftwaffe* finally made an appearance. On that date, Fifteenth Air Force bombers were up in mass to attack oil refineries in and around Blechhammer and Odertal, Germany. The bomber force, consisting of six groups of B-17s and eleven groups of B-24s, certainly generated the attention of German fighter controllers, and the fighters of the 15th Air Force were about to experience their largest air battle in quite a few days.

The 52nd FG went into action just south of the target area when the 5th FS encountered a large formation of about 45 Me 109s and 30 Fw 190s. The mission summary noted: *"These E/A were in typical irregular formation. The E/A turned 180 degrees right and started an attack from six o'clock. The P-51s broke into the E/A. Some E/A stayed at altitude but others dived down to just above the clouds at 9000 feet. Inasmuch as the P-51s were greatly outnumbered some of them were unable to do anything but break repeatedly.*

Lt. Palumbo's P-51D, WD-T seen from the right side. It carried the name "Georgia Peach" on the other side of the nose. (Credit: Paul Ludwig)

The E/A appeared to be both aggressive and skillful."

Despite the fact they were greatly outnumbered 11 of the 5th FS Mustangs fought the German fighters and when it was all over four Messerschmitts and two Focke-Wulfs had been shot from the sky. Three of the kills were claimed by Capt. Bob Karr, who raised his total to six and became the Group's newest Ace. He described his big day as follows: *"I chased one to about 18,000 feet and opened fire at long range, getting hits on the fuselage, cockpit and engine. The pilot bailed out before I closed in. I picked up another and got hits on the engine. The plane started smoking and hit the overcast at 8000 feet. My wingman saw large pieces of the ship fall off. Tagging on to another I got into a Lufbery circle with him. Finally I got inside him, scored some hits and saw the pilot bail out at 11,000 feet."*

The scoring continued when Lts. Charley McCloskey and Vincent Tranquillo found some other targets. McCloskey reported: *"A whole bunch came at me and started to make a pass. I called the flight to break and went into a diving spiral, pulling out at 15,000 feet. Approaching a Fw 190 from the rear, I fired a long burst but didn't observe any hits until I was almost on him—then got him good. As I passed by, he exploded on my right. Climbing back to about 25,000 feet on the pullout, I saw a P-51 with a Me 109 on his tail. I dropped in on him, clobbered him hard, and saw him spinning out of control through the overcast with his left wing smoking."* The last kill of the day occurred when Lt. Tranquillo dived on a straggling Fw 190 and opened fire. *"On the second burst I got a hit on the canopy and the ship went out of control and spun down burning."*

In addition to the 5th FS kills, fighters of other 15th AF groups claimed another 17-3-6 for a grand total of 23-3-6 for the day. The six victories by the 5th FS pushed the 52nd Fighter Group's total of enemy aircraft destroyed in aerial combat to 403.

The next several days provided a fairly heavy schedule of missions for the Group. Six escort missions were flown between 18-26 December and the *Luftwaffe*, except for two biplane trainers, failed to make an appearance. The crew of the biplane paid a heavy price for their foolishness. This kill occurred on 26 December when the 52nd FG escorted bombers to Bechhammer and Odertal. As the Mustangs headed back to Madna after overseeing a successful bombing attack, a pair of Mustangs of the 4th FS were at 11,000 feet when they observed two biplane trainers circling the airfield at Sisak. The trainers were at about 200 feet and apparently preparing to land when the P-51s closed in for a closer look, and after three passes to insure that they were enemy aircraft, F/O Henry E. Simpson, Jr. gunned one of them out of the sky.

The Group's last casualty of 1944 came on 27 December during a strafing mission along the Vienna-Linz railway. The Group was searching out targets of opportunity. Various rail and industrial targets were hit as well as some unusual ones. Dave Emerson of the 2nd FS included an aircraft junk pile along with a locomotive and a factory in his targets strafed. In spite of the blistering attack, German Flak gunners in the vicinity managed to zero in on Lt. Daniel Adams' (2nd FS) ship, and bring it down. Lt. Adams died in the crash.

Two escort missions, flown on 28 and 29 December closed out operations for 1944, but the primary enemy on these missions was the weather. Dave Emerson, 2nd FS, was quoted in the *American Beagle Squadron* that the weather was so bad on the 29th that the unit returned to Madna on the deck through rain and muck, with the ceiling at 100 feet in some places. Tom Thacker also mentioned the deteriorating weather during the last half of December in his unpublished history of the 52nd: *"By this time, the Battle of the Bulge was underway on the Western Front. The vile weather which became notorious for its duration extended from England to the Med. On Christmas Eve more than 20 heavies landed at Madna, some remaining to the New Year. Thus our Christmas Turkey was sliced rather thin in order to be shared with 200 unexpected guests."*

The dawning of a new year, 1945, did not bring a reprieve from the rotten winter weather and operations were again limited during the month of January. All accounts of the month recount the same theme, miserable weather and the lack of activity, in the air and on the ground. The 52nd Fighter Group monthly report under the heading of *"Outstanding Events"* stated. *"Few months have been filled with more inclement weather and less activity than January 1945 with its almost constant wind, rain, snow, sleet, and mud. It was, without a doubt, the toughest month spent by the Group at Madna airfield.*

"Only 17 missions were flown, and nearly all of these were reconnaissance and evacuation escort types. The men found such inactivity demoralizing and were saved

Lt. Robert "Rocky" Rhodes put his P-51B down in the River Rhine in Switzerland after it was damaged by flak during a strafing run. (Credit: J. Fred Baumann)

from complete boredom by the encouraging news of Russian victories along the east front, the regular Special Service amusements, such as moving pictures and stage shows, and their own indoor club activities.

"There were no really outstanding events during the month and not a single enemy plane was encountered during the few missions that were flown. For the most part, January was a month to be endured with a lot of suffering and inconvenience."

Even the shortage of missions and contact with enemy aircraft did not completely eliminate casualties during the month. On 9 January, Lt. Leslie Keeler, 5th FS, was killed when he ran into a mountain during a training flight and on the last day of the month, Lt. Bernell Whitaker, 5th FS, was forced to bail out over Hungary and became a POW.

There were a number of personnel changes during the month and included Lt. Colonel Wilmot replacing Lt. Colonel Charles Boedeker as Deputy Group Commander. Lt. Colonel Boedeker, his tour of duty competed, headed home during the month.

February 1945 began with a dramatic change in the weather and with it came an increased number of missions and a definite improvement in morale. The monthly historical report by HQ 52nd FG noted: *"After a long bleak winter during which operations were seriously curtailed, the approach of Spring, early even for this part of Italy, brought more activity to Madna airfield than there had been since last August. Almost daily missions were flown throughout the month, and although no enemy planes were encountered, some locomotives and other rolling stock were destroyed or damaged during strafing attacks."*

Escort missions were flown on 1 and 5 February to targets in Italy and Czechoslovakia, and various selected pilots flew special missions, such as escort for reconnaissance aircraft during the first few days of the month. Lt. Claude Bennett, 2nd FS, fell victim to a Flak burst on the mission of 5 February and bailed out safely and became a POW.

On 7 February 1945 the 52nd FG carried out a successful strafing mission in the vicinity of Vienna. In these attacks pilots of the Group destroyed four Ju 88s and one He 111 and damaged several other enemy aircraft on the ground. Then the pilots turned their attention to rail and production facilities in the area and destroyed six locomotives, a factory and two radar stations in the process. One pilot, Lt. Herbert McKinsey, 4th FS, was lost when he flew into the target he was strafing.

One of the 4th FS's young pilots, Lt. Hugh Ottley, wrote about the various missions of February. During the month he flew his 13th through 19th combat missions and had these observations about escort and strafing missions of this period of the war: *"Most of our missions were long-range heavy bomber escorts, lasting most of the day. We would be going into the mess hall for breakfast as the bombers were overhead, formed up and heading north. After breakfast, we had our briefing, went to our aircraft and then took off. We would overtake the bombers over the north coast of the Adriatic, stay with them over the target, and come back with them to the coast. Usually our fuel was low (at this point), so we'd return to base. After our debriefing, we stepped outside and watched for the returning bombers. For us, typically it was about a five hour trip while the bombers logged about nine hours.*

"Nearly all of the targets on the bombing missions were over heavily defended areas and Flak was so intense that it had the appearance of a severe thunderstorm. We usually flew about 6000 feet above the bombers and were luckily out of the Flak. It was very unnerving to see the bombers fly into the thick cloud and either explode or descend trailing smoke. I didn't envy the bomber crews. They were a brave bunch.

"Occasionally, we participated in strafing missions. On one in particular, we spotted a freight train coming into a small town. The locomotive stopped on a road crossing in the center of town, which made it difficult to get a shot at him. We dove down and flew straight down main street between the buildings. For a split second I glanced to my right and there, standing in a second story window, was a well dressed, elderly woman. I shall never forget how she looked. Then with a burst of my six guns, the locomotive blew sky high. This was my first locomotive kill."

During the next two weeks of the month nine escort missions were flown to various targets and

A shaky image of Lt. Edward Borosky of the 2nd Fighter Squadron, and his P-51B, serial number 43-106816, named "Me", and coded QP-W. (Credit: American Beagle Squadron)

without contact with enemy aircraft. One pilot, Lt. Clarence Mains, 5th FS, was lost when his engine failed over the Adriatic and he crashed into the sea.

The mission of 22 February 1945 found the 52nd Fighter Group a role in one of the major offensives of Operation Clarion, the purpose of which was to destroy or disrupt the German transportation system, industrial targets, oil facilities and communications. On this date 800 aircraft of the 8th, 12th and 15th Air Forces struck numerous targets in southern Germany. After escorting the bombers to targets in Bavaria, the Mustangs went down to strafe and found numerous targets and intense Flak. Lt. Bill Eddins commented on his day: *"The 2nd FS provided target cover for the bombers and then went down through a hole in the overcast and strafed rail targets. By the time we began strafing, the Germans had been under attack for an hour or more and were ready for us. Mel Bryant fired a long burst at a locomotive without producing a boiler explosion. Apparently the engineer had time to blow down the boiler or perhaps it had been hit by other planes earlier. Bryant's plane was hit by light Flak, knocking out the engine. He bailed out and was captured."*

Hans Zachmann. 2nd FS, destroyed two locomotives and escaped the murderous Flak, but Edward Borosky was not so lucky. He and John Ondocsin were attempting to strafe trains near Augsburg and were caught in a cross-fire as they flew down a valley. Both aircraft took immediate hits from 20 mm Flak and Borosky went down, crashing in flames along the tracks. Ondocsin was lucky to escape as his Mustang took a 20MM hit that went through the left wing, into the left side of his canopy and out the other side before it exploded.

The 5th FS also took casualties. Lt. Priestly Cooper was shot down by Flak and killed, and Lt. Robert F. *"Rocky"* Rhodes limped into Switzerland in his badly damaged Mustang. *"Rocky"* Rhodes, a young 2nd Lieutenant, was on his sixth mission as a member of the 5th FS, and was flying P-51BVF-U, *"Little Ambassador"*, the former mount of Squadron Ace, Jim Empey, on what turned out to be his last mission. Rhodes had made his first strafing run against a train that turned out to be a Flak train and managed to escape that trap, but was not as fortunate during his next strafing run over a nearby airfield. His pass over the airfield was a part of the Squadron's second pass and this time the Flak gunners were ready and waiting. During the attack *"Little Ambassador"* took hits in the engine and tail section and as Lt. Rhodes attempted to climb, he realized that the elevator was damaged. After a struggle to reach altitude he radioed for help, requesting an escort back to friendly territory, but received no replies from undamaged pilots. As he attempted to find an escape route, he unknowingly crossed over the Swiss border. In an attempt to reach France he followed the River Rhine upstream until his engine seized up and he decided to put down on the gravel riverbank. He hit the riverbank at about 100 mph, ripping off the scoop and right flap, before sliding into the river. Finding the water only about three feet deep, he waded to shore and learned that he was in Lichtenstein. From there he was handed over to the Swiss authorities on the other side of the river. After a few weeks stay in Switzerland, he was taken to France and turned over to the American authorities. From here he made it to England and then back to the USA.

During the remainder of the month, the 52nd FG flew four escort missions and one strafing mission. There were no combat losses on these missions, but the 5th FS lost another pilot, Lt. Bruce Bucher, who was killed on a training flight on 28 February.

February 1945 had turned out to be the busiest month in some time for the 52nd Fighter Group and its strafing attacks had inflicted quite a bit of damage to the enemy. It flew 42 missions of various types and operated on 23 days. The list of destroyed tactical targets included locomotives and rail cars, rail stations, barracks, radar installations and aircraft.

Chapter Twelve

"A crack at Berlin"

The Final Campaign

March–May 1945

"Redgie Sisbet" was assigned to Lt. E. Palczewski, 4th Fighter Squadron, code and serial unknown. Note the replacement landing gear cover. (Credit: Hugh Ottley)

The flying weather continued to improve in March 1945 and even the *Luftwaffe* decided to come out of hibernation during the first few days of the month. The Group began the month of operations with a renewed vigor, even as rumors of a move were circulating around Madna. On 1 March the Group traveled to southern Germany on an escort mission and for the first time in two months the 52nd encountered German aircraft. The dogfights were of a limited number, but that did not stop the 52nd FG from adding to its scoreboard. Two German aircraft were downed on the mission, a Me 110 by Capt. J.J. Meyers, 2nd FS, and a unidentified enemy aircraft by Lt. Thomas Watkins of the 4th FS.

The action increased when the 52nd FG flew a strafing mission to Germany on 2 March, and found a number of targets in the air and on the ground. The mission was to attack suitable rail targets on the rail line stretching from Linz in Austria to Passau, Plattling and Regensburg. Forty-nine aircraft participated in the mission and upon reaching Atter Lake, the formation split into three separate attack units. The 2nd FS would strafe in the Linz/Passau area, the 4th FS in the Passau/Plattling area, and the 5th would strike the Plattling/Regensburg area.

The 2nd FS found only a moderate amount of traffic in its zone of attack, but struck what they found with a vengence. Lt. Bray led eight of the Squadron's Mustangs in the attack and they drew intense and accurate Flak as they approached the target. Bray honed in on the first of three locomotives observed and put it out of operation with well placed bursts. The rest of his flight then worked over the remaining two locomotives and heavily damaged them. Bray then turned his attention to another locomotive pulling 15 boxcars, destroying the locomotive and damaging at least 10 of the boxcars. Flak took its toll too, however, and Lt. William R. Dorsman was killed after taking hits and crashed into a hillside. After completion of their strafing runs Lt. Bray and his flight headed back towards Madna and encountered three Fw 190s and seven Me 109s in the Wels, Austria area. Bray bounced two of the Focke-Wulfs that were separated from the rest of the enemy aircraft and shot one of them down in flames. The second Fw 190 managed to escape the same fate when Lt. Bray ran out of ammunition and had to break off his attack. In the meanwhile the third Fw 190 found itself in the sights of Capt. Hans Zachmann and was quickly shot down.

The 4th and 5th Fighter Squadrons hit their respective target areas and also took a substantial toll of German rolling stock. The 5th FS headed back to base without any interference from the *Luftwaffe*, but the 4th did find some enemy aircraft on the way home and claimed a Fw 190 and a Me 109 destroyed and one 190 damaged. The confirmed kills were credited to Lts. Edmund Palczewski and Arnold Sobczak, and the damaged credit went to Lt. Frederick Straut. In addition to the 4-0-1 score in aerial victories, the 52nd FG destroyed 11 locomotives, two ammunition cars, six oil cars, two trucks, an oil barge, and two steam boats and damaged numerous other targets.

After several uneventful escort missions over the next two weeks, the Group returned to Germany on another strafing mission. The mission of 19 March 1945 turned out to be a successful, but costly mission. The mission was a fighter sweep in the area west of Mühldor and Landshut, Germany. The squadrons split and operated separately upon arrival in the target area, first sweeping the area in search of enemy aircraft and then down to the deck for strafing. All three squadrons went into action against ground targets at about the same time and destroyed three locomotives, six box cars, and damaged numerous other targets. The 4th and 5th Squadrons escaped the intense Flak, but the 2nd FS was not so lucky. Two of its pilots, Maj. James Curl and Lt. Donald Heider, were killed, and Lt.Boyd Nippert became a POW.

As three pilots of the 5th FS finished their strafing attack and headed west at 300 feet they observed a long-nosed Fw 190 D 500 feet above them, headed east, and turned after it. As the three P-51s began to close on it, the *Dora* dived to about 300 feet. When it came within range, Lt. Warren Lockwood opened up on it and scored hits on the canopy and right wing. The canopy quickly came off and the pilot bailed out, only to die when his chute failed to open. This victory was the 52nd Fighter Group's 410th aerial victory of the war. Before the mission was completed two other encounters occurred, but both were indecisive. One of them was an attempted bounce by an Me 262 on a flight of three Mustangs, but the P-51s quickly outmaneuvered the jet. Realizing that he had failed in his attack, the German quickly left the area.

Following this costly raid which included the death of its Commanding Officer, Maj. William R. Sefton was given command of the 2nd FS. At about the same period Maj. Hadley B. Eliker replaced Lt. Colonel Ralph Watson as Commanding Officer of the 5th FS. Lt. Colonel Watson then assumed his new duties as Deputy Commander of the 306th Fighter Wing.

The missions of 20, 21, 22, and 23 March found the Group escorting bombers to targets in

Germany and Austria and all were uneventful. Numerous encounters with piston-engined and jet fighters were reported in assigned areas of other Fifteenth Air Force fighter groups during this period, and a total of nine enemy aircraft were shot down. The claims included one Me 262 destroyed and five damaged on the mission of 23 March.

On 24 March 1945 the 52nd FG took part in what is described as the longest mission flown in Europe, a 1,600 mile round trip to Berlin and back. The mission was quite eventful for the 31st and 332nd Fighter Groups which ran into swarms of enemy aircraft and shot down nine, eight of which were Me 262s. For the 52nd FG it was a very long range milk run as they flew escort for heavy bombers hitting the Daimler-Benz tank factory in southeastern Berlin. The 52nd FG was led by Colonel Malcolm on this historic mission and his pilots reported that the bombers they escorted did an effective job against their target. The comments of two the 52nd's pilots appeared in a press release: *"Capt. Barnett Chaskin, 4th FS stated 'The big babies really clobbered hell out of Berlin. The bomb clusters were dropping smack into the target area, with explosions clearly visible at 10-second intervals. Fires were raging and huge columns of smoke ascending." Capt. Leonard Potterbaum, 5th FS, stated that he was: "Too busy looking for Flak and enemy aircraft and worrying about my gas supply to get much of a look at Berlin. But you couldn't miss the huge clouds of smoke boiling up over the target area. He added, 'The heavies were really rolling them down the alley today."*

Perhaps the best assessment of the Group's performance on this mission to Berlin is from Lt. J. Fred Baumann, 5th FS. He stated: *"Our job was to guard those bombers from fighter attack, and that is precisely what the 52nd Fighter Group did that day— we covered them as they came into the area like a protective blanket. The jets came up and the 332nd and 31st Fighter Groups did manage to shoot down a few apiece; however no enemy fighters approached our bombers. Our score was zero, but the bombers made it OK, as far as the enemy fighters were concerned. That was our job!"*

The final note of the press release noted previously went on to state: *"Despite the length of the mission – over six hours – the pilots seemed less tired upon their return than is frequently the case on missions of shorter duration. All had been eagerly awaiting a 'Crack at Berlin' and today they had their wish. As Colonel Malcolm put it in summing up the results of the day's flight, 'It was really worth the effort, for it was what we'd all been waiting for – a crack at Big B."*

After another uneventful mission to Czechoslovakia on 25 March, the Group finally got another chance to engage the *Luftwaffe* on 26 March. The 52nd was to provide escort on penetration, over the target, and during withdrawal for four B-24 groups of the 47th Bomb Wing attacking the Bruck Leithe east and west marshalling yards in Austria. No enemy aircraft were encountered during penetration or over the target but as the formation was withdrawing from the target area elements of the 2nd FS observed two flights of Fw 190s far below. The enemy aircraft were heading north along a

Lt. W. L. Speicher's, P-51D "Barbara" of the 5th Fighter Squadron. This aircraft, because of the six Swastikas and Crew Chief's name, S/Sgt Hahn, painted under the cockpit, is believed to be 44-13469, VF-B, previously assigned to Captain Bob Karr. (Credit: Everett Jenkins)

Colonel Marion Malcolm takes a last look a his map prior to a mission. (Credit: Thomas Thacker)

Lt. Fred Baumann and his crew chief pause for a photograph prior to a mission to Germany, March 1945. (Credit: J. Fred Baumann)

Lt. David Griffith's P-51D of the 2nd Fighter Squadron, named "Bodacious Varmit", was coded QP-V, serial number 44-63563. The name of the aircraft is derived from a character, Sut Tattersall, from the comic strip "Barney Google". (Credit: David Griffith)

railroad track and four of the Focke-Wulfs were observed to dive earthward and begin a strafing attack. Four Mustangs peeled off and dived after these enemy aircraft and the remaining four Mustangs headed down after the second flight of Fw 190s. In the ensuing dogfight four of the Focke-Wulfs were shot down. Two were credited to Capt. John J. Meyers, one to Lt. Herbert Toombs, Jr. and the fourth Fw 190 was shared by Lts. Oscar Bushwar and Paul Westphal. For his actions in this engagement Lt. Toombs was awarded the Distinguished Flying Cross. The citation stated in part: *"As the bombers were being escorted on withdrawal, the leader of Toombs flight called in a bogie at 10,000 feet and took the flight down to look it over. It was a B-24. Then Toombs saw four Fw 190s flying north in a loose 'V' at about 4000 feet in the area east of Papa, Hungary.*

"After calling his leader Toombs dived on these aircraft. As he approached them he saw that they were starting a strafing attack along the railroad that apparently was in the control of the Russians. He closed to about 650 yards and fired, but saw no strikes. The enemy aircraft split-essed, leveled off on the deck and started to fish tail and make occasional tight turns. Despite this evasive action Toombs stayed with the 190, closed to about 200 yards, fired short bursts and saw hits on the wings. Then he fired a long burst and saw strikes on the fuselage and around the cockpit. Parts of the plane flew off and the pilot then jettisoned the canopy and bailed out.

"After the E/A crashed and Toombs rejoined his flight, more 190s were seen. He immediately turned and chased one, at about 2000 feet, encountering light Flak as he did so. When the E/A was within range Toombs fired a short burst, only to find that just one gun was firing. He called for someone else to continue the attack on this E/A and then broke off his attack."

Capt. Meyers continues the description of the dogfight. *"We each picked a plane and went after him with everything we had. I got my first at about 1000 feet when he was trying to gain altitude. Smoke began pouring from his engine and he rolled over on his back and plunged into the ground. I saw the plane explode. The second victory came harder. I latched onto him just after the first plane hit the ground, but we were all over the sky for about 30 miles in a northwesterly direction before I finally got him. The plane blew up in the air."*

Based upon the description of these 190 in the mission summary, *"they were painted a dark green, some with a dull yellow tail, painted like ours, with yellow stripes on the wings and a yellow spinner."*

They were, in all probability, from 102/2 *Vadászbombázószázad* (Fighter-Bomber Squadron), Hungarian Air Force. The mission report describes the enemy pilots as quite experienced. All of the 2nd FS Mustangs returned safely from this engagement, although one of them landed with an explosive 20 mm shell lodged in its tail. It was very carefully removed!

The approach of spring did seem to somewhat brighten the spirits of the 52nd's personnel in general. The monthly diary reported, *"Delightful weather, more activities, and especially the sensational advances by Allied armies on both the western and eastern fronts have combined to noticeably heighten morale of the entire group. Disappointment among enlisted men over the quota reduction for rotation was somewhat overcome by the announcement that temporary duty furloughs have been extended to 45 days. It was pointed out that, however high the morale may be for the moment it would prove only transitory unless definite provisions are made soon to hasten homeward those men who have been overseas for more than two and a half years. The pilots, who have been flying quite regularly since the advent of almost continuously clear weather, are now eager to complete at least 40 missions before the collapse of Germany."*

With the arrival of April 1945 the weather continued to improve and combat operations increased accordingly. Tom Thacker remarked rather poetically about the advent of a beautiful spring: *"Perhaps we were getting a little war-weary as we rolled into April. However, with spring at hand, the mud dried up, the grass became green once more, flowers bloomed and there was a definite air of enthusiasm once again. The impending move northward plus reasonable assurance that the war in Europe was nearly over contributed to that feeling."*

So good was the flying weather during April that the 52nd Fighter Group would fly 80 missions during the month, the largest number of missions in one month since the Group converted to Mustangs. With the *Luftwaffe* virtually defeated and the need for strategic missions into Germany and the Balkan countries greatly reduced, the 52nd FG's primary mission during April became a tactical one. Most of the missions were in support of bombing or strafing missions in the north of Italy, Austria and Bavaria in an attempt to hinder the retreating German forces.

The first mission of the month nearly had tragic overtones to it, when some of the Group's Mustangs accidentally strafed two hospital trains. The trains had not been clearly marked as hospital trains, but as soon as the pilots noticed the faded Red Cross markings the attack was immediately broken off. Other legitimate targets were observed and before they left the area 25

VF-M and VF-4 of the 5th Fighter Squadron awaiting their next mission to Germany, March 1945. (Credit: J. Frank Baumann)

Captain Hans Zachmann, 2nd Fighter Squadron, receiving congratulations from his Commanding Officer, Major William Sefton, after completing his 60th and last mission. (Credit: Hans Zachmann)

Lt. George Angle, 5th Fighter Squadron, smiles for the cameraman in his "Mustang du jour". Angle was never assigned his own P-51 during his stay with the Squadron. (Credit: George Angle)

locomotives were destroyed and 11 damaged. In addition to the locomotives destroyed, the 52nd's pilots damaged two enemy aircraft on the ground, and some 70 rail cars were heavily damaged. The 4th FS showed the way by destroying 17 of the locomotives. Capt. Paul Steinle was high scorer on the mission with five locomotives destroyed and two enemy aircraft damaged to his credit.

With the Germans in full retreat in northern Italy the need for tactical strikes increased and on a number of occasions the Group's Mustangs were sent in small separate formations to attack a number of different targets. One example of this type of mission was reported as follows: *"Strafing-wise, Nazis in Italy continued to keep their troops and convoys off of the roads during daylight hours, providing slim pickings for 18 P-51s of Colonel Malcolm's 52nd Fighter Group which conducted an armed reconnaissance in the north eastern Italian section this morning. Total claims for the Group were one enemy motorcycle and rider killed, one truck damaged and a motor launch shot up on the Adige River."*

Another mission in early April was described in the daily report as a twilight armed reconnaissance of the Udine, Italy area by eight Mustangs of the 2nd Fighter Squadron. The report noted: *"Despite adverse weather which narrowed their target area these Mustangs destroyed one locomotive, 48 box and tank cars, 5 troop laden trucks, two scout cars, a motorcycle and damaged one tank or tank destroyer. Accounting for the only locomotive of the day was Lt. Carroll F. Morrison, Jr."*

As these two missions indicate, no target was too small for the marauding Mustangs to strike. It was now the goal of the 15th AF fighters to harass and intimidate the retreating Germans into surrendering, and these constant strafing attacks were slowly achieving their purpose.

On 6 April the Group mounted a strafing mission along the railroads, stretching between Munich, Pilsen, and Linz. On his last combat mission Hans Zachmann, 2nd FS, closed out his tour of duty by destroying one locomotive. During the mission Lt. Raymond Mills, 2nd FS, suffered a bout of vertigo when entering a thick bank of cloud and bailed out over Austria. He was later rescued, and his aircraft was the last Mustang lost in combat by the Group.

On 11 April the Group was escorting B-17s which were targeting bridges in Northern Italy. Destruction of these bridges, it was hoped, would cut off the escape routes of retreating German forces trying to make it back into Austria and Germany. The approach to the target and the target area was clear of enemy aircraft but as the 52nd FG began its return trip, Lt. Ben Hall, 2nd FS, spotted the elusive Ar 234 that had been reported as operating in this area for the past several days. The jet was poised to bounce a flight of twelve B-17s. Hall and his wingman, Lt. Cecil E. Cooper, Jr., were shepherding a crippled B-17 when they first noticed the jet's approach and went after it. The mission summary described the action in a terse manner, saying: *"Giving chase, Hall cut the Nazi plane off when it attempted to run and closed to within 800 yards when he saw strikes on the*

The 2nd Fighter Squadron flight line at the unit's new base at Piagiolino airfield. QP-V in the foreground is David Griffith's "Bodacious Varmit". (Credit: Air Force Museum)

left jet. This slowed the enemy aircraft and Hall was able to pull up to 300 yards where he saw more bursts take effect and the plane started to burn. As the 234 went into a shallow dive, Cooper placed a few bursts in vulnerable parts of the ship and it was seen to hit the ground and roll over several times, still burning fiercely."

This Ar 234 B 'T9+DH', flown by *Lt.* Günther Gniesmer of *Kommando Sommer*, was the only aircraft of this type shot down by a Fifteenth Air Force pilot.

During the next few days the base was buzzing about continued rumors of the 52nd FG moving closer to the front lines, and in the middle of all this speculation, the news of President Franklin D. Roosevelt's passing cast a cloud of gloom over Madna. On 15 April memorial services were conducted for President Roosevelt, attended by more than 500 of the Group's personnel. Then as Tom Thacker put it: *"We lowered our flag to half staff and went on with the job of winning the war."*

When the 52nd went into action on 16 April 1945 it had its biggest day in terms of aerial victories in quite a while. The mission was a fighter sweep into Bavaria and Austria and the pilots were looking for targets in the air and on the ground. The enemy aircraft were all accounted for by pilots of the 4th FS when they ran into a mixed bag of German aircraft and downed five of them. Colonel Malcolm and Capt. Barnett Chaskin each destroyed an Me 109, Lt. James. J. Gentile an Fw 190, Lt. John Lang a Ju 88, and Lt. Arnold Sobczak an unidentified twin engine aircraft. In addition to these kills numerous other targets on the ground were destroyed in the areas of Munich and Linz and Wels. The five aerial victories were the 52nd Fighter Group's final kills of the war and brought its grand total to 425.

During the next four days the Group's aircraft flew missions to northern Italy and on the ground the news got hotter and heavier about the upcoming news. It was no longer a rumor, a move was about to take place. Ground personnel began breaking camp and preparing for the move to Piagiolino airfield. The move would take the Group about 180 miles northwards and the base was located about 14 miles south-west of the town of Fano. From this new airfield the 52nd could more easily carry out daily armed reconnaissance missions in support of the US Fifth and British Eighth armies.

The monthly report noted: *"Because of swift advances made by Allied armies on all European battle fronts, the strategic operations of the 15th Air Force gave way to tactical work and with this change, there was a corresponding tactical turn to the Group's operations during April.*

"Flying their last mission from Madna on 21 April, the Group's pilots landed on the new airstrip at Piagiolino during the afternoon of the same day after completing their missions. Not a single hour of operational time was lost in making the move.

"For three days, April 20, 21, and 22, a fleet of C-47s of the Troop Carrier Command shuttled back and forth between the two airfields transporting personnel and equipment. On the first day 119 aircraft loads were

S/Sgt Harry Greig inscribing a message to Generaloberst Heinrich-Gotfried von Vietinghoff, Commander-in-Chief, German Army Group C, and Commander South West in Italy on a bomb carried by Major Sefton's P-51D prior to a dive-bombing attack on 29 April 1945. (Credit: USAF)

The 52nd Fighter Group's B-25 hack looked 'refreshed' after its olive drab and gray camouflage was stripped away and the yellow Group tail markings were added. (Credit: Thomas Thacker)

transported with 100 C-47s participating.

"Prior to the air movement long convoys of motor trucks carried full loads day after day, continuing to do so for more than a week until by April 24 the entire Group had been moved."

From its new base the 52nd FG flew its final missions of the war. On 24, 25, 26 April the Group's aircraft flew escort/strafing missions to northern Italy and Austria, and on 27 April elements of the 2nd FS flew a POW pick-up mission to Yugoslavia. The mission was aborted, however, after bad weather in the pickup area turned the C-47s around.

To finalize the transition from strategic to tactical missions, P-51s of the 2nd FS flew the Group's first dive-bombing mission 29 April 1945. The four bomb carrying Mustangs, each carrying two 250-lb bombs, and four other escorting P-51s were led on this mission to the Udine, Italy area by Major William R. Sefton in search of targets of opportunity. For Sefton this mission was nothing new since he had spent 11 months flying A-36s as a dive-bomber pilot with the Twelfth Air Force. Near the Piave River the small attack unit spotted a German convoy consisting of about 40 vehicles, but just as they prepared to dive upon the target, P-47s cut them off. When the Thunderbolts finished with their attack there were no remaining targets, so Major Sefton and his bomber flight used their bombs to destroy a section of highway in front of where the convoy was attacked.

One week later, on 7 May 1945, the 52nd Fighter Group flew its last mission of the war and all there was left to do was celebrate victory in Europe! For the men of the Group it had been a long and very successful campaign, and now the most urgent mission in most of their minds was, '*when will I go home?*' The Group did not shut down operations in Italy immediately. At war's end the unit began a slow, phased shutdown and finally in August 1945, the last of the Group's personnel departed for the United States.

The 52nd Fighter Group scored a total of 425.33 confirmed victories, probably destroyed 33, and damaged 137 enemy aircraft in aerial combat. The 15th Air Force did not give credit for enemy aircraft destroyed in strafing attacks, but if it did, the Group's total score would increase by at least 200 destroyed. In its long campaign, the 52nd Fighter Group produced 21 Aces who accounted for 147.33 of the Group's aerial victories. Victory was not gained without cost, however, and over 100 of its personnel paid the supreme sacrifice to the effort to achieve it and hopefully, to bring a lasting peace and freedom to a war ravaged world. The 52nd Fighter Group was deactivated in November 1945.

The hoped for world peace, as we know, did not come about at the end of World War II. The Soviet Union soon thereafter began to threaten the security of the world and in November 1946, the 52nd was reactivated as the 52nd All Weather Fighter Group. It is still in existence today as the 52nd Fighter Wing, based at Spangdahlem Air Base, Germany. The present day 2nd Fighter Squadron is based at Tyndall AFB, Florida, flying F-15s. The 4th Fighter Squadron is based at Hill AFB, Utah, flying F-16s, and the 5th Fighter Training Squadron is at Vance AFB, Oklahoma.

12/ 311 The tail codes say it all. Mustangs of the 5th Fighter Squadron lined up to announce Victory in Europe. (Credit: Ralph Watson)

APPENDICES

Appendix 1
The Ground Personnel of the 52nd Fighter Group

Appendix 2
Commanding Officers

Appendix 3
Aces of the 52nd Fighter Group

APPENDIX 1
THE GROUND PERSONNEL OF THE 52ND FG

S/Sgt. Stephen Jacobs, 5th Fighter Squadron, working on a tire for his P-51C Mustang. (Credit: Thomas Thacker)

In almost any endeavor a man's success is largely due to the equipment he has to work with and the support of others. This was certainly the case of the 52nd Fighter Group, or any other military unit for that matter, when it came down to engaging and destroying the enemy air forces in aerial combat. The pilots were well-trained and highly skilled aviators, but it also took the skills of the maintenance crews and other ground personnel to insure their success.

Closest to the pilot was his skilled and dedicated ground crew that looked after their aircraft in a fashion close to a mother's love for her child. They worked extremely hard to make sure that the aircraft was in tip-top condition so that when they loaned it to their pilot to fly a mission he would not have to worry about mechanical failure in addition to the weather, Flak and enemy fighters. The pilot virtually placed his life in the hands of the men who maintained the engine, airframe, radios, instruments and guns of the plane he flew and the bond between the pilot and his ground crew was strong.

The ground crews of the 52nd Fighter Group were exceptional in their devotion to *"keeping them flying"* and on numerous occasions had to perform near miracles under less than perfect working conditions to insure their aircraft was ready for the next mission

Two shining examples of this excellence were P-51B, "Old 7" of the 2nd Fighter Squadron, and P-51D *"Georgia Peach"* of the 4th Fighter Squadron.

The 2nd Fighter Squadron's "Old 7" was P-51B 43-7061 and was part of the first batch of Mustangs received by the squadron in late April 1944. This Mustang served several pilots during its long career and its guns accounted for at least eight enemy fighters destroyed. During its long combat career Old 7 flew at least 125 combat missions and amassed 778 hours of flying time, including more than 600 hours on combat missions, without a single crack-up or sign of battle damage.

It's first crew chief was S/Sgt. Vincent Reagan and its first assigned pilot was Capt. Arthur Johnson, who reached Acedom in this bird which was named *"Marie"* and coded QP – M during this period. Johnson flew *"Marie"* during its first 256 hours, and downed six e/a while flying this Mustang. When Capt. Johnson received a new P-51D, *"Marie"* was assigned to Capt. William DeForest, who renamed it *"Myrtle"* and its codes were changed to QP–7. DeForest flew the aircraft an additional 200 hours before receiving a new P-51D.

At this point a new crew chief , S/Sgt James Lynes, Jr., took on the responsibility of keeping *"Old 7"* in the air. During its next two hundred hours of flight time several pilots used this aircraft and one of them scored two kills in it.

By December 1944 it was the oldest ship in the squadron and became a training aircraft for new pilots to transition in , and Sgt. C. G. Jones, became her crew chief. Under the care of Sgt. Jones, *"Old 7"* was refurbished and certified for another 180 hours and the old war horse returned to combat duties in January 1945 with Lt. Thomas Hoover as its assigned pilot. So proud of *"Old 7"* were the officers and men of the 2nd FS that they petitioned the Air Force to send her back to the United States for a War Bond tour. Their efforts failed, but it did not diminish the squadron's love of this old Mustang and its respect of the men who kept *"Old 7"* in the air.

The 4th Fighter Squadron's P-51D, 44-13323, coded WD-T, was a *"late-comer"* to the war compared to *"Old 7"*, but the work of crew chief,

From left to right: S/Sgt Elmer Dalebreaux, Crew Chief, and Sgt. C. G. Jones, Asst. Crew Chief, for Captain "Sully" Varnell's "Little Eva III". (Credit: C. G. Jones)

S/Sgt Reagan, Crew Chief, on the wing and Captain Bill DeForest in the cockpit of "Old Number 7", now named "Myrtle". (Credit: Robert Curtis)

Sgt. James F. Watson, 2nd Fighter Squadron, loading the guns on Captain Fred Ohr's P-51D "Marie", 9 August 1944. (Credit: Thomas Thacker)

"Old Number 7", the 2nd Fighter Squadron's pride and joy. (Credit: C. G. Jones)

S/Sgt. Mike Krot and his crew enabled this Mustang to complete 98 consecutive missions without an abort. Like its counterpart in the 2nd FS, this aircraft went through pilot and name changes. Its first pilot, Capt. Lester Steinke, named it *"Vicious Aloysius"*, and was renamed *"Georgia Peach"* when Lt. Rocco Palumbo became its pilot. On the right side of the nose it always bore the name *"Miss Marie"*, after S/Sgt. Krot's girl friend. During its combat tour, which lasted from 23 June 1944 until the end of the war, the *"Georgia Peach"* amassed a total of 719 hours flying time, of which, more than 600 hours were combat time. This example of the dedication of the ground crews reportedly established the MTO record for maintenance.

These are only two examples of the excellent work turned in by the ground crews of all three squadrons of the 52nd Fighter Group, and they certainly illustrate one of the reasons that their pilots were so successful.

Beyond the flight line there were many other ground activities that supported the pilots. These support units, that include the Engineers that maintained the airfield, the fuel crews, machine shop and sheet metal workers, the Quartermaster supply sections, all played a very important role in insuring the 52nd FG functioned properly. Right along with these sections in importance were the Mess Sergeants and their cooks, the unit mail clerks, both had an impact on morale. The Chaplains also played an important role in maintaining morale by providing spiritual guidance when needed by the men, and the unit medics were vitally important in helping heal the physical wounds.

The ingenuity shown by these men throughout the war in improving conditions at their airfields, most of which were newly established airstrips with none or little permanent facilities was remarkable and is certainly a tribute to the American soldier of World War II. A few examples are the improved tents made from drop tank crates built by the officers and men that certainly improved daily living conditions, stone mess hall and Chapels provided a better atmosphere for dining and religious services. Bars and clubs sprung up at the bases, using whatever materials available and the squadron artists decorated them with a variety of artwork, and were an important part of life at the base.

"Georgia Peach" with Crew Chief, S/Sgt Mike Krot on the wing and Lt. Palumbo seated in the cockpit. (Credit: Paul Ludwig)

Lt. Palumbo and S/Sgt. Krot posing with their Mustang, this time showing the name "Miss Marie" on the right side of the nose. (Credit: Paul Ludwig)

Two views of the 52nd Fighter Group's stone chapel erected at Madna. (Credit: Thomas Thacker)

Sgt. Clarence Watson, machinist, poses with an Italian-made lathe mounted in a German mobile machine shop, under its new management – the 52nd Fighter Group. (Credit: Paul Ludwig)

The 4th Fighter Squadron portable shower unit at Madna, September 1944 (Credit: Paul Ludwig)

Two views of HQ detachment officer's area clearly showing the walls of the tents constructed from drop tank cases. (Credit: Paul Ludwig)

Sheet metal worker, Pvt. Chester Mullins, shows off some of his tools of the trade needed for repairing the skin of battle-damaged 52nd Fighter Group aircraft. (Credit: Paul Ludwig)

Sgt. Kenneth Parkinson, a 4th Fighter Squadron baker, checks his oven in the Squadron mess hall, Madna, 20 September 1944. (Credit: Paul Ludwig)

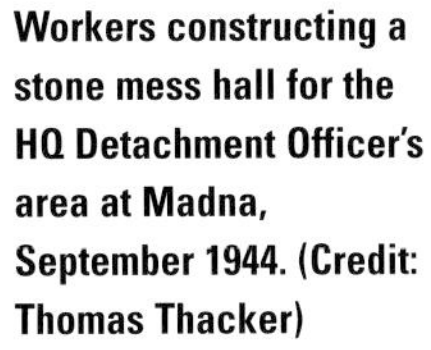

Workers constructing a stone mess hall for the HQ Detachment Officer's area at Madna, September 1944. (Credit: Thomas Thacker)

APPENDIX 2
COMMANDING OFFICERS

Group Commanding Officers

Major Earl W. Barnes, 16 January 1941–14 May 1941
Lt. Col. Robert E. Schoenlein, 15 May 1941–26 February 1942
Lt. Col. Dixon M. Allison, 28 February 1942–28 February 1943
Lt. Col. Graham W. West, 1 March 1943–20 June 1943
Lt. Col. James S. Coward, 20 June 1943–31 August 1943
Lt. Col. Richard A. Ames, 1 September 1943–5 September 1943
Lt. Col. Marvin L. McNickle, 6 September 1943–24 February 1944
Lt. Col. Robert Levine, 25 February 1944–26August 1944
Colonel Marion Malcolm, 26 August 1944 until end of war

2nd Fighter Squadron Commanding Officers

1/Lt. Donald L. Wilhelm, Jr., 15 January 1941–summer of 1941
1/Lt. John Chennault, summer of 1941–mid December 1941
1/Lt R. C. Richardson, mid December 1941–17 January 1942
Major Ralph E. Keyes, 18 January 1942–9 December 1942
Major James S. Coward, 10 December 1942–5 March 1943
Capt. Arnold E. Vinson, 6 March 1943–2 April 1943
Major George V. Williams, 3 April 1943–14 August 1943
Major Bert. S. Sanborn, 15 August 1943–19 May 1944
Major Robert C. Curtis, 20 May 1943–18 September 1944
Major Fred Ohr, 19 September 1944–31 October 1944
Major Daniel J. Zoerb, 1 November 1944–3 December 1944
Major J. G. Curl, 4 December 1944–18 March 1945
Major W. R. Sefton, 19 March 1945–end of war

4th Fighter Squadron Commanding Officers

1/Lt. J. Francis Taylor, Capt. Thomas Holdiman, and 2/Lt. Duane Cutting
served as Commanding Officers during the period of 15 January 1941–26 May 1942
Major Robert Levine, 26 May 1942–23 June 1943
Major William Houston, 24 June 1943–24 February 1944
Capt. Lee M. Trowbridge, 25 February 1944–June 1944
Major James O. Tyler, June 1944–30 September 1944
Major James Wiley, 2 October 1944–May 1945
Lt. Col. Gilbert Pritchard, early May 1945
Capt. Paul Steinle, late May 1945

5th Fighter Squadron Commanding Officer S

1/Lt. Allan T. Bennett, Capt. John Erickson, 1/Lt Ward W. Hackett, 1/lt James Whisenand, Capt. George Holdiman
served as COs of the squadron during the period 15 January 1941–9 May 1942
Major George C. Deaton, 10 May 1942–1 May 1943
Major William J. Payne, 2 May 1943–24 November 1943
Capt. Everett K. Jenkins, 25 November 1943–3 May 1944
Capt. Edwin W. Fuller, 4 May 1944–August 1944
Lt. Col. Ralph J. Watson, August 1944–March 1945
Major H. B. Eliker, March 1945–end of war

APPENDIX 3
ACES OF THE 52ND FIGHTER GROUP

(Numbers in parentheses indicate the pilot's total aerial victories of which some were scored with other units.)

Capt. James S. Varnell	2nd FS	17
Major Robert C. Curtis	2nd FS	14
Capt. J. Barry Lawler	2nd FS	11
1/Lt. Sylvan Feld	4th FS	9
Capt. Arthur G. Johnson	2nd FS	8.5
Major James O. Tyler	4th FS	8
Major Norman McDonald	2nd FS	7.5 (11.5)
1/Lt Calvin D. Allen	5th FS	7
1/Lt Dwaine R. Franklin	5th FS	7
Capt. Daniel J. Zoerb	2nd FS	7
1/Lt James E. Hoffman	2nd FS	6.5
1/Lt William F. Hanes, Jr.	4th FS	6
Major Fred F. Ohr	2nd FS	6
Capt. Robert A. Karr	5th FS	6
1/Lt. Richard Lampe	2nd FS	5.5
Capt. Arnold E. Vinson	2nd FS	5.33
1/Lt. James W. Empey	5th FS	5
1/Lt. Richard L. Alexander	2nd FS	4 (5)
1/Lt. Victor N. Cabas	4th FS	4 (5)
Lt. Col. Ralph J. Watson	2nd & 5th FS	2 (5)
Capt. James E. Peck	2nd FS	1 (5)

BIBLIOGRAPHY AND SOURCES

This history would have been impossible to write, without the following materials so graciously provided to the authors:
From the 2nd Squadron: *The American Beagle Squadron* by Lawrence Burke and Robert Curtis.
From the 2nd Squadron: *The Men of the American Beagle Squadron* by Carlton Hogue.
From the 4th Squadron: A diary written by Emil Torvinen.
From the 5th Squadron: A history of the 52nd Fighter Group prepared and written by Col. Tom Thacker, USAF, (Ret.)
Group and Squadron daily diaries.

Books, Manuscripts, Reports and Diaries

Burke, Lawrence G. and Robert C. Curtis. *The American Beagle Squadron*, Lexington, Massachusetts: The Lexington Press, 1987.

Chandler, Clifford H, Jr., Major, USAF. Report No. 88-0500, *History of USAAF Spitfire Operations in the Mediterranean (31st and 52nd Fighter Groups)*, Air Command and Air Staff College, Maxwell Air Force Base

Collier, Richard and the Editors of Time-Life Books, *World War II, The War in the Desert*, Illinois: Time-Life Books, 1977.

Craven, Wesley Frank, and James Lea Cate, *The Army Air Forces In World War II. Volume II. Europe - Torch to Pointblank*, Chicago: The University of Chicago Press, 1949.

D'Este, Carlo, *Patton, A Genius For War*, New York: Harper Collins Publishers Inc., 1995.

______. *Eisenhower, A Soldier's Life*, New York, Henry Holt and Company, L.L.C., 2002.

Hammel, Eric, *Air War Europa*, California: Pacifica Press, 1994.

Hogue, Carlton, *The Men of the American Beagle Squadron*, Sunnyvale, Texas: Lakeside Printing, 1993.

Hoover, R.A. "Bob" and Mark Shaw, *Forever Flying*, New York: Pocket Books, 1996.

Ludwig, Paul A. and Malcolm Laird, *American Spitfire Camouflage and Markings, Part One*, New Zealand: Ventura Publications, 1998.

______. *American Spitfire Camouflage and Markings, Part Two*, New Zealand: Ventura Publications, 1999.

MacCloskey, Monro Brig. Gen, *Torch, and the Twelfth Air Force*, New York: Richards Rosen Press, 1971.

Massimello, Giovanni and Giorgio Apostolo, *Italian Aces of World War 2*, Wellingborough, UK: Osprey Publishing, 2000.

Maurer, Maurer. *Air Force Combat Units*, Washington, D.C.: Zenger Publishing Co. Inc., 1961.

______.*Combat Squadrons of the Air Force in World War II*, Washington, D.C.: Zenger Publishing Co. Inc., 1969.

Office of Air Force History, *USAF Credits for the Destruction of Enemy Aircraft, World War II*, USAF Historical Study No.85. Montgomery, Alabama: Albert F. Simpson Historical Research Center, 1978.

Olynyk, Frank, *Stars & Bars*, London: Grub Street, 1995.

______. *USAAF (Mediterranean Theater) Credits for the Destruction of Enemy Aircraft Air-to-Air Combat World War Two*, Published by the author, 1987.

Pyle, Ernie, *Here Is Your War*, Cleveland, Ohio: The World Publishing Company, 1945.

Salmaggi, Cesare and Alfredo Pallavisini, *2194 Days of War*, New York: Mayflower Books, 1977.

Shores, Christopher and Hans Ring and William N. Hess, *Fighters Over Tunisia*, London: Neville Spearman, 1975

Thacker, Thomas L., Col., *Fifty-Second Fighter (Formerly Pursuit) Group*, Fairborn, Ohio: A manuscript prepared at home by Thacker.

Torvinen, Emil, *The Fourth Fighter Squadron – WWII History*, A manuscript prepared by Torvinen from his diary.

Articles

Curtis, Robert C. February 1944 Fighter Sweeps.

______. Sweetland and Muencheberg – *The Deadly Encounter*.

______. *A Fresh Look at a Fighter Pilot's Recollection of His Last World War II Combat Mission*, Aviation History magazine, March, 2000, pages 18 - 20 and 71 - 72.

Ludwig, Paul, *U.S. Spitfire Operations, Part 1, Northern Europe*. Norwalk, Connecticut: International Air Power Review, Volume 2, Autumn/Fall 2001

______. *U.S. Spitfire Operations, Part 2, The Mediterranean Theater*. Norwalk, Connecticut: International Air Power Review, Volume 5, Summer 2002.

Shores, Christopher F. *Yankee Spitfires. Air Classics*, Volume 14, Number 6, June 1978, (June 1978), pages 50-59.

______. *Yankee Spitfires. Air Classics*, Volume 14 Number 7, (July 1978), pages 32-44 and 64-67.

Thacker, Tom, Col. USAF (Ret.). *Spitfires and Stukas in North Africa*.

______. Gibraltar and Operation Torch.

______. Hungarian Attempt to Surrender in World War II.

______. Spinning the P-43 "Lancer."

______. Piggyback Rescue

______. Sinking of the Italian Ocean Liner Rex

______. Duckworth

Letters and photographs

Agha-Zarian (373rd FG for details of Sid Feld's last tour of duty), Richard L. Alexander, Dixon M. Allison, Alvin M. Anderson, George Angle, Mason L. Armstrong, Walter W. Barrett, Elbridge C. Bates (373rd FG), Shirley Baumgartner, Beth Berry (for John J.), Lt. Col. Dean H. Bishop, USAF (Ret), Steve Blake, John K. Blythe, Frederick E. Bullock, Brig. General Victor N. Cabas, USAF (Ret), Lt. Col. William B. Canning, USAF (Ret.), Jerry Cogal, Marshall J. Cowan, Colonel James S. Coward, USAF (Ret), Robert C. Curtis, Ted Damick, Colonel R. H. Damico, 373rd FG, USAF (Ret), George Deaton, Charles DeVoe, Morris Dodd, James Dolsen, Frank W. Dorfmeyer, Lt. Col. Fred K. Durni USAF (Ret), Sandra Ellis (daughter of Norm McDonald), Lt. Col. James W. Empey USAF (Ret), Miguel Encinias, Jeff Ethell, John Fawcett, Joe Fregosi, Robert D. Fulks, Lawrence Fullington, Jr., Lt. Col. Richard C. Gartner USAF (Ret), W. E. Garske, Al Gelo, Richard Gibian, Sr.(373rd FG), Fred Gombert, Jon Guttman, David Griffith, George Hahn, Floyd Hansen, Lt. Col. Marvin R. Haskins USAFR (Ret), Tom Hawley, Carlton H. Hogue, A. P. Holloway (31st FG), Everett K. "Pop" Jenkins, C. G. Jones, Peter Kassak, Lloyd H. Kempf, Lt. Col. Ralph E. Keyes USAF (Ret), Glen E. Klocke, Robert A. Klug, Malcolm Laird, R. C. Lampe, James R. Larson, Paul Lehmann, Robert Levine MD, Robert H. Liebl, George A. Lindahl, Hugh Looney, Lin Lundgaard, Colonel James F. McCarthy, Jr. (373rd FG) USAF (Ret), John A. McGeever, Alwin E. Miller, Carl Molesworth, G. E. Morris, Joe Dale Morris, Joe E. Myers, Fred F. Ohr DDS, Hugh L Ottley, Richard Potter, Glen Race, Joe Randerson, Jack L. Reed, James M. Richardson, O. Richmeyer, Robert W. Rivers, Kelly & Lillian Rodgers, Stanley Rollag, Bert S. Sanborn, Samuel W. Scalzi (373rd FG), Richard E. Schorse, Frank Sherman, Samuel L. Sox, Jr., Jeri Sprecher, Stan Staples (461st BG), Clayton Sutphin, Dwayne Tabatt, Raymond J. Teliczan, Sr. Thomas L. Thacker, Neil Toppen, Emil G. Torvinen, Carl N. Turner (373rd FG), Lt. Col. James O. Tyler USAF (Ret), Ralph J. Watson, Edward Werbe PhD, Fred A Wiersma, W. A. Williams, Homer G. Wise, Hans Zachmann, William E. Zins, Colonel Daniel J. Zoerb USAF (Ret)

INDEX